Hard Times in the Lands of Plenty

Hard Times in the Lands of Plenty

Oil Politics in Iran and Indonesia

Benjamin Smith

Cornell University Press
Ithaca and London

First published 2007 by Cornell University Press
First printing, Cornell Paperbacks, 2007

Printed in the United States of America

Library of Congress Cataloging-in-Publication Data

Smith, Benjamin B., 1970–
    Hard times in the lands of plenty : oil politics in Iran and Indonesia / Benjamin Smith.
        p. cm.
    Includes bibliographical references and index.
    ISBN 978-0-8014-4439-5 (cloth : alk. paper) —
ISBN 978-0-8014-7277-0 (pbk. : alk. paper)
    1. Petroleum industry and trade—Political aspects—Iran.
2. Petroleum industry and trade—Political aspects—Indonesia.
3. Iran—Politics and government—1941–1979.   4. Indonesia—
Politics and government—1966–1998.   I. Title.

HD9576.I62S65 2007
338.2'7280955—dc22

                                                    2007010665

Cornell University Press strives to use environmentally responsible suppliers and materials to the fullest extent possible in the publishing of its books. Such materials include vegetable-based, low-VOC inks and acid-free papers that are recycled, totally chlorine-free, or partly composed of nonwood fibers. For further information, visit our website at www.cornellpress.cornell.edu.

Cloth printing   10 9 8 7 6 5 4 3 2 1
Paperback printing   10 9 8 7 6 5 4 3 2 1

Contents

Acknowledgments

All significant projects accrue sizable debts, and this one is no exception. During the writing of this book, I have piled up IOUs to a great many individuals and organizations that provided financial, intellectual, institutional, and personal support. To a large degree, I am merely what Charles Tilly described as the "shyster" of the stone soup fable, taking objects of value from others, throwing them into my own shabby pot, and producing something good in the end only because my friends and colleagues gave up their valuable ingredients to me so that I wouldn't have to stand on a street corner with a sign reading "Will break new ground in social science for food." First of all, I owe special thanks to Jay Speakman, who during my sophomore year of college unknowingly convinced me to make the academy my professional home for life.

Research for this book was conducted under grants from the Ford Foundation, the Social Science Research Council, the American Institute for Iranian Studies, and the Harvard Academy for International and Area Studies. The Graduate School and Middle East, Southeast Asia, and International Studies centers of the Henry Jackson School of International Studies, the departments of Political Science and Near East Languages and Civilization at the University of Washington provided crucial support. (The Thomas and Judy Smith Foundation for Wayward Scholar-Sons, with a pool of grant recipients totaling one, was indispensable as well.) I am grateful to all for allowing me to pursue several years of research. The Harvard Academy for International and Area Studies under Sam Huntington's kind leadership provided a fabulous intellectual home, first to ignore the book for a year while I worked on other things and learned a great deal from my colleagues (thanks especially to Scott Desposato on that count, even though he kept calling me a "softy") and then to revise the nascent manuscript and start calling it "my book."

In Iran, I collected archival data from the Institute for Political and International Studies in Tehran. I conducted additional archival research on Iran at the Persian Collection of the Hoover Institute Library at Stanford University, the Iranian Oral History Project at Harvard University, and the Foundation for Iranian Studies in Bethesda, Maryland. I conducted interviews for the Iran case study in Tehran and Isfahan as well as in Los Angeles and Seattle. In Indonesia, I collected archival data at the Center for Strategic and International Studies in Jakarta, the National Library in Jakarta, the Biro Pusat Statistik (Central Statistics Bureau, BPS) in Jakarta, the Yogyakarta regional branch of the National Library, the Yogyakarta BPS regional branch office, and the Center for Population Studies at Gadjah Mada University in Yogyakarta. Additionally, I undertook research at the Southeast Asia Collection at the University of Washington libraries and the Institute for Southeast Asia Studies in Singapore. I also conducted interviews in several branches of the provincial government of the Special District of Yogyakarta, including the Dewan Perwakilan Rakyat Daerah (Regional Peoples' Representative Council), the Office of Employment, and the Social-Political Affairs Office.

Individuals under the compunction of no official obligation who read chapters or outlines, provided empirical or theoretical insights, and otherwise helped make this a much better work include Ichlasul Amal, Mehrzad Boroujerdi, Lance Castles, Larry Diamond, Tulia Falleti, Herb Feith, Barbara Geddes, Sam Huntington, Ahmad Karimi-Hakkak, Terry Karl, Charlie Kurzman, Bill Liddle, Miriam Lowi, Val Moghadam, Vali Nasr, Rizal Panggabean, Misagh Parsa, and Lisa Wedeen. Larry Dodd's advice about revising the manuscript helped immensely to sharpen the argument; thanks are also due to the two anonymous reviewers for Cornell University Press for their superbly insightful recommendations. Eva Bellin waived her anonymity as a reviewer for Cornell and provided me with a set of amazing comments and criticisms that rivaled in length some of the chapters in this book. Thank you, Eva—I truly hope the final product reflects the great suggestions you took the time to craft.

Special thanks go to Jason Brownlee, Dan Slater, and David Waldner: they were crazy enough to read all or nearly all of the book from many hundreds of miles away. David acted with complete selflessness and amazing insight. Jason and Dan along the way became two of my best friends, a great unexpected consequence of studying dictatorships and the "devil's excrement."

The Dehkhoda Institute for Persian Language Studies at Tehran University hosted me in the summer of 1998, making possible some very fortuitous research discoveries. The generosity and hospitality of Rector Ichlasul Amal and Professor Samsu Rizal Panggabean at Gadjah Mada University enabled me to get done much more than I had thought possible. Rizal's open arms at the Center for Security and Peace Studies provided me with a comfortable and intellectually stimulating office away from home (and has continued to do so ever since), where among others Lance Castles and the late and great Herb Feith asked curious questions and hammered away at my preconceptions until I abandoned them and developed "post"-conceptions that fit reality better.

My academic mentors deserve massive thanks. Steve Hanson refused to let me ignore the roles of ideology and world-historical factors, and I thank him as well for giving my theoretical arguments such close attention. Tony Gill pushed me constantly to pay close attention to micro-mechanisms (for instance, people and the things they do) and to make my arguments ever more precise and (I hope) clear and in general greatly helped to turn my unwieldy project into something that looks a bit more like social science. Erik Wibbels was extremely helpful and has my gratitude for so much assistance. He expended, in my view, way too much time on my writing, but I appreciate the help.

Finally, Joel Migdal has gone so far above and beyond the call of duty that I could never imagine completing this thing at all without his guidance. Joel pushes his students immensely hard but never in any one direction; he forces them to chart their own path and not his. He spent countless hours marking up my grant proposals, conference papers, and chapter drafts. Joel demands clarity of thought and word over what he calls the "narrowly constructed world of rigor" and, while I probably look and sound more "rigorous" than he would prefer, it is to his credit that he consistently pushed me to pursue my own direction. Above all, he is exemplary in all ways of what students imagine becoming when they idealize about academia: a person of character and exceptional intellect who can talk microeconomics, postmodernism, Gramsci, and how to live the good life. Most important, Joel is still the model to which I look as I chart my course. Much of what is good in this book is his fault; much of what is not is a result of me being too stubborn to take his advice.

Patricia Woods, my colleague and ex-wife, deserves tremendous thanks. Anyone who has been around me while I try to complete something like this book will know that it isn't often very gratifying. Patricia put up with me anyway and gave me crucial moral, emotional, and intellectual support, without which I'd still be throwing away drafts of the first chapter. Her suggestions improved my thinking and writing in innumerable ways, for which she has my respect and gratitude.

My parents, Tom and Judy Smith, who also appear in the second paragraph of these acknowledgments, deserve special thanks for helping to guide me to a career I love. I cannot remember either of them pushing me in any vocational direction since I wanted to be a scuba diver when I was about six. Somehow, though, they still managed to coax me into pushing myself along the way to becoming what I like to tell them—a geophysicist and a biochemist—is a genuine "hard scientist." After all, atoms and phosphates never get moody or impulsive (that we know of), so they behave more predictably. Take that, you guys: there has never been a nationalist isotope, and no formula ever tried to pass itself off as the Father of Indonesia's Development. Thanks: really.

My daughter, Kyra Miriam, deserves the greatest thanks of all for inspiring me from day one. I wrote chapter 5 in a daze during the first month after her birth, often while she slept on my chest (thanks to Baby Bjorn™ for making that possible). As the book moved through the review process, she moved through the infant to toddler process, from sleeping twenty hours a day to rushing me at my desk like a linebacker to insist that I get up and do something more fun. I am writing this paragraph late at night in my office, after playing hooky from the book to play with her all afternoon. Easy choice, that; she has filled all corners of my life with joy. It is with much love that I dedicate this book to her.

Hard Times in the Lands of Plenty

Introduction

This book is concerned with the politics of oil wealth and how it shapes the abilities of rulers in oil-rich countries to deal with social dissent. Autocrats in some oil-rich countries managed to ride out the political crises brought on by the 1973–74 and 1979 booms and 1986 bust, while others were not so lucky. Despite the extensive literature on oil wealth and politics, we still lack a general explanation for why some oil-rich regimes survive boom- or bust-generated political shocks while others collapse, upending their domestic stability, oil exports, and sometimes the international political economy. In the following chapters, I provide one—the first response that takes in all of the contemporary oil-rich developing countries to provide a comprehensive perspective on oil wealth and regime survival. In doing so, I challenge the contention of the classic rentier state/resource curse theory that oil rents have the same effects on particular institutions. By contrast, I argue that oil rents have effects on institutions that vary systematically according to the circumstances of oil's entry as a major export commodity. Where rentier state/resource curse theorists have asked whether a country is oil-rich, I ask *when*.

The conditions under which oil revenues, or "rents," become available to rulers powerfully shape the subsequent uses to which rulers put those rents. More specifically, oil's effects on state institutions and on regime viability depend heavily on the circumstances surrounding the initiation of "late development" in oil-exporting countries, in which the state takes the commanding role in the economy, garnering whole sectors for itself and directing extensive public funding and legally granted privileges to private actors in other sectors. During this period, late development promised to reshape fundamentally the way that citizens bought, sold, and produced goods and organized themselves. More specifically, this book attends to the politics of oil wealth and the challenges faced by political regimes that use it to accomplish economic transformation while also staying in power. As we shall see, it is very difficult to manage both when the context is the volatile global market for oil.

The world oil market has been at the heart of many of the major political upheavals of the last thirty years, and sharp changes in the price of oil have been catalysts for change. The so-called Third Wave of Democratization washed over many authoritarian regimes in developing countries whose dependence on increasingly expensive oil imports helped to erode their economic growth and legitimacy (Huntington 1991). Scholars of the Soviet Union have noted the central role of the oil booms in undermining the economic viability of the Eastern bloc in the late 1970s and early 1980s (Bunce 1985). In the industrialized West, the retrenchment of welfare states took place under leaders who came to power on promises to clean up the fiscal mess exacerbated by the 1970s oil shocks (Pierson 1994). Finally, several studies have highlighted the destructive effects of oil wealth on the economic policies and institutional capacities of exporting states (for example, see Gelb 1988; Karl 1997; Chaudhry 1997; Vandewalle 1998). The second oil shock of the 1970s, in 1979–80 (the first was in 1973), was caused in large part by the loss of much of Iran's oil production during its revolutionary crisis. The 1979 shock, like the Libyan price hike of 1971, caused a major shift in global market prices as a direct result of domestic political events in an exporting state. The politics of oil wealth inside individual exporting countries can have great effects far from those domestic settings.

In the exporting states, the shocks brought huge revenue windfalls, but the results were no less dramatic than in the importing states that retrenched, democratized, or collapsed. In many cases, the booms tripled or quadrupled the discretionary revenues available to leaders. Rulers' attempts to spend this windfall—and the currency valuation brought about by the windfall itself—caused inflationary and Dutch disease shocks, paradoxically causing a crisis in countries that should have been enjoying the fruits of a commodity boom.[1] Moreover, in many cases, the economic problems caused by the booms created political crises by sparking price-hike protests or opposition aimed at curbing official corruption. A few regimes

---

[1] Dutch disease refers to the effect that a commodity boom can have of causing a shift in private investment away from other sectors in the economy. An oil boom, for instance, can damage agriculture and industry in an exporting country by providing powerful incentives to shift resources out of other areas of the economy or by increasing the value of national currencies, which has the effect of making other exports less competitive in global markets. See, for example, *Economist* 1977 and Corden and Neary 1982.

collapsed during these crises; most of the others weathered hard times to emerge with newly consolidated authority. In this book, I develop an explanation of the effects that oil wealth, and the oil booms in particular, exerted on the politics of exporting states during the period of about 1960 to 1980—both before and during the booms that made oil such the major factor in the economy. The evidence suggests something that neither aggregate statistical analyses nor case studies of individual countries have yet illustrated: that oil wealth has political effects that vary, effects that vary systematically in ways that go beyond the particularities of individual countries.

In the chapters that follow, I address the following questions: Why did the oil booms of the 1970s have such heterogeneous effects on regimes in exporting states? In some countries, serious political crises toppled rulers, whereas other rulers rode out equally taxing challenges. Why has oil wealth undercut regimes in some exporting states but apparently bolstered regimes in others? The economic effects of the booms are generally thought to have led to substantial middle- and upper-class opposition to the Shah's regime in Iran, but very similar effects in Indonesia produced much less widespread dissent. Why does oil contribute to the building of weak states in some countries and strong ones in others?[2] In Iran, the administrative and extractive capacities of the state deteriorated substantially between 1960 and 1977, whereas it was precisely during the boom years that the New Order government in Indonesia invested most dramatically in the institutions of state. I propose an answer to these questions that looks further back in time than the oil booms and the leaders' proximate responses to them.

In particular, I focus on the initiation of late development as a crucial historical moment. When I refer to "late development," I mean a set of policies in which "the state explicitly nurtures the development of private sector capital and labor, relying on a variety of means—financial, social, political, and infrastructural" (Bellin 2002, 3–4) as well as more directly interventionist policies such as the creation of state-owned industrial enterprises and state-granted monopolies in key sectors.[3] Late development also denotes industrialization in the context of a world economy already populated with industrialized states (Gerschenkron 1962). Success at playing "catch-up" becomes the benchmark for judging government effectiveness

---

[2] As will be clear in the pages that follow, I define *state capacity* as the ability to extract, regulate and monitor, and mobilize.

[3] There is a vibrant controversy over just what *development* means—even what *late development* means. I do not mean to brush off the normative and empirical questions surrounding these concepts; rather I want to make it clear that here I refer to the specific policies outlined above and their political consequences.

at managing the economy and moving the country from "backwardness" to modernity.[4]

My major theme is that we should ask not *whether* countries become oil-rich, but *when*. More specifically, does oil wealth precede or follow late development? If mass-based opposition movements at the initiation of late development are already in place, this has a powerful effect on rulers' decisions about coalition and institution building. Where late development begins before states gain access to substantial oil revenues and there exists powerful opposition, rulers face what are essentially "forced moves"—to survive early on, they must build robust coalitions and state institutions that can effectively gather revenues and exert social control in local settings. Rulers who initiate late development with established access to oil revenues with little or weak opposition, conversely, have the widest initial array of potential options and can opt to use oil-funded patronage in lieu of a deeper politically based coalition. They can also elect not to develop the extractive institutions of state and not to pursue the aggressive expansion of infrastructural power into local settings. The early choice of options has counterintuitive implications for the long-term survival prospects of such rulers.

As I explain in chapter 4, during the period under discussion, the fiscal and political constraints on rulers at the onset of late development—including whether or not they had significant access to oil revenues—exerted powerful effects on the decisions they made about building institutions and coalitions. Those decisions in turn defined the scope of their options for dealing with later revenue shortages, political challenges, and the revenue windfall created by the oil booms of the 1970s. Where previous studies focused almost exclusively on the institution-eroding effects of oil wealth, I show that, under certain conditions, oil wealth can facilitate both institutional development and strong political coalitions. Moreover, the analysis of data from twenty-one oil-exporting developing countries in chapter 5 suggests, in fact, that it does so more often than it doesn't. In short, previous studies of oil and politics have generally focused their attention on a small number of cases at one end of a spectrum of oil-induced political effects: Algeria, Iran, Nigeria, and Venezuela, what I refer to as the "big four" of rentier state studies. At the other end of the spectrum are countries like Indonesia, Iraq, Malaysia, Syria, and Tunisia, where oil seems to have strengthened at least some political institutions and provided rulers with the resources to manage political crises effectively. To foreshadow the ar-

---

[4] Generally speaking, late development in oil-exporting states has taken the form of import-substitution industrialization. It has frequently been combined, in such countries as Indonesia and Malaysia, with export-led policies or market-oriented policies or both.

gument that I develop in chapter 2, it is the presence or absence of substantial access to oil rents and of powerful, organized opposition that is determinative of regime resilience during subsequent crises.

Although much of the discussion has concentrated on the handful of political crises that followed the 1986 oil bust, the boom years were no less volatile. A number of oil-rich states experienced major social protests in the late 1970s, at the precise moment when they should have been riding the wave of revenue windfalls. For many protesting groups, inflation caused by the booms was the explicit motivation for challenging governments. In Iran, a prominently weak oil state, the protest movement that emerged in early 1977 ultimately brought down a monarchy backed by 700,000 soldiers. In Indonesia, too, protests emerged in 1977–78 aimed at achieving greater public participation in the politics of Suharto's "New Order." These protesters, however, were much less successful than their counterparts in Iran. By late 1979, Suharto's New Order was again riding an oil revenue windfall, whereas the revolutionary movement that sent the Shah into exile earlier that year had begun to consolidate what would become the Islamic Republic of Iran.

The differences in these two regimes' abilities to govern through crises went beyond their capacities for dealing with and containing social dissent to larger issues of state capacity. By the mid-1970s, the Iranian government derived almost none of its income from direct domestic taxation. Over the previous fifteen years, its ability to assess and collect taxes had drastically deteriorated, to the point that in 1969 a proposal to increase taxes on domestic commerce proved wholly unfeasible because the agencies that would have been responsible simply could not muster the capability to send out tax collectors. In Indonesia, by contrast, the revenue shortfalls that confronted Suharto's government in the early 1980s met a different response. In 1983, the New Order regime adopted a major tax reform as a way of mitigating the decrease in oil revenues with little difficulty, in stark contrast with abject extractive failures in Saudi Arabia (Chaudhry 1997) and elsewhere. Moreover, by 1986, when oil prices dropped more substantially, the government had both begun to tax with much more efficiency and to encourage private investment in manufacturing. These policies reduced the state's reliance on oil revenues and mitigated the short-term prospects for economically motivated protests. Both sets of policies were possible because of prior investment in government capacity. At first glance, these two states seem to have been affected in widely different ways by their oil wealth. But why?

The Questions at Hand and Current Answers

Scholars in comparative politics, political economy, and development economics have done much to explain how and why oil wealth can contribute to poor economic performance, democratic breakdown and authoritarian politics, even civil conflict. In general, however, they have not treated systematically to what is often a central, if implicit, claim—that oil wealth is a cause of political instability. Neither the resource curse nor the rentier state literatures deal systematically with this issue except inasmuch as they often attribute a monocausal power to oil.

The academic literature on oil and politics has not yet given us a way to understand the range of possible effects caused by oil wealth. If we look across the exporting countries, oil wealth seems to have shaped their political trajectories in different ways, sometimes weakening state institutions and regimes and at other times plausibly contributing to increased institutional capacity and regime longevity. While scholars have tended to look at the cases with instability and weak institutions, the states on the other side of the spectrum are often described in exceptional terms, as outliers or anomalies ill-suited to the "mainstream" analysis of oil and politics.

Let us return to Iran and Indonesia. Despite the dramatic divergence of their trajectories in 1979, I posit that the experiences of Iran and Indonesia are representative of broader political trends in oil-rich countries. The conventional wisdom notwithstanding, we have seen great variance in the degree to which regimes in these countries have been able to direct windfall revenues to bolster their own political positions. On one hand, regimes in Ecuador, Nigeria, and Iran collapsed during the boom years, and regimes in Congo and Nigeria (again) collapsed after the bust. On the other hand, some regimes have displayed remarkable durability during the same period: Suharto's New Order in Indonesia lasted 32 years, Saddam Hussein's Ba'ath regime in Iraq lasted until the 2003 U.S.-British invasion despite two major interstate wars, a longstanding Kurdish rebellion, and ten years of international sanctions. The Partido Revolucionario Institucional in Mexico surrendered the presidency to an opposition as late as 2000, after a tenure that had lasted seven decades. Perhaps most strikingly, none of the Gulf Arab monarchies has faced a serious challenge to its rule since independence, this despite a growing dissident movement in Saudi Arabia and periodic opposition movements in the smaller Gulf states. The historical record suggests that, if oil is as important to politics in exporting countries as scholars have come to believe it is, it can "do" different things. What remains is explaining how and why it can do different things across a wide range of country settings.

This book does not treat durable regimes in oil-rich states as anomalous. By leaving out the assumption that durable regimes in rentier states must be analytical glitches, I construct a systematic answer to these questions and show that both stable and unstable polities and both strong and weak states are logical outcomes of a dependence on oil exports. In other words, where other theories have sought to assign monocausality to oil wealth, I present a theory that can account for its varying effects on regimes. In my view, this is best accomplished by discarding the assumption that oil, or more accurately the world oil market, is a purely structural variable. By this I mean that it is not simply a macroeconomic constraint on state leaders. It is always potentially a sizable political resource that can be skillfully wielded by politicians both to bolster regimes and to build state capacity.[5] Because it is a highly flexible form of revenue, oil wealth does not exert its effects structurally. Rather, its effects depend on how rulers incorporate it into the domestic political economy.

A foundational building block of my argument is that, where oil has been generally conceptualized as a structural variable in comparative studies, we ought to look at ways in which its effects might be quite malleable. Oil export revenues are not like taxes or conditional foreign aid because, in nearly all cases, they accrue directly to the state and are highly flexible or discretionary. Because no process of accountability structures their use, oil revenues are a tremendous political resource that, in most exporting countries, finds its way into the hands of a very few individuals in mostly authoritarian regimes. Instead of assuming that in all circumstances oil wealth must exert a single set of effects, I argue that, when political leaders have been forced to engage a different set of structural constraints without the benefit of oil revenues, they may later use such revenues in ways that political scientists have disregarded in current studies. It is crucial to understand the process by which oil becomes a political resource in the hands of state leaders if we are to understand its effects.

To be sure, there are many studies that illustrate how the politics of oil wealth is filtered through local political realities and shaped by historical legacies (see, for example, Chaudhry 1997; Crystal 1990; Karl 1997; Katouzian 1981; Lowi 2004; Okruhlik 1999; Vandewalle 1998). On the other hand, some studies based on aggregate data analysis point to the systematic effects of oil wealth (Ross 2001c; Sachs and Warner 1995). The first group traces the processes through which oil revenues enter into and shape the polities of individual states, creating outcomes contingent on the in-

---

[5] For an extended study of how politicians in Indonesian, Malaysia, and the Philippines manipulated the domestic effects of another commodity market—timber—see Ross (2001a).

teraction between rents and local settings; the latter group seeks broad correlational trends. How, then, to reconcile the observations that (a) oil wealth's effects may vary according to context and (b) oil has systematic effects? By integrating case study analysis, carefully constructed structural comparison, and aggregate analysis, this book outlines a theoretical framework for resolving this question to demonstrate that history matters and that it does so in systematic ways amenable to general explanation.

Long-term regime viability in rentier states depends on a set of prior variables that revolve around the initiation of late development. I take a dynamic, sequential approach to analyzing the onset of late development in which the political effects on the capacities of institutions and durability of regimes depend on the timing of late development relative to confronting political opposition and gaining access to significant discretionary revenues from oil. Regimes in many resource-rich states and across the developing world began late development in response to political and economic crises as a way of escaping their dependence on commodity exports and, often, as a central component of state building projects. Typically, they used revenues from the sale of commodities to fund economic diversification projects that revolved around state investment in or outright ownership of major industrial projects. In many cases, they adopted development programs in the face of serious political challenges and without the external oil revenues that were to arrive later.

In terms of the causal sequences of oil and late development, I argue that, when oil rents are not available to rulers when they begin late development, they pursue institution building as a less preferred but unavoidable

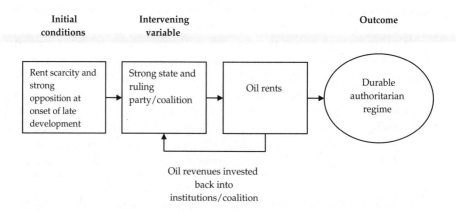

Figure I.1. Hard times and late development: Oil politics as a function of institutions

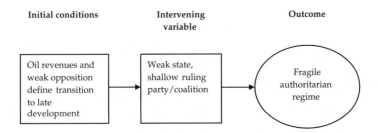

Figure I.2. Plentiful oil rents, weak opposition, and late development: Oil politics as a cause of institutions

alternative strategy. When oil rents do become available to rulers who had to live without them earlier, they usually tend to be invested in further institution building. Thus, oil wealth becomes a part of the domestic political economy as an intervening variable whose effects are filtered through preexisting institutions (see figure I.1).

Conversely, when oil revenues are a central part of the political environment surrounding the onset of late development, they exert an independent causal effect on the institutions themselves, shaping how the state takes shape. In such cases, oil is a causal variable that exerts its effects in part by influencing the capacity of institutions (see figure I.2). So this is not solely a story about oil states. Rather, I integrate the experiences of oil exporters into theoretical treatments of state building and of the broader political economy of development to develop and test new hypotheses about the role of oil wealth.

This argument draws on both economic and historical theories of institutions and institutional change. At the onset of late development, a micro-level conception of leaders' desire to consolidate their economic policies at the lowest possible political cost drives the theoretical analysis, and I derive hypotheses from politicians' likely actions during this period. Once these state leaders make decisions, however, they take institutional form and subsequently take on a life of their own. Often, they have unintended consequences that affect regime viability in later periods.

Once decisions take institutional form, the role of agency changes. As institutions solidify and develop over time, they change the array of possible options available to the same leaders who created them in the first place. Here, I draw heavily on historical institutionalist conceptions of path-dependent change, positing that it is the institutional legacies of the early development period that constrain and enable state leaders during subsequent economic and political crises. As I outline below, the effects of the oil windfalls of the 1970s had their origins in decisions about state building in the 1960s.

In this analysis, then, I move beyond static structure-agency debates to engage a temporally dynamic conception of institutional development. Put briefly, the very institutions that state leaders have much freedom to construct during initial periods powerfully shape their later options for dealing with economic and political crises. The institutional paths influence the likelihood that regimes will be able to weather such crises. To return to the central question at hand, why do some regimes manage to weather those crises while others come apart at the seams? Why does oil exert seemingly contradictory pressures on regime viability and state capacity?

Strategies of Inquiry

I approach these questions using a number of methodological and analytical tools. First, rather than simply assessing the logic of rentier state theory, I subject it to extensive empirical scrutiny. After all, if its predictions hold up well across the developing world, there would be little reason to proceed any further. As a first cut at the theoretical conclusions reached by current studies, I test the rentier state and resource curse hypotheses in a broad cross-national setting in chapter 1. I constructed a dataset of economic, social, and political indicators for 107 developing states between 1960 and 1999. My goal in this first set of time-series analyses is to gauge whether in fact oil-rich states have tended over time to be less stable than other developing states and thus whether the rentier state and resource curse literatures serve as a good predictor of broad trends. I assess the independent effects of oil wealth on regime durability, levels of political protest, and civil war.

Another common theme in rentier state theory is that the magnitude of the 1970s oil booms promoted instability and political crisis in exporting states. To investigate this question, I tease out the independent effects of the oil booms and bust volatility on the twenty states most dependent on oil export revenues. The results are surprising. All else being equal, oil wealth tends to produce regimes that are more rather than less durable, and regimes in oil-rich countries face significantly lower risk of collapse than those in oil-poor countries. I also find that sub-regime change indicators of political instability—political protests and civil conflict—occur at significantly lower levels in states dependent on oil exports. The results also indicate that post-boom and even post-bust rentier states were no less stable than they were before the booms. In short, the systematic effect that the windfall revenues were presumed to have—provoking political crises—does not pan out.

These findings call into question much of the conventional wisdom concerning rentier states and the resource curse and suggest a need for developing theories that can account for multiple effects of oil wealth. What they do not do is tell us why it is that some oil states seem to have grown so much stronger precisely during the periods that we should have expected them to display weakness. In other words, chapter 1 does not provide any answers to the questions that this book addresses. Instead, it provides a cross-national approach to reviewing the literature, establishing that in fact the questions I raise in this book are in need of answering. These are questions to be answered by looking for causal mechanisms that tie macro-phenomena such as oil wealth and late development through intervening variables—institutions and state-society relations—to outcomes—the ability of rulers to foresee and forestall widespread challenges to their authority.

To my mind, structured, focused comparisons and especially most-similar analyses offer the best way to test theories of this kind. In addition to making it possible to test theories in a close empirical setting and to confirm their implications in small causal steps, most-similar analysis can avoid the selection bias problems of a most-different approach to showing the effects of a structural variable like oil. Structured comparisons also make it possible to compare not just countries as cases but also distinct periods and specific institutions across cases, a strategy that can increase confidence about findings at the same time that it increases the number of discrete observations.

I pursue a most-similar comparison with maximum outcome variation for two reasons. First, it is a way of moving beyond the deterministic but broadly questionable findings from single and most-different case studies. Second, it is an opportunity to probe causal sequences not captured by the causally incomplete implications of large-N analyses that I used to assess previous understandings of oil and politics. The overarching methodological structure of this portion of the research is a comparison of two cases over time in which many socioeconomic, political, and historical factors are held roughly constant but in which outcomes varied dramatically and in which—at the onset of late development—two key factors varied between the cases. As I explain below, these processes were path-dependent, in the sense that initial decisions took certain options off the board for later consideration and made other courses of action so costly as almost to ensure they could not be followed.

To trace these processes—from executive-level meetings to informal contacts between state elites and social leaders to major institutional changes—I employ a variety of qualitative and quantitative research methods. First, I employ archival data, structured and open-ended interviews, oral histories, provincial- and national-level statistical data, and the analysis of elite memoirs as a way of grounding mid-range and meta-level theorizing in the events that I contend built on one another to produce the outcomes that are the focus of my research. I compare the two states at two distinct stages through the same three institutional lenses. Early interactions between regimes and social organizations, executive decisions about the role and scope of provincial government, the structuring of official parties, and other crucial processes give analytic shape to each case and together present what I hope is a compelling illustration both of the theory and of the means by which these two regimes got to where they were by the late 1970s.

Outline of the Book

In chapter 1, I introduce the issue of oil as a major factor in comparative and international political economy. Reviewing the literature on rentier states and the resource curse, I show how oil has been conceptualized in structural terms and develop from this literature a set of testable hypotheses related to political stability and regime durability. I test the major theoretical conclusions from the rentier state and resource curse literature and find that in general they are not supported by the data. In fact, durable regimes are the norm in oil-exporting states, even during the boom and bust years, and their durability does not appear to be a function of repression.

Building on these results, I develop in chapter 2 an alternative theory of oil and politics. I argue that, at the onset of late development, the strength of political opposition and availability of oil revenues shape leaders' decisions about coalition and state building. I develop a number of hypotheses and empirical implications of this theory, and I outline a most-similar comparative research design focused on assessing the theory against the experiences of Iran and Indonesia during the 1960s and 1970s.

The third and fourth chapters of the book trace the effects of oil wealth and late development from the 1960s to the late 1970s in Iran and Indonesia. These chapters illustrate the powerful trends that emerged from Suharto's and the Shah's early decisions about how deep and wide a coalition would be necessary, and how strong a state necessary, to confront the challenges posed by late development. They point to specific differences in the power of the ruling parties created by each regime to serve as its public face and electoral vehicle, for example. They outline how, after late development began, state building accelerated aggressively in Indonesia while it stagnated and even backslid in Iran. Tax revenues as a share of non-oil government revenues climbed steadily in Indonesia throughout the 1970s, even during the first boom, while they declined substantially in Iran. Over time, all of these systematic changes left Suharto and the Shah with very different political and institutional resources for managing political crises. Whereas Suharto had had many fewer options fifteen years earlier, by 1978 it was the Shah who faced a much narrower range of viable strategies for maintaining power. The outcomes in each case reflected these changing resources: Suharto had restabilized his regime by 1979, while the Shah fled into exile in January of the same year.

Chapter 5 of the book extracts the general implications of the Iran-Indonesia comparison and uses them to develop an original dataset of oil-exporting states that incorporates new variables for late development and opposition strength. Using those new variables, it tests the hypotheses derived from the case study chapters against data from twenty-one oil-rich states and finds powerful cross-national support for the propositions that (a) the circumstances surrounding late development created divergent effects of oil wealth and (b) they did so in large part by affecting the likelihood that rulers would craft powerful ruling parties to sustain their coalitions.

Chapter 5 also presents brief case studies of late development, oil wealth, and regime viability in Congo and Egypt. The experiences of regimes in these two countries confirm that the same basic causal mechanisms—fiscal and political circumstances at the onset of late development catalyzing institutional trajectories—appear to operate across a wide array of settings in shaping how oil, opposition, and late development interact to affect the survival of autocrats in oil-rich countries. In short, the investigation uses causal inferences developed through the in-depth comparison of Iran and Indonesia to draw general conclusions about the role that oil wealth and late development have played in shaping the long-term prospects for authoritarian regimes throughout the oil-exporting world. In doing so, it unites two major approaches to inquiry in comparative social science, combining the strengths of both methods to balance causal depth and complexity available from individual cases and the quest for theoretical generalizations.

In the conclusion, I summarize the findings from Iran and Indonesia and discuss the implications of the comparison. First, this project has import for the broader study of resource wealth and for the prospects for regime stability and growth in developing countries with rich oil or natural gas reserves. It frames commodity export dependence—a situation shared by over half of the world's developing countries—in the context of rapid state and market building during the last half of the twentieth century, incorporating the issue of natural resource endowment into theories of state formation. Where rentier states, and especially oil exporters, have long been treated as exceptional, I suggest that their experiences cast fruitful light on the study of postcolonial states more broadly.

Second, the crucial importance of timing and sequence in political inquiry is on full display in the effects of oil wealth on the politics of state building and development. The most important conclusion to emerge from this book is that the presence of oil wealth cannot be determinative on its own—how and, most important, when it is introduced is critical. Even powerful macro-structural variables like the global oil market can vary substantially in their impact depending on their temporal relationship to other domestic variables. Third, the origins of late development regimes are just as important to their long-term prospects for survival as the organizational shapes they assume. As the second half of the book illustrates, fiscal and political challenges to the late development process tended to compel rulers to build powerfully organized ruling parties to "house" equally robust ruling coalitions made up of important social groups. The recent resurgence of systematic studies of durable authoritarianism (for example, see Brownlee 2002, 2007; Geddes 1999, 2003; Levitsky and Way 2002; Ottoway 2003; Smith 2005) has brought the survival of autocracies back to the foreground of comparative politics. What it has not done is explain comprehensively why some of these regimes become so durable in the first place, nor why some develop into durable single-party regimes while others become less robust military or "sultanistic" ones. This study offers a theory to explain how fiscal and political challenges early in the life span of regimes help to shape their long-term prospects and, in doing so, makes a small contribution to our understanding of the remarkable longevity of many regimes that have bucked the third wave of democracy.

Finally, the book illustrates the complementarity of small-N qualitative and large-N quantitative analysis. In an era of debate over the "fragmentation" of comparative politics, I suggest that no such fragmentation is necessary or inevitable. Throwing in my lot with a growing number of scholars who eschew methodological debates in favor of maximizing the size of their "toolboxes" (see, for instance, Lieberman 2005; Coppedge 2005; Anderson 2005), I have pursued a pluralist approach to research methods. Integrated comparative analysis, as I like to think of it, can chart a path that blends explanatory depth—outlining specific causal mechanisms at work in individual cases—with explanatory breadth illustrating broad, systematic relationships while controlling for other plausible factors.[6]

---

[6] I borrow the metaphor from my University of Florida colleague Leslie Anderson (2005). Abraham Kaplan also put the metaphor to good use in *The Conduct of Inquiry:* "Give a small boy a hammer, and he finds that everything he encounters needs pounding" (1998, 28).

CHAPTER 1

Oil Wealth and Politics in the Developing World

Theories and Evidence

"Give me $18 a barrel oil, and I will give you political and economic reform from Algeria to Iran."

—*Thomas Friedman (2005)*

"The ratcheting up of oil prices brought immediate instability. Few regimes could weather such turmoil."

—*Terry Karl (1999, 40–41)*

The global oil market and its associated booms and busts have generated a large literature in political science. One contention in this literature is that political instability is a near-certain long-term outcome of oil wealth. Another line of argument maintains just the opposite, that oil makes authoritarian regimes stronger by funding patronage and repressive apparatuses. In this chapter, I conduct the first cross-national tests of these arguments and investigate the effects of oil wealth and the oil booms and bust on political stability. Drawing on data from 107 developing countries between 1960 and 1999, I estimate the effects of oil wealth on regime failure, antistate social protest, and domestic armed conflict. Thus, as a first goal this chapter addresses an analytical shortcoming in previous studies by separating regime survival empirically from both economic policy and regime type (democratic or authoritarian) and by focusing on the direct effects of oil wealth on several measures of political stability. I address the relationship between oil wealth and these outcomes both by comparing exporters to the rest of the developing world and by comparing oil-rich states across pre-boom, boom, and bust periods. The research presented here is a first step toward developing a theory that can account for both the weakening and strengthening effects of oil wealth on state capacity and regime viability. This first step, in which I assess the current state of theorizing on oil wealth and politics, is focused on marking broad trends rather than on presenting conclusive answers. I discuss in the next chapter the ways in which a return to structured comparative research focused on explaining variation rather than conformity of outcomes is likely to be the most fruitful strategy.

The results indicate that oil wealth is robustly associated with more durable regimes and significantly related to lower levels of protest and civil war. Moreover, the collapse of oil prices in 1986 exerted no significant negative effect on regime viability or civil conflict among oil exporters, even though regimes in the most oil export-dependent states faced significantly higher levels of antistate protest. Finally, oil's strengthening effect does not appear to be a function of repression. These findings suggest in turn that political scientists have some serious rethinking to do in the study of the effects of resource wealth on the viability of regimes. Where Luciani (1987, 1994), Karl (1997), and others argue that oil rents can create a long-lived but shallow stability in an otherwise weak state, I suggest that the persistence of authoritarian regimes in oil-rich states long after the bust of the 1980s—after access to patronage rents had dropped off dramatically—suggests that leaders in many of these states invested their windfall revenues in building state institutions and political organizations that could carry them through hard times. In short, I ask why, given the sudden collapse in 1986 of potential patronage rents by more than two-thirds of such regimes, so few faced serious challenges.

The answer to this question, I argue, is that in many of these states rulers came to power years before they could rely on oil revenues. More specifically, these rulers initiated late development as a part of state building and, when they could not rely on externally derived revenues such as oil profits, made substantive concessions to coalition partners and built institutions that could extract revenues domestically. Early concessions in these countries produced resilient regimes. Only when oil revenues formed a backdrop to late development did the most often theorized trajectory take shape. In these cases, leaders who could buy temporary legitimacy at the time of late development did so. The short-term political cost was lower, but leaders in countries like Iran paid the price for it later, when the boom-bust cycle led to economic crises that threatened regimes across the exporting world.

Oil Export Dependence and the "Three R's":
Rentier States, Repression, and Rent-Seeking

Most recent work on oil and stability falls into three broad categories of causal explanation: the "rentier state," repression, and rent-seeking theses. While scholars approach the political economy of oil from diverse methodological origins, the theoretical arguments about the structures and nature of the rentier state flow from the state's access to externally obtained revenues from the sale of oil. Moreover, the different approaches highlight many of the same weaknesses of exporting states, based on their susceptibility to the pitfalls discussed below. Let's examine the major arguments by which oil wealth is argued to produce political crises.

The Rentier State Thesis

As oil revenues increase to the point at which they dominate a government's revenue sources, the government evolves from an extractive state into a distributive one: "The bulk of the internal activities of the state are concerned with distribution" (Delacroix 1980, 18). For the most part, this line of argument draws on the logic of the extractive state, reasoning that compared with the taxing states of early Western Europe, a government that does not rely on domestic extraction for the bulk of its revenue must lack a crucial capacity. Beyond the collection of fiscal resources, the information generated by a robust tax bureaucracy weighs heavily on the viability of the state itself. In contrast to a tax-dependent state that must devote great energy to extracting its operating revenues from society, a distributive state simply must decide which social groups are to be the favored recipients of oil rents. Beblawi and Luciani note that oil revenues enable the state to "buy off political consensus" (1987, 7).

The rentier state thesis has a corollary: as state leaders have no need to extract, they have no need to represent. As a result, the kinds of iterated and multifaceted interactions between rulers and ruled that provide both public participation in policymaking and a means by which rulers keep an eye on the public tend to be weak, if they exist at all (Najmabadi 1987a; Vandewalle 1998). Chaudhry discusses the rapid dismemberment of the tax bureaucracy in Saudi Arabia following the first oil boom, using the microstudy of Saudi state extractive agencies to advance a more general argument about the decline of state capacity (1997, 143–47). In the rentier state thesis, oil is posited to obviate extractive bureaucracies and the relations with social groups necessary to collect taxes effectively. Skocpol argues that reliance on oil wealth made it possible for the Pahlavi regime in Iran to maintain an impressive degree of autonomy from its society: "Suspended above its own people, the [Shah's regime] did not rule through, or in alliance with, any independent social class" (1982, 269). However, that autonomy proved shallow in the face of mass-based mobilization against the state in the late 1970s. Together, these effects produce weak state-society linkages and ought to produce subsequent instability both during booms, when politicians are likely to flood the domestic economy with revenues, spending unwisely and spurring destabilizing inflation, and busts, when weak state institutions prove unable to continue patronage and extract revenues from domestic sources.

In addition to the line of argument specifically linking oil price–induced economic crises to political problems, broader research in political economy points to a strong relationship between economic crisis and regime breakdown (for example, see Gasiorowski 1995; Haggard and Kaufman 1995; van de Walle 2001; Smith 2006). If economic crises linked to oil export dependence are like other crises, we should reasonably expect fluctuations in oil prices to produce the same sorts of political shocks that economic crises catalyze elsewhere.

Other rentier state theorists of oil argue that externally derived rents can actually prolong authoritarian regimes (Beblawi and Luciani 1987). Karl's wide-ranging study of Venezuela and several other large "petro-states," which put forth the weak state theory of oil wealth, is the most ambitious comparative analysis of rentier states. She asserts that by distorting property rights regimes, the power of interest groups, and the role of the state in the market, oil wealth "creates incentives that pervasively influence the organization of political and economic life and shape government preferences with respect to public policies" (1997, 7). However, if revenues remain stable, Karl argues, oil wealth can contribute to long periods of stability, such that oil-based rent seeking can actually prolong regime life spans, even if in a shallow way that relies almost exclusively on rent patronage—"spending instead of statecraft" (20–21).

During boom periods, the ability of the state to placate important social groups by paying them off with oil revenues should allow regimes to survive long after they would otherwise be able to, despite the inherent weakness of rentier state institutions and coalitions (Crystal 1990; Chaudhry 1997). In addition, the vesting of groups in the continuity of the regime contributes a social base to the rentier regime bargain, provided that the money does not run out and the economy remains fairly stable (Luciani 1987, 7; Karl 1997, 57–58). This line of argument suggests that oil-dependent regimes should evince significantly greater levels of stability during pre-boom and boom periods and greater instability during the bust of the late 1980s. On the other hand, the Dutch disease phenomenon, in which booming sectors such as oil raise a currency's value and discourage agricultural and manufacturing exports by likewise raising their prices on international markets, ought plausibly to create the basis for political crisis by damaging the viability of key non-oil sectors (Gelb 1988, 87–89; Davis 1995, 1768). Thus, the economics of Dutch disease might well provoke political crises during boom periods despite a growth in patronage revenues. In addition, the magnitude of rent seeking leaves regimes in rentier states extremely dependent on economic performance and thus vulnerable during both boom and bust periods.

The Repression Thesis

Ross suggests that oil revenues make it possible for regimes in exporting states to invest in repressive apparatuses that can keep them in power despite social opposition (2001a, 349–51). His analysis suggests that oil wealth is correlated with military spending, which is in turn associated with authoritarianism. This analysis, however, finds an uncertain relationship between oil and what would be an obvious measure of military expansion, the number of military personnel.[1] Bellin takes up the repression question and develops a causal argument related to the strategic value of oil for superpowers (2004). Superpower interests in access to oil combined with the frequent presence of oil wealth in Muslim-majority countries renders regimes in these countries less vulnerable to external pressure to liberalize or at least not to repress.[2] Subsequently, the ability and will of rulers to repress contributes to what Bellin terms the "robustness of authoritarianism." A testable implication of this theory is that highly repressive regimes that confront opposition during a crisis are more likely to survive. That is, regimes in oil-rich states survive because they repress.[3]

Oil Rent-Seeking, Distributional Inequity, and Greed-Motivated Rebellion

The "oil-as-spoils" thesis maintains that the presence of oil revenues or other extracted natural resources in a country causes political instability by presenting an attractive set of spoils to potential rebels or state-break-

---

[1] Also, no empirical connection between military expenditure and repression is established, raising the possibility that many oil states invest in their militaries simply to protect themselves from potential external threats. Below, I explain my own attempt to assess the repression effect using a proxy for state repression derived from Polity's Autocracy measure.

[2] Ross finds a simple bivariate correlation of .44 between oil exports as a share of GDP and Muslims as a share of a country's population (2001a, 338–39).

[3] In practical terms, if oil wealth bolsters authoritarian longevity by funding repression, then including a measure for repression ought to reduce the effect of oil wealth in regression models.

ers or by creating resentment over unequal distribution of oil rents, which can spill over into conflict over the pattern of distribution. This thesis holds, first, that easily captured revenue sources such as oil present an attractive target to potential rebels and, all else being equal, raise the risk of civil war. Indra de Soysa counters scarcity-driven theories of civil war by arguing that greed-driven rebellion is more likely and, indeed, that it is significantly more likely in resource-rich states (2000). Collier and Hoeffler confirm this finding, but it is important to note that the independent effects of oil wealth are not tested in either analysis (1998). Second, the unequal distribution of rents can cause conflict when excluded groups attempt to force redistribution by resorting to violence, which can destabilize democratic and authoritarian governments alike. By a number of different mechanisms, in short, resource wealth in general and oil wealth in particular makes civil war more likely (Ross 2004a, b, 2005).

Wantchekon does not directly test this instability hypothesis but argues that instability is a causal mechanism tying resource wealth to nondemocratic rule. In his model, resentment over unequal distribution of resource rents promotes conflict, creating an instability that tends to undermine democratic government (1999).[4] It also can be a source of instability in authoritarian settings, as Okruhlik argues with reference to Saudi Arabia (1999). An observable implication of both of these theories is that both social protest and civil war ought to be more likely in oil-rich states than in other developing countries, even more so during the boom-bust cycles that create economic crises.

Theorizing the Political Effects of Oil Wealth

Despite a host of varying methodological and theoretical approaches, scholars of the politics of resource wealth have come to a loose consensus about several things. First, oil wealth tends to weaken state institutions and to produce shallow, fragile ties between rulers and ruled. Second, the volatility of the world oil market and its domestic effects on exporters means that the rulers presiding over those weak institutions and ties to society face tough times when price spikes or collapses create economic crises. Third, although oil wealth can bolster regime longevity by making possible expansive coercive capacity and rent-purchased social bargains, sudden price drops can liquidate those advantages, leading to antistate mobilization,

---

[4] It is important to note that, other than the experience of Nigeria, from which the instability mechanism is induced, the effect of resource wealth on stability is not tested in Wantchekon's analysis.

armed domestic conflict, and regime collapse. It is not possible to test all of these propositions directly, but it is possible to test many of their implications.

Given higher levels of oil export dependence, we should expect several trends across the population of oil-exporting countries. To my mind, these are some reasonable implications of the rentier state literature for political stability:

H$_1$: Dependence on oil exports subjects states to wide fluctuations in the major source of revenues and to the weakening of state institutions. Because of these effects, oil wealth is likely to be associated with greater likelihood of regime failure.

H$_2$: The capacity to invest oil revenues in repressive apparatuses and in extensive patronage should counteract these destabilizing effects. As a result, highly repressive oil-rich states should fail less often than others.

H$_3$: The incentives for greed-motivated rebellion make the risk of civil war greater in oil-rich states. Distributional inequities generated by the political uses of oil rents suggest that oil wealth ought to be associated with increased antistate protest.

H$_4$: Boom and bust cycles tend to generate economic crises in oil export-dependent states. As a result, regime failure, civil war, and antistate protest should all be more likely during oil boom and bust periods.

In the next section I test these hypotheses in order. First, I compare oil-exporting states to other developing countries, testing the hypotheses that the former should be less stable across time. Second, I deal specifically with the effects of dependence on the export of a commodity whose prices have fluctuated dramatically since 1970. I test these by isolating the independent effects of the boom and bust years, respectively, and discuss my strategies for doing so in the next section.

Data, Methodology, and Models

The analyses presented here focus on the effects of oil wealth on regime failure, antistate social protest, and armed domestic conflict. The data are drawn from 107 developing countries between 1960 and 1999 for 4,280 possible country-year observations (see Appendix II). They allow for two analyses of oil states that have not yet been conducted. First, despite frequent assertions of the effects of oil wealth on stability, no large-N analysis has compared oil exporters to other developing nations in terms of relative regime durability. Second, small-N studies of oil states during and after the booms of the 1970s often focus exclusively on those periods. They have generally failed to ask whether such states were in fact less stable after the first boom than they were before it, seeking instead to point out simply that some regimes were unstable during the 1980s and early 1990s. The data cover fourteen years before the first oil boom of 1974 and thirteen years after the collapse of oil prices in 1986. In addition to allowing for a greater number of yearly observations than in an analysis limited to the 1970s and 1980s, the longer time period also makes it possible to see if, all else being equal, the population of oil states was prone to greater instability during and after the oil booms than before them.

Dependent Variables

While I am primarily interested in regime durability, it is important to recognize that political instability can take other forms. Two countries in which regimes survived might have very different levels of antistate protest or internal conflict; in such cases, regime durability data might obscure underlying instability. To obtain a more nuanced view of the effects of oil wealth, I use two additional dependent variables to measure political stability in each nation; thus, the dependent variables include regime failure as well as antistate protest, and internal conflicts in a given country-year. First, I measure political stability as regime failure (REGIMEFALL). I derive this variable from the Polity98 dataset (see Marshall, and Jaggers 2000) and code it "1" for each year that is given a value of "0" in the regime durability variable, or each intervening year between a change of 3 or more on Polity's regime type index. Second, I test the effects of oil wealth on antistate protest, measuring protest as the sum of peaceful demonstrations, riots, and strikes in a country in any given year (Banks 1998).[5] Third, to assess the civil war/conflict hypotheses of the resource curse literature, I test the effects of oil wealth on internal conflicts on a country's soil in any given year. CIVILWAR is coded, following Gleditsch et al. (2002), from "0" to "3":

---

[5] Given the possibility that oil wealth might affect these three types of protests differently, I estimated the protest models using each separate measure as a dependent variable. Across strikes, riots, and anti-government demonstrations, oil wealth has a consistently negative effect on their frequency, although in the case of strikes oil's effect falls narrowly outside the $p<.05$ significance range at $p<.051$ (z−score=1.95). There are also problems of reliability with Banks's data for these events. While the Cross-National Time Series data archive contains the most extensive cross-national coverage of protest events currently available, the protest results presented in the next section should be taken as preliminary findings pending the accumulation of further data.

"0" indicates no armed domestic conflict, "1" indicates a conflict with at least 25 battle-related deaths per year and fewer than 1,000 during the course of the conflict; "2" an intermediate conflict with at least 25 battle-related deaths each year and an accumulated total of at least 1,000 deaths, but fewer than 1,000 in any given year; and "3" a war with at least 1,000 battle-related deaths each year. The use of this measure, rather than a binary one, allows for testing of oil's effects on both the presence and magnitude of internal conflict.[6]

Independent Variables

The primary explanatory variables in this study are related to oil exports and to the booms and bust of the 1970s and 1980s. The oil dependence variable (OIL/GDP) is the ratio of the value of oil exports to gross domestic product in a given year (World Bank 2001).[7] It highlights both the role of oil as a source of export revenues and its importance in the domestic economy.[8] Its explanatory role is to assess whether, once other factors are accounted for, oil-exporting states tend to differ from non-exporters.

Another plausible conclusion from the rentier state hypothesis, however, is that the oil wealth that flooded the population of exporters in the 1970s and the price collapse of the mid-1980s may have caused a negative shift in their overall level of stability. I test this hypothesis—that the boom-bust cycle of the 1970s and 1980s made oil states less stable over time—by incorporating two interrupted time-series variables to account for the independent effects of boom and bust periods. I employ a strategy suggested by Lewis-Beck for testing the effects of crucial events in time-series data or, in comparative historical terms, critical junctures (1986). The first variable (BOOMEFFECT) is the product of OIL/GDP multiplied by a dummy variable, BOOM, which counts upward from "1" beginning in 1974 and

[6] Employing an ordinate measure of civil war also mitigates a problem with using only a binary measure, such as that used in the Correlates of War (CoW) project, alongside the Polity regime scores. The problem emerges with a binary measure because the Polity coding scheme takes intense domestic conflict into account when scoring levels of representation; subsequently, civil war, measured dichotomously, can be a partial cause of an independent variable that is then used to predict it.

[7] Measuring oil dependence in this way, rather than as a share of exports, overcomes the question of gauging the overall importance of exports to a given country's economy. However, to investigate the possible effect of oil revenues as a share of exports, I estimated each of the models using the ratio of oil exports to total exports instead of to GDP. In all cases, the impact of Oil/Exports was insignificant.

[8] This measure does not take oil consumed domestically by exporting nations into account. This type of oil production revenue raises many interesting questions; I thank one of the anonymous reviewers for bringing this to my attention.

ending in 1985 for any country that depended on oil exports for ten percent or more of GDP for at least five years between 1974 and 1999.[9] All other country-years are coded "0."

The second, BUSTEFFECT, is the product of oil exports as a share of GDP multiplied by a dummy variable for the bust (BUST) which counts upward from "1" beginning in 1986 through 1999, the final year of data. in the same states that had nonzero values for the boom effect. All other country-years are coded "0." The rationale for constructing the variables this way—with ascending values rather than constant ones—is that scholars generally agree that the political effects of the booms and bust built over time. The boom and bust effect variables take into account the highest levels of dependency on oil exports, the variation among those nineteen highly dependent states, and the accumulated effects of the booms and bust.[10] By constructing the variables this way, it is possible to assess both the hypothesis that the political effects of the booms and bust built over time and the argument that more dependent states suffered more from the fluctuations in oil prices and in their domestic economies than less dependent ones.

Control Variables

In addition to these variables, I incorporate a number of economic controls that are commonly held to affect regime durability and political stability so that I can adjust for these effects in order to isolate the independent effects of oil wealth. Per capita income, measured here as the natural log of per capita GDP (Gdppcln) in constant 1995 U.S. dollars, was included in early iterations of the models and was predicted to affect negatively the likelihood of protest, civil war, and regime failure. I also included inflation (Inflation), measured as the annual percent change in consumer prices (World Bank 2001), to account for its plausible positive effects on the protest activity and rebellions that could lead to civil war.[11] Finally, rates of economic growth (Gdpgrowth) are included, with the premise being that growth should increase the longevity of regimes and decrease the likelihood of civil war and antistate protest (on the economic causes of regime

[9] They are: Algeria, Bahrain, Congo (Brazzaville), Ecuador, Egypt, Gabon, Indonesia, Iran, Kuwait, Libya, Mexico, Nigeria, Oman, Saudi Arabia, Syria, Trinidad and Tobago, Tunisia, the United Arab Emirates, and Venezuela. Three exporting states—Angola, Iraq, and Qatar—do not appear on this list for reasons of missing data.

[10] The oil wealth variable is also included in the boom models; it captures the effects of lower levels of oil dependence.

[11] These two economic controls were insignificant and were thus excluded from the final set of estimations.

collapse, see Warwick 1992; Gasiorowski 1995; Remmer 1999; and Haggard and Kaufman 1995; on civil war, Fearon and Laitin 2003).[12]

I also include a number of social and political indicators. First, I control for regime type using a score (Democracy), taken from the Polity IV dataset (Marshal and Jaggers 2000) and calculated by subtracting the autocracy score from the democracy score in each country-year, for a range between -10 and 10. I expect that higher democracy scores should lower the likelihood of regime failure. Given that the vast majority of democratic developing states have become democratic during the "third wave," however, democracy in this sample of mostly newly democratized and unconsolidated states might be positively related to the likelihood of civil war (Huntington 1991). I also include the square of the democracy score (Democracy^2) as a proxy for regime coherence, following a strategy utilized by Hegre et al. (2002) to account for the empirically established U-curve relationship between democracy and conflict and for the effect of regime coherence independent of regime type.[13] Second, ethnolinguistic fractionalization (ELF85), measured here as the likelihood that in 1985 two randomly chosen individuals in a country would not speak the same language (Roeder 2001), is commonly asserted as a contributor to political instability (see, for instance, Horowitz 1985). Third, the rate of urbanization (Urbangrowth) has been theorized to produce instability when it happens too quickly (Huntington 1968). For instance, the new (and largely unemployed) urban poor that poured into Iranian cities during the late 1960s and 1970s is argued to have been a major factor in the Iranian revolution.[14]

Many of the cases chosen to illustrate how oil destabilizes domestic politics are either Middle Eastern or sub-Saharan African states—witness the heavy attention paid to Iran, Algeria, and Nigeria. One might reasonably infer that these regions are more prone to regime failure and civil war than others. To assess whether there is in fact something to this lumping of cases, I investigate a possible regional effect by using dummy variables for the Middle East (MEAST) and sub-Saharan Africa (SSAFR), coded "1" for each country that is included in these respective groupings by the World Bank (2001) and "0" otherwise.[15] I also include variables to account for the

[12] I also included unemployment and the ratio of government debt to GDP in initial estimations of the models. They were insignificant predictors of all three dependent variables and were subsequently excluded from the final models.

[13] As I discuss below, I also conducted tests in which I replaced Democracy^2 with a dummy variable for highly repressive regimes to separate the effects of coherent regimes from those of repression.

[14] That assertion has since been challenged by increasing evidence that the urban poor played a minor role in the uprisings of 1977–79.

[15] There is one exception. The World Bank codes Turkey as a European country; I include it in the Middle East.

population (LOGPOPTOTAL), the land area (LOGAREA), and the population density (LOGPOPDENSITY) of individual countries.[16] Larger populations should plausibly prove harder for regimes to control; Fearon and Laitin (2003) show that large populations tend to increase the likelihood of civil war, and Herbst (2000) shows compellingly the difficulties that state leaders in Africa have had in extending their authority over large areas. Population density should plausibly raise the potential for collective social action, but it might also make it easier for rulers to control their populations. I take the natural logarithm of all three of these variables for inclusion in the models.

Finally, many scholars point to individual countries' unique political histories as a factor in regime durability. Whether it is couched in terms of historical legacies or of repertoires of contention, the argument goes that nations with a history of instability or with many past transitions may be more prone to instability, making subsequent regimes more likely to fail. I include a past transitions variable (PASTFAIL), represented as the sum of all previous regime failure years according to Polity98 for each country-year.

Recognizing that each of the dependent variables could be highly dependent on past values, I employ lagged dependent variables in all of the models. A problem, however, as Achen (2000) notes, is that this strategy can make any outcomes overwhelmingly a function of values from the year before and can sometimes suppress the effects of substantive variables (in this case, oil dependence, ethnic diversity, past political history, and so on). The possibility of temporal relation among observations in models with binary dependent variables (such as the regime failure models used here) raises similar concerns. To mitigate this tendency, I followed a strategy suggested by Beck, Katz, and Tucker (1998) and included dummy variables for each country-year in the dataset, minus one, in the regime failure models. None of the year dummies were significant, the results did not change significantly, and the slight improvement in model fit was outweighed by the loss of degrees of freedom (39). Thus, I estimated the models with one- and five-year lagged dependent variables and also estimated the regime failure and civil war models with a trend dummy variable that begins at "1" and counts upward by one per year in each panel. As I discuss below, this strategy had the effect of correcting for temporal relations among observations while retaining the significant effects of the substantive variables and in-

---

[16] Controlling for population serves mainly to check the possibility of larger countries naturally experiencing more protests than smaller ones. Population was a significant predictor of aggregate protest levels, but it was highly collinear with population density and did not otherwise change the results except for squeezing out land area; thus, population is excluded from these models.

creasing the degrees of freedom.[17] In all cases, however, I present data below from the models that include a one-year lagged dependent variable; as I discuss, the more strenuous test has no significant effect except in the case of civil war, in which oil's effect falls just outside the .05 range of significance.

Results

Oil Wealth and Regime Failure

Addressing the question of how oil influences the durability of political regimes in developing states, the first model estimates the determinants of regime failure across 107 developing countries. Oil dependence is shaded darkly and, in the boom and bust models, the boom and bust effects are shaded lightly; all other variables are unshaded. Table 1.1 provides the results of the model using logistic regression. In these models, a negative coefficient indicates that a variable's effect is to lessen the likelihood of failure, where REGIMEFAIL takes a value of "1." To recall the hypotheses, the more common prediction from rentier state and resource curse theories is that increasing oil dependence should be associated with a higher likelihood of regime failure. The results contradict this hypothesis. Oil dependence exerts a robust and significant negative effect on the likelihood of regime failure, suggesting that longer-lived regimes in oil-exporting states appear to be the representative cases. It is important to note that, even when the models include a one-year lagged dependent variable, the positive effect of oil wealth on regime durability remains robust.

Democracy's effect is insignificant, as are ethnolinguistic fractionalization and economic growth. However, democracy's quadratic negatively affects the chances of regime failure in any given year, providing further confirmation of the U-curve relationship between regime coherence and conflict and suggesting that its reach extends beyond civil war to regime failure. As expected, past regime failures boost the likelihood of future ones. Interestingly, the sub-Saharan Africa dummy variable significantly decreases the expected likelihood of regime failure, while the Middle East dummy variable is insignificant. A number of demographic factors play a significant role in determining the viability of regimes. Urban growth is robustly associated with a greater risk of regime failure, providing some

---

[17] All models were estimated using Stata 7.0. I used Stata's VIF command to test for multicollinearity, and in no cases did independent variables exhibit significant collinearity except in the above-mentioned cases of population and population density.

TABLE 1.1.
Oil wealth and regime failure, 1960–1999

Independent variable	Model 1	Model 2
Constant	−2.575***	−1.427**
	(.517)	(.561)
Oil/GDP	−3.011**	−3.199**
	(1.528)	(1.590)
Democracy	−.024	.007
	(.020)	(.021)
Democracy^2	−.019***	−.021***
	(.004)	(.004)
ELF85	.169	.249
	(.468)	(.464)
Sub-Saharan Africa	−.933***	−.913***
	(.315)	(.313)
Middle East	−.150	.262
	(.449)	(.448)
Urban growth	.124**	.133**
	(.063)	(.061)
GDP growth	−.030	−.038*
	(.020)	(.020)
Past regime failure	.242***	.391***
	(.044)	(.049)
Population density$_{ln}$	−.137	−.144*
	(.085)	(.084)
Regime failure$_{(t-1)}$	1.791***	—
	(.226)	
Trend	—	−.058***
		(.014)
N =	1961	1925
Pseudo R^2	.198	.162
Log likelihood =	−362.11383	−371.7088
Likelihood ratio χ^2 =	178.77	144.11

Notes: Analysis is by logistic regression. Entries are unstandardized coefficients. Standard errors are in parentheses. ***, **, and * indicate significance at the .01, .05, and .10 levels, respectively.

support to the instability thesis advanced by revisionist modernization scholars (Huntington 1968, for example).

To summarize, regimes in oil-rich states enjoy a boost in longevity as a result of their access to oil rents when compared to other developing countries. Oil dependence is a positive predictor of durability, but at the same time it is negatively related to democracy, another positive predictor. This relationship hints at a different set of mechanisms keeping democracies and oil-rich autocracies in power. One possibility, investigated by Ross (2001a), is that repression helps to maintain oil-rich regimes through crises. To examine this possibility, I replaced Democracy^2 with a dummy variable for highly authoritarian regimes, coded "1" if the democracy score was between −6 and −10. Negative scores indicate not just an absence of political freedoms but also the regular use of coercion, so they help to fill in the causal gap between repression and regime outcomes. The effect of repression was to decrease significantly the risk of regime failure; the coefficient for the variable was −1.370 with a standard error of .342. Repression did not, however, reduce the effect of oil wealth, suggesting that factors other than spending on coercion are at work in the robust relationship between oil wealth and regime durability.

Table 1.2 presents the results for the effects of the booms and bust of the

TABLE 1.2.
Oil booms, oil busts, and regime failure

Independent variable	Model 1	Model 2
Constant	−2.572***	−1.390**
	(.515)	(.560)
Oil/GDP	**−6.606****	**−5.346****
	(3.113)	**(2.562)**
Boom effect	**.4378**	**.373**
	(.433)	**(.386)**
Bust effect	**.577***	**.531**
	(.328)	**(.328)**
Democracy	−.023	.008
	(.020)	(.020)
Democracy^2	−.019***	−.021***
	(.004)	(.004)
ELF85	.225	.262
	(.468)	(.464)
Sub-Saharan Africa	−1.017***	−.962***
	(.321)	(.316)
Middle East	−.214	.224
	(.448)	(.445)
Urban growth	.142**	.144**
	(.065)	(.062)
GDP growth	−.029	−.038*
	(.020)	(.020)
Past regime failures	.237***	.394***
	(.044)	(.050)
Population density$_{ln}$	−.149*	−.153*
	(.086)	(.085)
Regime failure$_{(t−1)}$	1.764***	−.060***
	(.226)	—
Trend	—	
	(.014)	
N =	1961	1925
Pseudo R^2	.201	.165
Log likelihood =	−360.375	−370.445
Likelihood ratio χ^2 =	182.24	146.63

Notes: Analysis is by logistic regression. Entries are unstandardized coefficients. Standard errors are in parentheses. ***, **, and * indicate significance at .01, .05, and .10 levels, respectively.

1970s and 1980s. To recall, the boom and bust variables account for the consequences of high levels of oil export dependency during sudden price fluctuations. While oil wealth continues to decrease significantly the likelihood of regime failure, the pernicious economic effects of the booms and bust do not seem to have had an effect on regime viability in either direction. The same controls that were significant in the first set of models—democracy squared, the sub-Saharan Africa dummy, urban growth, past political history, and population density—remain significant here, but regimes in the nineteen most dependent states do not seem to have suffered politically, even though for many of them the price of a commodity providing more than half of the GDP shrank by two-thirds in just a year.

Oil Wealth and Civil War

Table 1.3 estimates the effects of oil dependence on the likelihood of civil war using ordered logistic regression. As with the regime failure models, negative logistic coefficients suggest a negative impact on the likelihood of an event, in this case civil war. Included in table 1.3 are the results of models containing a one-year lagged dependent variable (column 1) and a less dominant five-year lagged dependent variable (column 2). Oil wealth only exerts a significant negative effect on the intensity of civil war in a given year in the model that includes a five-year rather than a one-year lagged dependent variable. This finding contradicts the "oil as spoils" thesis in which greater resource wealth is held to provide an incentive for rebels to launch rebellion aimed at seizing production facilities. It also contradicts recent findings by scholars of civil war who find a positive relationship between oil wealth and civil war onset, a different measure than the one I use here (see, for instance, Fearon and Laitin 2003; de Soysa 2000).

Ethnic diversity significantly increases the estimated likelihood of civil war, as predicted.[18] In one model (see column 2), democracy also exerts positive pressure on the likelihood of civil war. Although democracy is not a significant predictor in the model with a one-year lag, it is significant in the five-year lagged model. That democracy is positively related to civil war seems counterintuitive until one remembers that most of the democracies in the developing world have made the transition from authoritarianism in the last quarter-century. A number of studies have shown that semi-democracies are more likely to suffer civil wars (see, for instance, Hegre et al. 2001 and de Soysa 2000). Given this, it is unsurprising that in the developing

---

[18] This finding also runs counter to what Fearon and Laitin (2003) find and suggests that results may be partially dependent on how "civil war" is measured.

TABLE 1.3.
Oil wealth and the intensity of civil war, 1960–1999

Independent variable	Model 2	Model 3
Oil/GDP	**−1.519**	**−3.283*****
	(1.028)	**(.863)**
Democracy	.0199	.029***
	(.013)	(.011)
Democracy^2	−.010***	−.013***
	(.003)	(.002)
ELF85	.760*	1.957***
	(.398)	(.331)
Sub-Saharan Africa	-.215	−.895***
	(.263)	(.215)
Middle East	.562**	1.313***
	(.270)	(.216)
GDP growth	-.037**	−.067***
	(.017)	(.014)
Land area$_{ln}$	.199***	.260***
	(.059)	(.047)
Population density$_{ln}$	.225***	.399***
	(.079)	(.066)
Civil war$_{(t-1)}$	3.095***	—
	(.125)	
Civil war$_{(t-5)}$	—	1.142***
		(.064)
N =	1961	1926
Pseudo R^2	.553	.262
Log likelihood =	−644.93718	−1053.97
Likelihood ratio χ^2 =	1598.21	748.77

Notes: Analysis is by ordered logistic regression. Entries are unstandardized coefficients. Standard errors are in parentheses. ***, **, and * indicate significance at the .01, .05, and .10 levels, respectively.

world, early democracies are among the most at risk of civil war. Democracy's quadratic is robustly and negatively related to the likelihood and intensity of civil war, as it is with regime failure.

Interestingly, the sub-Saharan Africa dummy variable exerts a significant negative effect on the likelihood of civil war in the five-year lagged civil war model, suggesting, as was the case in the regime durability models, that the nearly fifty states in that region may be poorly represented by the handful of states in which civil conflict has been endemic. However, location in the Middle East (including Saharan Africa) raises the expected likelihood and intensity of civil war. Economic growth, unlike its effects on regime failure, exerts a significant negative effect on the outbreak and intensity of civil war. Finally, geographic and demographic factors such as total land area and population density continue to be important predictors of conflict: both area and density increase the likelihood and magnitude of armed domestic conflict.

TABLE 1.4.
Oil booms, oil busts, and civil war

Independent variable	Model 1	Model 2
Oil/GDP	−1.450	−5.065***
	(1.575)	(1.573)
Boom effect	−.092	.1941
	(.274)	(.227)
Bust effect	.077	.365*
	(.230)	(.189)
Democracy	.019	.029***
	(.013)	(.011)
Democracy^2	−.010***	−.013***
	(.003)	(.002)
ELF85	.767*	1.974***
	(.398)	(.331)
Sub-Saharan Africa	−.221	−.912***
	(.263)	(.214)
Middle East	.546**	1.276***
	(.272)	(.217)
GDP growth	−.037**	−.066***
	(.017)	(.014)
Land area$_{ln}$	.198***	.255***
	(.060)	(.047)
Population density$_{ln}$	.224***	.383***
	(.080)	(.066)
Civil war$_{(t-1)}$	3.096***	—
	(.125)	
Civil war $_{(t-5)}$	—	1.145***
		(.065)
N =	1961	1926
Pseudo R^2	.553	.263
Log likelihood =	−644.727	−1052.081
Likelihood ratio χ^2 =	1598.63	752.54

Notes: Analysis is by ordered logistic regression. Entries are unstandardized coefficients. Standard errors are in parentheses. ***, **, and * indicate significance at the .01, .05, and .10 levels, respectively.

Table 1.4 estimates the effects of the booms and bust on civil war. In short, as with regime failure, the economic turbulence of the late 1970s and 1980s does not seem to have affected adversely the likelihood or intensity of civil war in oil-rich states.[19] Oil wealth continues to lower the likelihood and scope of armed domestic conflict, although its effect is significant only in the five-year lagged model. In the model that uses a five-year lagged dependent variable, the bust effect is marginally significant at .10, but in the one-year lagged model it is not significant. In neither model is the boom effect significant.

[19] As mentioned above, Angola and Iraq are missing from the sample of highly dependent states. It is plausible that, were data available, their inclusion might affect the findings, since both states have been prone to armed domestic conflict since the 1970s.

As with the previous model, ethnolinguistic fractionalization, democracy (albeit only in the five-year lagged model), the Middle East dummy variable, land area, and population density exert a positive and significant effect on civil war. Democracy squared, the African dummy variable, and economic growth all have a significant negative relationship to the likelihood of civil war. Again, not even the economic unrest caused by oil price fluctuations produced any broad trends toward greater domestic conflict, suggesting that (a) regimes might well have been able to cope politically better than assumed, and (b) oil wealth has political effects that differ considerably from other kinds of resource wealth.

Oil Wealth and Social Protest

Tables 1.5 and 1.6 present the results of Poisson regressions estimating the effects that oil wealth and the booms and bust had on relative levels of antistate political protest. Again, oil wealth, as shown in table 1.5, is a powerful predictor of increased stability and lowers the expected level of protest significantly. One plausible conclusion from this finding is that repression is behind the lower levels of protest in oil-rich states, especially since democracy appears to increase relative levels of protest. To investigate the independent effects of repression, I replaced democracy's quadratic with the dummy for highly authoritarian regimes and re-estimated the models. Highly authoritarian regimes actually experienced considerably higher levels of protest than did others, and repression lowered the expected number of protests. However, it did not reduce the effect of oil wealth; this result is discussed in more detail in table 1.5. In any case, it appears that mechanisms other than repression drive the relative respite from protest that oil-rich states enjoy.

The Africa dummy, urban growth, economic growth, and democracy squared are all significantly and negatively related to the volume of expected protest activity. Interestingly, urban growth raises the likelihood of regime failure while lowering the level of antistate protest; this may be a two-stage effect in which urbanization produces pressure for democratization (which contributes to authoritarian breakdown) and, once democracy is consolidated but not highly coherent, maintains higher levels of social protest. Democracy, land area, and population density all exert significant positive effects on expected protest levels, although the land area effect is plausibly a function of larger countries having larger populations, other things being equal.

In one of the most interesting findings of all of these models, the most oil-rich states in the sample tended to face significantly higher levels of so-

TABLE 1.5.
Oil wealth and social protest, 1960–1999

Independent variable	Model 1	Model 2
Constant	−3.686***	−4.797***
	(.230)	(.232)
Oil/GDP	−1.829***	−2.248***
	(.301)	(.327)
Democracy	.017***	.020***
	(.003)	(.004)
Democracy^{2a}	−.002**	−.001*
	(.001)	(.001)
Sub-Saharan Africa	−.429***	−.427***
	(.068)	(.071)
Middle East	.099	.113
	(.079)	(.081)
Urban growth	−.142***	−.143***
	(.018)	(.018)
GDP growth	−.036***	−.044***
	(.004)	(.004)
Past regime failure	.009	−.013*
	(.008)	(.008)
Land area$_{ln}$	.286***	.355***
	(.014)	(.014)
Population density$_{ln}$	.317***	.431***
	(.020)	(.020)
Social protest$_{(t-1)}$	.057***	
	(.002)	
Social protest$_{(t-5)}$	—	.023***
		(.003)
N =	1681	1553
Pseudo R^2	.311	.269
Log likelihood =	−3348.830	−3391.064
Likelihood ratio χ^2 =	3024.94	2497.02

Notes: Analysis is by Poisson regression. Entries are unstandardized coefficients. Standard errors are in parentheses. ***, **, and * indicate significance at the .01, .05, and .10 levels, respectively.

[a] I re-estimated the models in tables 5 and 6 and included a dummy variable for highly authoritarian states instead of democracy squared, coding it "1" if the democracy score was between −6 and −10. Interestingly, it was a highly significant positive predictor of protest even when accounting for the boom and bust effects: its coefficient was .393 and the standard error was .099, with significance at p<.01. Given these results, the coefficient of democracy squared here is properly interpreted as indicating that only highly democratic, rather than both highly authoritarian and highly democratic, polities experience lower levels of social protest. The simple bivariate correlation between highly authoritarian government and regime failure is −0.096.

cial protest during the bust period. However, regimes in these states did not generally suffer during this period. Nor was civil war any more likely. Moreover, controlling for coercion showed that more repressive regimes actually faced more protest than regimes in other oil-rich states. It would be tempting to point to rent patronage as the answer to this puzzle, but by definition the bust period was one in which the oil revenues previously doled out in huge volumes shrank dramatically. In short, the explanatory failure of repression or continued patronage suggests that scholars of oil and poli-

TABLE 1.6.
Social protest during oil booms and oil busts

Independent variable	Model 1	Model 2
Constant	−3.684***	−4.790***
	(.231)	(.233)
Oil/GDP	−2.205***	−2.849***
	(.484)	(.566)
Boom effect	−.046	−.037
	(.084)	(.091)
Bust effect	.215***	.276***
	(.081)	(.089)
Democracy	.017***	.020***
	(.003)	(.004)
Democracy^2	−.002**	−.001*
	(.001)	(.001)
Sub-Saharan Africa	−.435***	−.432***
	(.069)	(.071)
Middle East	.082	.092
	(.080)	(.081)
Urban growth	−.138***	−.137***
	(.018)	(.018)
GDP growth	−.036***	−.044***
	(.004)	(.004)
Past regime failure	.008	−.014*
	(.008)	(.008)
Land area$_{ln}$	.286***	.354***
	(.014)	(.014)
Population density$_{ln}$	.316***	.429***
	(.020)	(.020)
Social protest$_{(t-1)}$	.057***	—
	(.002)	
Social protest$_{(t-5)}$	—	.023***
		(.003)
N =	1681	1553
Pseudo R^2	.312	.271
Log likelihood =	−3343.4264	−3383.7611
Likelihood ratio χ^2 =	3035.74	2511.63

Notes: Analysis is by Poisson regression. Entries are unstandardized coefficients. Standard errors are in parentheses. ***, **, and * indicate significance at the .01, .05, and .10 levels, respectively.

tics ought to look to other means by which regimes in these oil-rich countries maintained themselves through the tough times of the late 1980s and early 1990s.

A Non-numerical Summary

The conventional wisdom in rentier state and resource curse theory is that (a) oil wealth has similar effects on particular state institutions across many national settings and (b) the effect is generally to weaken those institutions.

My analysis of oil-exporting countries in the developing world calls these arguments into question and suggests that we have some rethinking to do. First, governments in oil-rich states, at least for most of the last half of the twentieth century, fared better than their oil-poor counterparts in terms of survival, even when they confronted economic crises. They appear to be slightly less prone to civil war and significantly less vulnerable to destabilizing antistate protests.[20] Further, it does not appear to be the case that all of these effects occur because rulers in oil-rich countries have poured their revenues into coercion or because they simply buy off their populations. In sum, there is a kind of black box here: the oil-exporting world is home to some of the most durable autocracies in modern history, and we lack an explanation for why that is so.

Durable authoritarian regimes in oil-rich states are not the outliers that the rentier state and resource curse theories have made them out to be. Rather, regimes like Suharto's in Indonesia, which lasted thirty-two years, Saddam Hussein's Ba'athist regime in Iraq, which lasted thirty-five years,[21] and the long-lived monarchies of the Persian Gulf appear to be more representative of broad trends of regime durability than the "big four" favorite cases of Iran, Nigeria, Algeria, and Venezuela.[22] More importantly, despite what Luciani (1987) and others have argued, the durability effect appears to have occurred independent of consistent access to rents with which regimes can buy legitimacy, since the busts created no trend toward regime crisis or instability in exporting states.

This trend of regime durability, its robustness throughout the oil bust period, and the absence of repression in determining the result all suggest that there is more to the durability of regimes in oil-rich states than patronage and coercion. Even when access to oil rents dropped dramatically, regimes in these states do not appear to have suffered much. Repression similarly fails to provide a full account of how it was that regimes in oil-rich states managed to lose much of the discretionary windfalls of the 1970s, face more protests, and still fall considerably less often than regimes in other developing countries. The most important conclusion reached here is that longevity—even through volatile price shocks—is the domi-

---

[20] To reiterate, the civil war debate is unresolved, and my results here are but one set from a large number of often contradictory studies. As Humphreys (2005) and Ross (2004b) have suggested, the contradictions may well stem from the sensitivity of these findings to model specification or how we measure civil war or both.

[21] Saddam Hussein officially became the president of Iraq only in 1979, but he had become the de facto ruler in 1968. It is also useful to remember that the regime did not end as a result of internal unrest.

[22] At least one critic has questioned Karl's categorization of Venezuela as an example of an unstable petro-state, noting that by most measures it was one of the most stable states in Latin America until the 1990s (see Ross 1999).

nant trend among oil exporters. This conclusion is bolstered by the significantly lower likelihood of civil war and the volume of anti-government political protest in oil-rich states.

That regimes in oil-rich states tend to fare better than others despite the volatility of their revenue base—even during the oil bust of 1986 and beyond—suggests two plausible mechanisms of regime maintenance that belie the weak-state assumptions associated with oil wealth. First, many of these regimes may have had robust social coalitions that went much deeper than the simple purchase of legitimacy. Second, regimes such as these may have built institutions that could provide nonrepressive responses to organized opposition. In short, such regimes may well have avoided the substitution of oil for statecraft, and there is little to guide scholarship in the study of how oil wealth and strong institutions might mix. Theories to explain, and studies to trace, the processes through which regimes in oil-rich countries might have indeed built strong states are currently in short supply.

Methodologically speaking, that most theories draw heavily from the experiences of the big four suggests that scholars should throw their nets more widely and devote more comparative attention to cases that, while less politically exciting, may help us understand the dynamics of oil wealth and political stability. As Karl notes, many such states account for a much smaller share of the world's oil supplies than the big four do (1997, 19). This, however, is insufficient justification for excluding them. If the goal is to explain the effects of oil on domestic politics, it makes more sense to select cases based on the role of oil in the domestic political economies of exporting states rather than on any country's clout or lack thereof on the global market.

Nonetheless, despite aggregate tendencies toward stability among the population of oil exporters when compared to nondependent states, it is clear from the continued scholarly attention paid to the big four that oil wealth can help to undermine political stability and undercut regimes in exporting states. Richly detailed case studies show clearly that oil has been significant in perpetuating weak institutions or stymieing reform in a number of exporting states; that they appear to be outliers is no reason to discard them. In concert with broad trends that belie the experience of these apparent outliers, the wide variation in levels of stability in oil-dependent states suggests that oil wealth might exert varying effects on regime durability and domestic conflict.[23] Large-N statistical analyses are unlikely to

---

[23] Herb (2005) makes this observation with regard to oil's effect on democracy, noting that it is argued simultaneously to have made Venezuela's pacted transition to democracy possible and to have stifled democracy elsewhere.

provide an answer to this question, as they are more useful for establishing correlations than explanations; case studies focused on the commonalities of unstable states have done little more to help us understand the nuances of oil politics.

I believe that a major part of this problem has been the way that scholars have conceptualized oil: as a structural variable willfully exerting its own effects. Despite wide variation in their approaches to the study of oil politics, both statistical and small-N/case study methodologists have underplayed the importance of timing. A number of recent works (Lowi 2004, Herb 1999, Bellin 1994, Okruhlik 1999) have hinted at this, but none has yet provided a comprehensive theory to explain how oil revenues might "do" different things depending on the context in which they do them. These works are a crucial reminder that oil revenues are filtered into domestic political settings by politicians with their own interests at stake, and those interests might be shaped in different ways depending on the circumstances of oil's entry into a political economy.

To foreshadow the theory developed in chapter 2, several states that rely on oil revenues now or that relied heavily on them during the 1980s and 1990s were oil-poor when they had to consolidate. The recently departed Suharto regime in Indonesia, Mahathir's government in Malaysia, Mubarak's Egypt, and several others have combined oil wealth with impressive durability and the ability to deal adeptly with numerous crises. Thus, one avenue of research that looks especially promising is the analysis of regimes for which oil wealth came along after rulers had already had to hand out other resources—power and influence among them—in order to survive. The late arrival of oil to such settings may have added a layer of substantial patronage rents to an already robust regime project, helping to explain the extraordinary durability of some regimes in major exporting countries. A broader focus on the conditions under which oil revenues become available to political leaders is a promising first step toward constructing theories of oil and politics in which politics remains important.

Uncertain Conclusions and a Return to the Literature

Why is it that despite a dramatic drop in their profits from oil sales in the mid-1980s, few of these exporters suffered major political crises? The ability of many regimes in rentier states to survive such serious fiscal calamity deserves a level of attention it has not yet received. In my view, two flawed conclusions—first, by small-N studies that predict instability and ignore contrary cases and, second, by large-N studies that assume a link between instability and other factors—persist because of methodological problems.

Small-N studies fall into the dual traps of selection bias (Geddes 1991, 2003; Lieberson 1992) and misuse of Mill's method of difference (Tilly 1997). In the first case, researchers choose cases that evince the outcome they want to explore and then conclude that other cases without the desired outcome must be exceptions or anomalies. In the second case, they use the method of difference to conclude, when dealing with cases with many differences but a major similarity like dependence on oil exports, that outcomes must be driven by that one shared variable.[24] Large-N studies tend to fall victim to an equally common trap, the conflation of correlation and causation and the assumption of plausible but untested mechanisms. The result is compelling connections linking oil wealth to both authoritarianism and economic stagnation, even as the relationships between these outcomes and the viability of regimes remain entirely undetermined. There remain two problems, then. One is to explain why it is that there is so much variation in the ability of regimes in oil states to weather crises, and a sample of cases with the same outcome is unlikely to produce that explanation. The second is to find the mechanisms at work behind the large-N finding—that, ceteris paribus, oil states tend to be more stable than others. I think the answer is not in abandoning case studies but selecting them more carefully for reasons other than conformity of outcome.

The Revisionists

A group of scholars has begun to challenge the rentier orthodoxy, and, given the results outlined above, their contributions to the study of oil and politics merit detailed attention. Where rentier theory tends to structural determinism, especially in small-N or single-case studies, these studies have shown how history and agency can shape oil's impact in domestic settings.

Miriam Lowi disputes the centrality of oil as the prime culprit in Algeria's political instability: "narrowly-based authoritarian rule, plus weak institutions of conflict management preceded the inception of oil-based development" (2004, 97). When oil coincided with "the 'national question'—who are we, and what do we want to achieve together," it reinforced preexisting tendencies in the trajectory of state development, and it was

---

[24] I do not treat this problem in detail here; see Tilly (1997) for a thorough discussion. Mill himself went to great lengths to explain how his method of difference could almost never be of use in the social world because there were too many variables at work and too much interaction between variables. See Mill (1860), ch. 10 § 8. In empirical terms, developing states in which the major export is oil tend to share many other traits, including their rough places in the global economy, attempts to "catch up" rapidly via late development, a colonial past, disadvantaged integration into global markets, and ethnic diversity, to name a few. All of these raise the question of oil's true centrality.

only in combination with this trajectory that the oil bust of the mid-1980s provoked a major regime crisis (85). Institutional trajectories and the developmental pathways down which states travel are at the heart of Lowi's analysis.

Michael Herb's elegant comparative study of why monarchies succeed or fail in the Middle East also points to the need to factor in prior institutional arrangements before reaching any conclusions about the effects of oil (1999). Where rentier state theorists point to their disproportionate oil reserves as the cause for the longevity of the Gulf monarchies, Herb points out that two—Kuwait and Saudi Arabia—had in place institutionalized means of succession well before the oil booms. Those institutions consisted primarily of regularized practices of dynasticism, and oil merely allowed the ruling families to extend familial privileges to a greater number of individuals, stabilizing what would have otherwise become contentious battles over succession. The remaining Gulf monarchies learned from their neighbors after independence and adopted similar systems. It is the act of vesting more and more citizens in the continuity of the monarchic system, rather than simply access to oil rents, that drives the impressive durability of these monarchies—note the crucial role played by agents and domestic institutions in mediating the effects of oil revenues. To tie Herb's discussion more directly to oil, it is as a resource that strengthened preexisting dynastic institutions rather than one that substituted for them.

Gwenn Okruhlik, although included in the "mainstream" rentier theorists above by virtue of arguing that oil is a destabilizing force, provides a nuanced account of how it does so (1999). Regional disparities in the distribution of oil rents in Saudi Arabia, in her argument, provided the resources necessary to mobilize dissent against the ruling al-Saud. Thus, it is politics rather than oil per se driving the analysis and, in particular, decisions made by the ruling family about which regions to favor and which ones to marginalize when it came to distributing oil rents. As she says, "Money does not spend itself" (297). Nor does it exert its effects in a vacuum; as other revisionists have noted, Okruhlik argues that "oil enters into an ongoing process of development" (309).

Together, these new accounts of oil and politics provide us with a starting point for reconceptualizing oil and for theorizing how it might affect regime durability and state capacity. Historical legacies and prior institutional structures all take center stage in these studies, and it is arguably clear that, over and above their theoretical differences, they imply empirical regularities. In particular, they imply, first, that politics is central to the effects of oil wealth; because oil revenues do not spend themselves, closer attention is due the interests of rulers under various conditions. Second, the absorption of oil revenues into ongoing development programs and processes can produce differential effects, but we lack a general account of how differential effects are produced across oil-exporting states. Despite these commonalities, these studies lack a means for unifying their insights into a comprehensive account of how resource wealth affects regimes and states over time. In the next chapter, I draw on the insights outlined here as well as prominent theories of institutions and change to develop a theory of oil wealth and regime durability and outline a research design and the methods with which to assess the theory.

CHAPTER 2

Explaining Regime Durability in Oil-Rich States

Oil, Opposition, and Late Development

"History will not blame oil. It will blame people."

—*Pat Utomi (2002)*

The oil booms of the 1970s dramatically increased the revenues available to state leaders in exporting countries (see figure 2.1). The quintupling of oil prices led to a radical shift in capital flows from developed to exporting nations and gave rulers in oil states huge discretionary budgets. Governments in these states injected the windfall revenues into their domestic economies in very similar and problematic ways, and in a short period much of the exporting world saw specific effects related to inflation, the booming oil sector, and exchange rate effects occurred in much of the exporting world in a short period (Gelb 1988; Auty 1990). Following the booms, the early 1980s saw a gradual decline in export earnings, with the harshest shock coming with the price collapse of 1986. Rulers in all of these countries were confronted with severe capital deficiencies, powerful vested interests, unsustainable industrial projects, and other economic problems that often provoked political crises.

Yet rulers in these countries fared quite differently during these volatile years. In Algeria, Iran, Nigeria, and Venezuela, which many scholars considered to be exemplary but which I demonstrated to be outliers in chapter 1, oil's economic impact seems to have helped to undercut regimes. In other countries, including Egypt, Iraq, Indonesia, Malaysia, and Tunisia, oil seems to have helped regimes to hold on to power, even through the crises of the boom and bust periods. As I explain below, the keys to explaining these variations lie in the onset of late development—it was at this critical juncture that rulers established institutional and structural patterns of state involvement in their respective economies and societies. I argue that

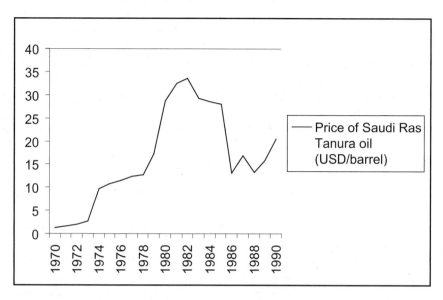

Figure 2.1. World oil prices based on Saudi crude, 1970–90

Note: The per-barrel price of oil leaving Ras Tanura, a port on the eastern coast of Saudi Arabia, is the traditional benchmark figure for the world oil market.

we must place the entry of oil into politics in the context of late development in order to understand its later effects on regime viability.

Studying the onset of late development and its legacies within a carefully chosen sample of oil-exporting states presents an opportunity to assess how oil became a part of the state building project and how it subsequently affected regime longevity. In this chapter, I adopt a framework for analyzing the role of oil in state building and development. The approach I outline below helps to move beyond other explanations that focus on structurally determined, voluntarist, or ad hoc causes by accentuating the centrality of leaders' decisions at critical junctures in the statebuilding process on institutional development, state-society relations, and subsequent trajectories of change. To adapt Pat Utomi's statement at the opening of this chapter, history will not blame oil; history will blame people for creating histories of oil.

This approach also incorporates the insights of revisionist rentier state theorists, for whom prior institutional configurations, agency, and historical legacies are crucial to explaining the effects of oil revenues. By integrating these contributions into a theory that can account for multiple effects of oil wealth, I hope to move the study of the politics of resource wealth beyond both structurally determined rentier theory and case-by-case refutations of it. The theory is grounded in two ideas specific to dependence on oil wealth. The first is that oil wealth is a political resource in the hands of politicians, rather than a structural variable that moves individuals in preset directions. The second is that the use and effects of oil in domestic politics depend heavily on the circumstances under which oil enters a domestic political economy.

I outline in greater detail in this section how I think the questions of oil and regime durability are best answered, but, to begin with, let us think about state building as a process that unfolds over time. Effects observed at one point are likely the result of state-building decisions made earlier—perhaps much earlier—rather than the static effects of decisions made during one "snapshot" view of history (Pierson 2000a, 2003). To borrow Pierson's geological analogy, regime durability during a crisis is much like an earthquake, whose causes manifest over time but lead to outcomes that happen quickly. Rather than explain how well regimes can weather political protests by pointing to the most proximate decisions that state leaders make during periods of protest, such an approach demands a close look at how they built (or did not build) political organizations and institutions in the years preceding those protests.

A Historical-Causal Framework

In economics and political science, path dependence has become something of a fad. It often assumes a folksy logic, something like "one damn thing follows another" (David 1985, 332). More than simply asserting that history matters, though, the logic of historical causation can be extremely useful for analyzing temporal processes in which causes are often temporally remote from their effects. To take one example, confronted with two photos of elite runners near the end of a marathon, one might posit that the winner triumphed because she exhibited a superior stride at a crucial stage late in the race. However, that superior stride did not emerge from nowhere; it was almost certainly the result of a long-term training regimen, extensive efforts to improve technique, and good genes. Thus, while the sporting equivalent of comparative statics would tend to focus on runners' technique late in a race, the more historically minded of us would look to past patterns of training.[1] Either because of lengthy causal chains in which one set of events sets subsequent ones in motion, or because events at a

[1] Thanks to Jason Brownlee for suggesting this analogy.

critical juncture lead to decisions that produce institutions or structures, causes present only at the outset can continue to exert their effects over long periods of time (Pierson 2003, 195–98; Stinchcombe 1968, 118–21).

Here I refer to the type of historical causation in which initial conditions lead to institutional persistence (and to a certain role for oil) that helps to shape actors' choices further along in time. I refer to this path of institutional persistence as a trajectory (see Aminzade 1992, 462–69); below I explain how different decisions and actions during a critical juncture created distinct political trajectories. In comparative political economy, historical moments of dramatic change in the economic development of individual states have often taken center stage as the critical junctures that determine not just economic but political outcomes as well. For Barrington Moore (1966), the commercialization of agriculture was such a juncture; for Alexander Gerschenkron (1962), the onset of internationally oriented industrial production; for James Mahoney (2001), liberal economic reforms; and for David and Ruth Berins Collier (1991), the incorporation of organized labor into national politics. I analyze a different economic juncture here— the initiation of late development—and hypothesize its effects on institutional trajectories. What draws these disparate historical moments together analytically is that in each case countries embarked on a path of economic transformation that fundamentally changed, and in most cases powerfully increased, the role of the state in the economy and in society. When they did, the decisions and subsequent policies of state leaders had powerful effects on political institutions.

The historical-causal framework I use here traces the processes of state and regime building across time by employing three analytically discrete concepts. At the most abstract level, these are the initial conditions that provide the options available at the juncture and provide incentives for rulers' choices; the critical juncture itself, at which rulers make choices; and the subsequent trajectories of structural or institutional development that emerge from rulers' choices. Critical junctures are points in time at which a number of options are available to actors; often the choices are made necessary by the inadequacy of current institutions to deal with some problem at hand, hence the juncture. Such junctures are "critical" because, once decisions are made, they become progressively more difficult to reverse. An equilibrium emerges from the juncture, and that equilibrium tends to reinforce itself. Arthur (1994) and Pierson (2000b) refer to this type of equilibrium as one generated by "increasing returns."[2]

---

[2] Note that in Arthur's work the words "critical juncture" do not appear. Rather, such moments are called "small events," not because they are unimportant but because they fall below the radar screen of economic theory and are thus untheorizable. I argue here, as many juncture theorists do, that they can in fact be theorized.

Whereas path-dependent analysis is often used to explain suboptimal outcomes (from the point of view of the actors who made decisions at the juncture), there are also path-dependent outcomes that are optimal, at least from the point of view of decisionmakers. As I outline in the coming chapters, Suharto in Indonesia made what looked during the critical juncture period to be vastly suboptimal decisions (for him and his regime) about coalition building and domestic revenue extraction. He gave up real policy authority to a number of social groups and expended significant political capital to build institutions for domestic revenue collection. Those initial decisions set in motion a trajectory of strong institutions and ties to organized social forces that, over time, paradoxically turned his early setbacks into strengths.

Initial conditions determine the type of trajectory that emerges from a critical juncture. These conditions shape the choices available to actors during the juncture itself, alternately constraining and enabling the number and scope of options. Thus, actors are not entirely free to choose as they please, but, as is always the case when institutions undergo flux, they can exercise more autonomy than they can once institutions are in place. In short, then, what makes a critical juncture distinct from other periods is that it generates choice points that "put countries (or other units) onto paths of development that track certain outcomes and that cannot be easily broken or reversed" (Mahoney 2001, 7). Before the juncture, a much more extensive set of options is available; afterward, institutions and structures, now much more stable and defined, considerably narrow the range of choices available. Institutional or structural trajectories are the "paths" down which countries travel after a critical juncture. Reversals are not, strictly speaking, impossible, but they are made very difficult by the "entrenchments of certain institutional arrangements" (Levi 1997, 28). Thus, it is not only institutional conditions that can lock in outcomes; structural ones can too. Indeed, initial structural conditions in this case generated outcomes by encouraging certain kinds of decisions about institution building.

Why Is Late Development the "Critical" Juncture?

In this study, I classify the initiation of late development, here defined as a phase incorporating full-scale industrialization in which the state actively takes the largest role in the economy, as a critical juncture for developing states. During this economic transition, rulers attempted nothing less than to redefine completely the way that the people they governed made, consumed, and distributed goods. It was critical not just because of the changes it produced in the state's role in the society and economy, but also because it was a crucial moment in the state-building process itself (Bellin 2002; Chatelus 1987). I focus on the initiation of late development because in each of these countries and in late-developing states more generally, the large-scale policy intervention of the state politicized the economy, created new economic winners and losers, and fundamentally changed the role of the state in society. The "big push" initiated in Iran and Indonesia and many others in the developing world required whole new state agencies and the construction of new relationships and new modes of confronting social groups. The juncture in each country took place under different conditions, and the initial conditions of that juncture produced powerful effects on long-term political development.

Those effects hinged on the changes that late development induced in domestic political economies. The simple public, political act of declaring and then embarking on late development directly implicated specific rulers and regimes in the health of the economy. In the postcolonial world, dozens of regimes put their national ambitions to the test by attempting to accomplish industrial transformation. Despite the long-term impact of initiating these state-led development programs, researchers have paid relatively little attention to its specific attributes and effects. The political and fiscal difficulties with which late development is inaugurated can tell us a great deal about the likely course of ensuing institutional development, as it strongly influences the decisions made by state leaders in the early stages of late development. The incentives and constraints imposed by political and fiscal pressures encouraged decisions that affected the absorption of oil revenues into state budgets and then strongly shaped states and their relations with organized social groups. Thus, the sequencing of major political and fiscal challenges relative to the onset of late development sheds light on why it was that some regimes were able to "deflect" the destabilizing effects of the oil booms and others were not. More broadly, the intersections of internal trajectories and international shocks underscore how pre-existing domestic political and economic configurations produced varying responses to the oil booms of the 1970s (Collier and Mahon, 1993; Collier and Collier 1991; Gourevitch 1986).

A Theory of Oil, Late Development, and Regime Durability

The model I develop below suggests a counterintuitive answer to why rulers in oil-rich countries had such different experiences dealing with boom- and bust-related crises: that the most vulnerable regimes with respect to social forces during the early years of late development seemed to be the most adept at fending off later challenges. I hypothesize that, at the onset of late development, (1) access to externally derived revenues such as oil wealth and (2) the strength of organized political opposition created incentives for rulers' decisions that can explain much of the political trajectories that they followed during later boom and bust periods. In short, where it becomes available only after a difficult consolidation period, oil wealth can facilitate, rather than hinder, institutional development and coalition building. This point is a crucial one for the study of oil wealth and politics. As I showed in chapter 1, this trajectory appears to be the prevalent trend among oil exporters, even though we have no compelling explanation for how it is that resource wealth might bolster state building or long-term regime viability during crisis.

Historical Causality, Rational Choice Theory, and Critical Junctures

As mentioned above, I believe that close attention to the inception of late development can tell us a great deal about later paths of institutional development and about a regime's ability to weather periods of protest. It is in the context of prior decisions about state institutions that oil affects politics, so that *when* a regime begins to rely on oil revenues is more important than the atemporal question of *whether* it does. State-led development programs that precede rather than follow the onset of oil wealth and that are inaugurated in an atmosphere of political challenge create incentives for state leaders that may trump the destructive effects of petro-politics for a long while. In developing the line of argument below on the importance of political opposition, I consciously incorporate late industrialization and questions of oil revenues into a larger body of work on the political economy of development (Bates 1981, 1988; Migdal 1988, 2001b; Geddes 1994; Waldner 1999). The political exigencies of staying in office or, in Migdal's language, "the politics of survival," compel decisions about major economic change that are often largely driven by non-economic considerations (1988, 206–37). The stakes involved in staying in power, especially the strength and organizational clout of political opposition, strongly affect rulers' decisions about building a ruling coalition. The question here is this: How does political opposition affect the politics of making the state the biggest player in the economy?

In situations like these, politicians want not only to accomplish their policy goals—even goals like development that are often born out of a deep commitment to a vision of the nation's future—but also to remain in power (Migdal 1988; Geddes 1994, 1999). After all, nothing can be accomplished if one is overthrown. Thus, a broad array of literature on the political economy of development proceeds on the assumption that leaders act as though they want to stay in power. Whether they can or not depends on how skillfully they deal with potential social challengers, gather and mobilize resources, and build institutions to protect themselves (Gandhi and Przeworski 2001; Bertocchi and Spagat 2001; Wintrobe 1998). Given this desire to stay in power, economic resources like oil revenues should be thought of as part of a broader political economy rather than constitutive of it, one means among many with which rulers can coopt social groups or build institutions. Finally, the degree to which they need to do so depends on the degree and scope of organized opposition to rulers.

Thus, the availability of oil revenues stands alongside the level of organized opposition to a regime as a major influence on the likely course of institutional development. Trends of continuity from the past persist, to be sure, but the initiation of state-led development programs shifts trajectories of institutional change in crucial ways. During this period, state leaders assess the sociopolitical landscape—weighing short- against long-term planning, choosing domestic and international enemies and allies, and making choices about whence and from whom to extract both economic and political resources. It is in this context that theoretical tools from institutional economics are useful. Grounded as they are in the instrumental rationality assumptions of microeconomics, they allow us to model systematically the origins of various institutional configurations in the goals and strategies leaders use to achieve them. Further, the context of the radical changes in state economic policy—a time of uncertainty for institutions, both formal and informal—is arguably an analytical domain in which rational choice theory is among the best suited, for it provides a concrete and precise way to derive expectations about various choices and courses of action under conditions of high uncertainty and even higher stakes for given choices. In cases such as these, structural conditions can be readily assessed and analyzed, as can institutional constraints. In brief, where existing institutions and modes of politics offer no "easy" way out, political leaders are in my view most likely to act instrumentally, so deriving hypotheses about their behavior should be most feasible.

It seems reasonable to suppose that leaders want to consolidate their development programs and would generally prefer to do it in the least costly way. Their preferences and strategies are central to explaining why institutions of the state and patterns of state-society relations take the early forms they do. My argument presumes that leaders would rather not have to make substantial concessions to social groups and, where possible, would prefer to pay them off with easily obtained external revenues like those based on the sale of oil. It also presumes that leaders would rather not have to tax: contra Levi's extraction-driven state (1988), I follow Chaudhry in assuming that politicians would actually prefer never to have to make the sorts of bargains with domestic groups that can pay taxes (1997). Thus, the no-tax, no-concession dynamic is the preferred choice. If this option is not available, the much more politically costly option of tax-and-concede may be necessary.

Nonetheless, assigning preferences ex ante and studying institutional change as a matter of comparative statics—comparing data points A and B and inferring what took place in between—misses a large part of the picture: how those preferences come to be formed over time by the experiences of development, state building, and subsequent patterns of institutional change. On the other hand, historical institutionalists in comparative politics (Steinmo, Thelen, and Longstreth 1992; Thelen 1999; Pierson 2000a; Migdal 1997; Katznelson 1997; Mahoney 2001) have stressed the need to view institutions (1) dynamically, as configurations that continually shape not only the strategies but the goals of actors as well and (2) as the results of power struggles rather than efficient mechanisms for coordinating aggregate preferences.

After the initial period, past decisions, given physical form in state institutions, alternately constrain and enable future policies in ways that can only be understood by tracing the processes of institutional development, a methodological tool that has since been incorporated into rational choice research (Levi 1997; Bates et al. 1998) but that finds its origins in historical institutionalism (Katzenstein 1985; North 1981, 1990). This project seeks to explain this variance by analyzing a critical juncture in the formation of states in the developing world—the onset of late development—that required a dramatic retooling of state institutions and of state-society linkages. The degree of fiscal and political challenge to these development programs weighs heavily on the types of decisions made about where to invest in institutions, however, and whether or not to build a social support base around development. Variation of these two factors—rent access and opposition strength—suggests the following four hypotheses about initial decisions and political trajectories as a function of enacting late development.

> **Hypothesis 1a:** Where state-led development begins without significant external revenues, such as from oil, leaders confront fiscal scarcity, which compels tough decisions oriented toward investing in extractive agencies to collect revenues domestically.

> **Hypothesis 1b:** Where easy access to external revenues, such as from oil, precedes the initiation of state-led development, leaders confront no necessity for powerful institutions. Early decisions are likely to be oriented to shifting the focus of government from extraction to redistribution.

Hypothesis 2a: Where state-led development begins in the face of a well-organized opposition, state leaders are likely to build early alliances with powerful social groups and to make significant concessions to those groups in return for their support. These coalitions give regimes political "breathing space" as well as a long-term capability to monitor these groups, even if later they oppose the regime.

Hypothesis 2b: Where state-led development begins without an organized opposition, state leaders are unlikely to make any serious attempt to build strong coalitions in favor of development policies. Over time, the likely disengagement from active contact with social groups leaves regimes with little reliable information about discontent and little ability to foresee it.

These hypotheses suggest a number of possible outcomes on the measures of state capacity and regime viability, and they are presented in the stylized model in table 2.1.

Implications of the Theory

What the hypotheses do not suggest are explicit means for testing them. Developing observable implications of a broad theory like this one—and illustrating the mechanisms linking initial conditions, choices, and trajectories to outcomes—is likely to produce a more accurate picture of how state capacity and regime viability develop over time. It is important to seek a way to assess state capacity with regard to social control if we are to

TABLE 2.1.
A working model of development trajectories

	Demanding consolidation —organized social opposition	Undemanding consolidation— disorganized or weak social opposition
No access to oil revenues during consolidation	**Strong and flexible state institutions** **Strong regime with powerful ruling coalition and robust party**	Reasonably strong administrative state Weak regime coalition
Oil-dependent during consolidation	Relatively weak administrative state Powerful pro-regime coalition, robust party	**Weak and oil-dependent state** **Weak regime with weak ties to society**

understand varying levels of it (Migdal 1988, appendix; Arbetman and Kugler 1997; Shafer 1994; Jackman 1993). Measuring the strength of authoritarian states relative to society, there are three main areas in which they exercise social control: information and regulation via fiscal *extraction*, legitimation via *mobilization* of official parties and ideologies, and *administration* of social institutions in local settings with central political authority. Taken together, these three indicators should give us a reasonably accurate view of state capacity and of patterns of state-society relations. Consequently, in the next two chapters my empirical analysis focuses on the effectiveness of tax bureaucracies, on the organization and utilization of official state parties, and on the efficacy of local government. It is in areas like these in which individuals and groups actually interact with the government on a daily basis—demands made in both directions, resources taken and redistributed, loyalty needed, loyalty offered for a price—that studying a country's state institutions can tell us something about its state-society relations. The nature of those relations, in turn, can tell us a good deal about a regime's likely overall ability to foresee when and whence social dissent is likely to emerge and its ability to use a combination of rewards, sanctions, and symbols to forestall its materializing. Together they should provide us with a thorough picture of how it is that regimes exercise social control.

Taxation

Information about who is part of a society, what they do to earn a living, where they live, and so on—all this is one of the benefits of the larger information-gathering project of a centralized tax bureaucracy. The sources of state revenues have powerful effects on the long-term development of political institutions (Chaudhry 1997; Levi 1988; Lieberman 2003; Tilly 1975, 1990; Weber 1978; Vandewalle 1998). During the process of state building, the extraction of taxes entails making decisions about from whom and how to acquire the money and politicizes those decisions by mandating bargaining with social groups over the representation-taxation equation, which generates revenue as it builds patterns of interaction between state and society. Thus, not only the information engendered by a robust tax bureaucracy but also the consequent capacity to keep an eye on social groups powerfully affects an authoritarian state's ability to exercise social control (Levi 1988). Further, suddenly imposed extractive grievances may, in the right circumstances, provoke violent resistance from social groups. We might recall that Skocpol's compelling model of social revolution begins with agrarian monarchies getting themselves into trouble by attempting to extract ever larger sums from the peasantry to pay for armies that had been overextended in foreign wars (1979).

Following Kiren Chaudhry's lead, assessing the level of taxation before and during the first oil boom may tell us a great deal about changes in the extractive capacities of the Indonesian and Iranian states, not to mention their abilities to monitor potential political crises. Moreover, as she points out, "the decline of a tax bureaucracy has unintended consequences that bode ill for the long-term development of all parts of the bureaucracy. Extractive institutions are the base of administration; without them, regulation and distribution are impossible" (1997, 33). If she is right, comparative assessment of extractive capacities will highlight larger issues of state capacity. However, despite the often powerful theoretical arguments about extractive capacity as a central determinant of political change, it can not tell us everything. As attractive as the single-function models of taxing states may be, we need to look at states as more than tax agencies with institutional hinterlands. To begin with, we ought to look at the means by which effective political loyalty is guaranteed (or compromised) by official political parties, which have often played more important roles in late developers than extractive institutions.

Ruling Parties and Regime Coalitions

The above model suggests that official parties, no less than other state institutions, ought to vary in capacity according to the circumstances under which the regimes began late development. After a difficult initiation period, we should expect political leaders to build a party apparatus capable of genuinely vesting individuals in the regime's continuity as a way of building support "walls" against the opposition. In concrete terms, recruitment efforts are likely to be aimed at individuals by offering job longevity, payoffs, and the like in return for loyalty to the party. Even where the official ideology clashes with that of an important social group, we ought to see real efforts at cooptation using other—material—means.

After an easy initiation of late development, we ought to see largely the opposite—in general, less dedicated efforts at recruitment. For instance, rather than beat the streets in pursuit of individual recruitees, party leaders are likely to pursue less dogged strategies such as signing on whole organizations—businesses, schools and universities, government agencies—so that individuals located in those organizations might have no direct contact with the party itself. In such cases, official parties may serve as little more than mouthpieces for governments. Absent a compelling reason to give them teeth, there is no incentive to vest parties with genuine institutional power and plenty of reason to worry that strong parties might become alternative power sources. Implicit in these two hypotheses about party building is the assumption that looking at gross membership figures will tell us little—what we must do is go to ground, analyze the ways that official parties actually interacted with citizens and attempted, with varying degrees, of success to ensure their loyalty. At election time, the regime would expect their votes; between elections, their political acquiescence in return for material favors.

Local Government

Studying the state in terms of its relationship to society precludes an exclusively center-based approach to analysis. Elite decisions are crucial to be sure, but even more important in assessing state capacity is how those decisions are carried out at the local level (Hyden 1980; Migdal 1988; Migdal, Kohli, and Shue 1994). Two specific questions emerge from this line of thinking. First, how capable are local agencies and institutions of enacting the decisions handed down from the commanding heights of government—how sure can state leaders be that their institutions and decisions trump local ones? Second, how willing are they—how strong a hierarchy exists to ensure earnest compliance with central decisions?

A difficult initiation period is likely to compel state leaders to make difficult decisions focused on long-term institutional development. Having faced a tough struggle to consolidate their power, they are likely to work hard to increase the power of local government while trying to tie it as closely as possible to central control. On the other hand, after a painless initiation to late development funded by ample revenues derived from export earnings, state leaders are not likely to pay much attention to local government. After all, with so little need to extract revenues from society, they will perceive little challenge from below. Thus, rulers are likely to give relatively little attention to building local government, so that over time it is likely to deteriorate, eventually becoming incapable of extracting much in the way of either revenues or information.

This multifaceted approach to assessing state institutions and state-society relations may give a more complete picture why certain regimes survive while others do not. Analyzing states through these three lenses makes possible an assessment of their capacities across a much broader range of measures than if the focus were solely on extraction, mobilization, or administration. Moreover, it enables us to explain how states and regimes may "score" well in some areas and poorly in others—in other words, how the different parts of the state apparatus and regime support structure come to demonstrate such varying capabilities. Finally, it allows for the testing of concrete and observable implications of a broad theory and for the elucidation of theoretically coherent trajectories.

This approach also makes it possible to avoid assuming capacity across similar-looking formal institutions and to concentrate on the "practices" embedded in institutions (Migdal 2001a). Where a pure institutional approach might take for granted the functions and capabilities of given sets of institutions like local government or official parties based on their existence alone, this cross-case focus on sets of institutions shows how institutions that look the same on the surface might in fact have very different capabilities to extract, mobilize, and administer. This state-in-society corrective to institutionalism is crucial if we are to understand not just how the choice of institutions enables autocrats to survive (e.g., Gandhi and Przeworski 2001; Geddes 1999) but also how choices related to building those institutions may be obscured by a too-formal approach to studying them.

An important requisite of studying states this way (Migdal, Kohli, and Shue 1994; Migdal 1997) is in-depth treatment of their institutional peculiarities. I am arguing here that formal similarities in the institutional configurations of states can hide serious substantive differences in the way they work. Vindicating that contention requires the kind of close attention to how institutions like official parties work in practice that can only be met with field research. I return to this issue in more detail in the conclusion, but for now I want to state simply that we can not understand the means by which regimes like the Shah's or Suharto's either failed or succeeded at eliciting support by analyzing their state apparatuses as typologies. "Single-party" or "patrimonial" status applies to both of the regimes, and yet such labels tell us little about the day-to-day strategies of regime maintenance—the practices of the state that reveal its underlying coherence or weakness (Migdal 2001a, 15–16; Smith 2003b).

Research Design, Case Selection, and the Conduct of Research

For a number of reasons, comparative politics has witnessed a "return" to the comparative method in recent years (see, for instance, Coppedge 1999, 2001; Collier and Mahoney 1996; Bennett 1997; and Bennett and George 1997). First, even if one takes for granted that more cases are necessarily better, a particular problem in the study of developing states is the lack of easily available quantitative data appropriate for answering the questions that many scholars find important. Generalization can run into a data problem if by generalization one takes statistical testing as the best first cut.

Second, it is far from obvious that what some call the "statistical world-view" is always the best starting point (McKeown 1999). Comparative-historical analysts are increasingly pointing to the analytical advantages of studying relatively small numbers of cases at close range: better definition of cases and of apparent outliers (Ragin 1997), the establishment of causal chains that are often lost in large-N analysis (Bennett 1997), and the ability to account for differing historical circumstances (Rueschemeyer and Stephens 1997), to name but a few. Third, contradictions between small-N conclusions and large-N findings, like the contradiction discussed in the conclusion, suggest that for many questions we have not gotten as far in the process of theory building as we had hoped. Fourth, cross-national statistical results, such as the repression- and patronage-independent relationship between oil wealth and increased regime durability that I outlined in the conclusion, raise serious questions about mechanisms that often go assumed but untested. In this case, there is no way to tell from this broad result how it is that oil states as a group seemed to fare so well during the bust: we are missing the mechanisms of explanation.

With causal uncertainties such as this, it is only by engaging carefully chosen cases in depth that we can hope to find the answers. First, the comparative method can lead to the empirical confirmation of theorized mechanisms tying macro-causes to macro-outcomes; indeed, a focus on historical causation can trace the links between cause and effect over time. Second, case studies, and especially carefully constructed comparative studies, make it possible to test carefully each sub-hypothesis in a larger causal argument at close range, assuring validity before moving outward to confront issues of generality. Given a common interest in confirming the validity of theoretical arguments in a limited setting before taking them as given in a broad cross-national study, small-N comparative studies are a promising means of getting at questions like the one at hand here. By studying the characteristics of oil wealth and late development within a most-similar research design (Przeworski and Teune 1970), it should be possible to trace the long-term effects of oil in such countries and to make more precise statements about what sorts of states and regimes are likely to emerge from varying types of antecedent conditions.

Methodologically speaking, reorienting the study of resource wealth in this way suggests an avenue for fruitful research. Carefully constructed comparative studies, especially using cases chosen for maximum variation on the dependent variable—which I define here as regime resilience during the crises of the boom-bust years—seem the best bet to provide the requisite detail to uncover causal mechanisms, to elucidate political trajectories, and to provide the validity of conclusions necessary to overcome the dual problems of selection bias (Geddes 1991) and prediction as explanation (see for example Elster 1989). In particular, a structured comparison in which other factors—ethnic diversity, the structure of political rule, past political history, and the oil booms, to name a few—can be held fairly constant presents in my view the most likely means of teasing out the ways in which oil comes to exert different effects on the durability of authoritarian regimes. How it does so is an important empirical question; there are ample cases for analysis if we restructure questions about oil and politics to remove the assumption that oil can act in some monolithic way to shape political outcomes. In the next section, I outline the rationale for pairing Iran and Indonesia.

The Case for the Cases

The pairing of Iran and Indonesia poses a particularly compelling puzzle, as the two states exhibited significant similarities in the structure of political rule, economic policy and focus on rapid industrialization, and integration into the world economy. Each country was flooded with oil revenues during the first oil boom in 1973–74. Major social protests against authoritarian governments in both countries erupted in 1977, suggesting widespread unpopularity. By the end of 1979, however, Suharto's New Order government in Indonesia had reestablished political control, while the Shah of Iran fled into exile. In Indonesia Suharto would rule for another twenty years, whereas in Iran the next two decades were dominated by Islamist revolutionaries, as is the case today. Why did these two regimes show such dramatically different abilities to control social opposition? More generally, why do some rentier states exhibit major weaknesses in the face of social opposition while others successfully maintain power throughout both boom and bust periods?

Late Development in Two Large Oil-Rich States

Rulers in both Iran and Indonesia embarked their respective countries on a program of rapid, state-directed late development. The Shah of Iran, and President Suharto of Indonesia both hoped to use late development to catapult their countries into modernity and, further, to cement their own rule by banking on the quick arrival of prosperity. In Iran and Indonesia, this transition to late development took place during the 1960s (1961–64 and 1967–70, respectively).

In 1961, Mohammed Reza Pahlavi, the Shah of Iran, began the White Revolution, a sweeping socioeconomic reform program aimed at modernizing Iran by transferring land ownership from elites to peasants, accelerating industrialization, mobilizing women into politics through enfranchisement and a state-controlled women's movement, and expanding the country's educational system. The steady rise of oil revenues to the Iranian government made this ambitious program fundable without the politically costly new extraction of revenues from Iranian society. Although the Shah faced limited and diffuse opposition from landowners, the *ruhaniyun* (Shi'a religious leadership), intellectuals, and the bazaar community, by 1963 he had successfully consolidated his White Revolution regime and had done so without facing any serious threat to his rule. In the process, he took away the political power of the landowners, undid the economic centrality of the bazaar, and exiled the Ayatollah Khomeini. By 1964, the Shah had fundamentally changed the social landscape and the role of the state in it, beginning a new period in Iranian society and politics. The post-1964 political economy in Iran was an era of "full-scale capitalist development" (Halliday 1979, 27).

In 1965, General Haji Mohammad Suharto in Indonesia used a coup attempt by army officers alleged to be pro-Communist to lay claim to the reins of state. Between October 1965 and March 1966, when President Sukarno surrendered sweeping official powers to him, Suharto and his supporters in the Indonesian armed forces had to create order from a chaos in which nearly half a million people died, in part at the hands of the army itself but also by Islamic, nationalist, and student organizations and state-supported unions. All of these groups rampaged against suspected Communist Party sympathizers and demanded assistance and cooperation from Suharto's incipient government. Sukarno's perceived pro-Communist leanings during the early 1960s had nearly destroyed Indonesia's oil exports to the West, making Suharto's early rule difficult by paralyzing a key revenue-generating sector at a time when huge costs lay immediately ahead. Nonetheless, by making substantive political concessions to, and building a coalition of, students, nationalists, and Islamists, Suharto was able to consolidate his regime, eliminate from the army and the government most of the remaining supporters of Sukarno and the Indonesian Communist Party, known as Partai Komunis Indonesia (PKI), and embark on a program of rapid development that rivaled the Shah's in Iran. By 1970, his New Order seemed to be as well entrenched as the Shah's White Revolution.

Clearly, there is a prima facie case for comparing these two states during late development: both began the phase at roughly the same time, there is dramatic variation in these regimes' abilities to cope with the political turmoil of the boom years and, finally, there is also variation in the independent variables that I argue are crucial to explaining long-term regime viability. To my mind, however, there are still a number of alternative arguments that deserve attention, both structural (such as socioeconomic characteristics) and historical (past political legacies, the context-specific "fixed effects" that remain so elusive in statistical studies). In particular, the historical logic of my theoretical argument rests on the assumption that other junctures in the development of these two states are not what lay behind the variation. With that in mind, in the sections that follow, I address both kinds of rival arguments in these two cases. Recognizing that the historical discussion is rather lengthy, let me offer some analytical guidance at the outset. Briefly put, Iran and Indonesia shared a remarkable set of political legacies on the eve of late development, but I do not ask the reader to take my word for it. I treat those legacies in some detail in the pages that follow precisely because, in my view, it is a crucial step in showing that the juncture I posit as central is, in fact, central, and not merely one of many that jolted the Indonesian and Iranian states along toward the oil boom years. Skeptics (see, for example, Geddes 2003) rightly point out that "critical juncture" analyses sometimes neglect to establish the "critical-ness" of the junctures upon which their analyses depend. What follows is an analysis of the historical processes prior to late development to establish the foundation for the coming chapters.

Social and Structural Factors

Iran and Indonesia after World War II shared many traits that might otherwise provide a compelling explanation for political outcomes. First, each of these countries had a history of ethnic or regional separatism in those years: Iran faced Turkish (Azerbaijani) and Kurdish secessionist movements, and Indonesia confronted challenges from Acehnese, Sumatran, and Irianese separatists. Urban growth occurred at nearly identical rates in Iran and Indonesia (World Bank 2001). In each country, Muslims make up just over 90 percent of the population. Both Iran and Indonesia have high levels of ethnic diversity and rank almost identically on "ethnolinguistic fractionalization" indices, with a 75 percent likelihood that two randomly chosen individuals will not speak the same language (Roeder 2001). Each of these countries made the transition to late development in the 1960s: Iran between 1961 and 1963 under the Shah, and Indonesia between 1967 and 1969 under Suharto. In the late 1960s and early 1970s, the World Bank singled out Iran as a benchmark for the developing world and noted that Indonesia had made great strides toward reversing the economic ruin of the late Sukarno years.

Both Iran and Indonesia had a period of constitutional democracy before the 1960s in which political representation and participation were genuine and vibrant albeit somewhat chaotic. Near the end of that period a nationalist leader emerged in each state—Mohammed Mossadegh in Iran and Sukarno in Indonesia—whose polarization of politics was a major catalyst for the ascent to power of the Shah and Suharto, respectively, both of whom came to power with the aid of British and American intelligence. Both Suharto and the Shah, by the first oil boom in 1973–74, had established close relations with the United States by virtue of staunch anti-Communist stances and encouragement of extensive western investment, and the New Order and Pahlavi regimes had ambitiously set out to integrate their countries into the global economy. These regimes were neopatrimonial and authoritarian, relied heavily on the military and patronage networks alongside capitalist development strategies and coercion, and attempted to use official state parties to legitimate themselves in their respective societies. Each made the state the leading force in the national economy. In the 1960s, rulers in both Iran and Indonesia embarked on massive economic development programs aimed at transforming their respective nations into major regional powers. The 1973–74 oil boom flooded both economies with revenue from abroad and caused an inflationary crisis in Iran and Indonesia.

Well before the oil bust of the early 1980s—in 1974 and 1977 in Indonesia, in 1977 in Iran—social unrest emerged that taxed the capacities of both countries to maintain social control. Yet, everything that the West knew about these two states at the time (and much of what scholars continue to find theoretically important about them), would have predicted stability for both the Shah and Suharto. In short, these were two authoritarian regimes that should have lasted for a long while, even given domestic dissent and the imminent oil bust of the mid-1980s.

A Shared Prelude to Late Development: Chaotic Democracy, Anti-Western Nationalism, and the Left

As with many developing countries in the 1950s and 1960s, Iran and Indonesia experienced the rise of anti-imperialist politics in the wake of colonial or quasi-colonial domination by a European power. Most generally, anti-imperialism was a response to economic exploitation by western powers. In Indonesia, it was directed largely at the country's former colonial ruler, Holland; in Iran, the animus was Britain, whose Anglo-Iranian Oil Company for much of the interwar period essentially ran the Iranian state under the informal protection of the British government. The need to map out an independent course in the world took center stage in domestic politics in both of these countries, playing an important role in the dynamics of parliamentary politics in the postwar era.

At this time, both Iran (until 1953) and Indonesia (until 1959) were constitutional democracies. In Indonesia, "civilians played a dominant role. The contenders for power showed respect for 'rules of the game' which were closely related to the existing constitution. Most members of the political elite had some sort of commitment to symbols connected with constitutional democracy." (Feith 1962, xi). In Iran, "the country was galvanized by lively but highly complex elections between rival candidates attached to diverse interests, espousing different views, and appealing to antagonistic social forces" (Abrahamian 1982, 186). Despite the vibrancy of democratic politics, however, in both countries the process was still quite chaotic, and political parties had fairly weak ties to solid social bases (On Indonesia, see Feith 1962, 124–29; Cribb and Brown 1995, 47–52; on Iran, see Abrahamian 1982, chaps. 4 and 5). In short, democracy failed to reach a stable equilibrium in both countries in the 1950s. Given a lengthy period of democratic instability, one might expect that subsequent authoritarian rulers promising to provide order and economic stability could count on pliant populations as long as economic performance continued to improve. Thus, as a constant across the two cases, it is possible to set aside this factor as a historical one that might explain the variation in outcomes across Iran and Indonesia.

Because of party fragmentation and the resultant inability of coalition governments to forge effective policy and because of the rise of the left-nationalist alliance, leaders arose in both countries who were dependent on this latter alliance. Sukarno, the first president of Indonesia and a hero of the independence movement, assumed nearly absolute power in the late 1950s by declaring a transition from parliamentary to "Guided Democracy." Mohammed Mossadegh, first elected prime minister of Iran in 1951, followed a similar strategy but, instead of suspending the power of parliament, chose to bypass it in favor of calling for mass demonstrations when parliament would not bend to his will. Like Sukarno, he attempted to gather much of the power of state in his own hands late in his tenure by declaring a state of emergency. While both of these leaders were democratically elected, each gradually relied more and more on populist-nationalist appeals and street mobilization as a counterweight to the difficulties involved in mobilizing legislative support. Mossadegh became famous for rallying his supporters in the streets of Tehran when the parliament or the Shah in his view behaved intransigently, and Sukarno in the last years of his rule frequently called for popular uprisings.

Both Mossadegh in Iran and Sukarno in Indonesia willfully polarized politics as a strategy of political survival, seeking to play leftists and nationalists against the military and conservative social groups, whether rural elites to religious leaders to foreign capital. Both men railed against what they called western neo-imperialism (a term lifted directly from English into both Persian and Indonesian as *imperialisme*) and used popular sentiment to build political capital. Mossadegh and Sukarno both came from elite nationalist origins and, as their personal legitimacy eroded in the face of economic crisis, came to rely on the organizational prowess of their countries' respective Communist parties, the Tudeh ("Masses") Party of Iran and the PKI.

The Cold War imperative of preventing the fall of major regional powers like Iran and Indonesia, when added to the economic necessity of maintaining their oil reserves in western-friendly hands, led to direct intervention by the United States and Britain in the domestic politics of both countries. In 1953 the CIA and British intelligence co-sponsored a coup against Mossadegh in Iran that was aimed at restoring the Shah to power and at removing Mossadegh as prime minister. The coup was motivated in large part by American and British worries about Mossadegh's reliance on the Tudeh for support and by his determination to nationalize Iran's oil industry and expropriate it from the Anglo-Iranian Oil Company. In the late 1950s, the CIA supported a separatist movement in northern Sumatra, not coincidentally the location of Indonesia's richest oil fields. As in Iran, the motivation was both political and economic, aimed at securing access to oil supplies in the face of what was perceived as Sukarno's reckless pro-Communist leadership. Then, in 1965 and 1966, the CIA provided quiet support for Suharto's efforts to purge the army and bureaucracy of Communist and Sukarno supporters, supplying logistical assistance and lists of suspected PKI sympathizers gathered by the CIA through the U.S. embassy in Jakarta (NSA 2002a; Sydney Morning Herald 1999). Iran and Indonesia, in short, entered the late 1950s under very similar circumstances, led by nationalists who maintained close working coalitions with their respective Communist parties and who railed against western economic neo-imperialism.

Fragmentation and the Rise and Fall of Parliamentary Politics in Indonesia

After winning independence in 1949 from Dutch colonial forces, Indonesia began its period of parliamentary democracy. The first parliament, which convened in 1950, was not elected but rather selected to represent Indonesian society broadly (Cribb and Brown 1995, 47). Two characteristics of the political parties that came to dominate Indonesian politics during this period are noteworthy for setting the stage for later conflicts over economic policy. First, a rough balance of power among the four largest parties—the Muslim party Masjumi, the Indonesian Nationalist Party (PNI), the Greater Indonesia Party (PIR), and the Indonesian Socialist Party (PSI)—made coalition cabinets a necessity, since no single party could hope to put together an outright majority. As in many other political systems in which the ruling coalition is consistently distinguished by multiple party members and hence by multiple veto points, the nature of coalition politics between a group of parties whose orientation ran nationalist, religious, and leftist made for policy that was little more than "a holding operation" (Cribb and Brown 1995, 61).

Second, the parties had no real organizational roots in Indonesian society. As appointed rather than elected representatives, members of parliament could point to no popular mandate to rule (Cribb and Brown 1995, 63). Thus, one impediment to decisive economic policymaking was that no single party, nor even any ideological "stream" within any of the larger parties, could point to popular consensus behind its vision of Indonesia's future. A second and perhaps more important problem was that parties served almost exclusively as patronage machines for bureaucratic employment. Because they functioned largely to this end, parties in general had shallow roots in society, which gave them little ability to respond or represent any real constituency.

During the early 1950s, then, parliament came to be associated with corrupt and unrepresentative politics, and the party system and even parliamentary democracy itself along with it. Sukarno, a mostly titular president with few real powers, and the military stood out in contrast as the two major political hubs that retained popular legitimacy. During the course of 1956, enthusiasm for democratic politics deteriorated, and political participation progressively more and more took the form of street protests and popular mobilization. Increasingly it also took the form of more extreme extra-party politics: in early October there was an attempted coup by army officers against Sukarno while he was out of the country on a state trip to the Soviet Union and China. In late October President Sukarno railed against the political parties, exhorting Indonesians to "bury them" if they could not overcome their inertia.

In February 1957 President Sukarno gave the speech that outlined his Guided Democracy. In it he claimed that parliamentary democracy had never fit well with Indonesian values. The competitive and zero-sum nature of the former, he argued, contradicted the principles that drove culturally authentic decisionmaking: *gotong royong* (mutual aid and cooperation) and *musyawarah* and *mufakat* (exhaustive discussion and consensus, respectively). In this speech, Sukarno sketched out his *konsepsi*, proposing a national council composed of representatives from important social groups rather than political parties—the *golongan karya* (functional groups) from which his successor's official party, Golkar, would emerge—and a cabinet appointed by Sukarno himself and comprised of members of all major parties (Cribb and Brown 1995, 77). In terms of addressing the power of social groups, the crucial implications of Sukarno's speech were that the PKI was likely to gain in any Sukarno-envisioned arrangement, as were Nahdlatul Ulama (NU) and the military (Feith 1962, 542–43).

President Sukarno got the chance to pose a concrete alternative to parliamentary politics a month later. On March 2, the commander of the armed forces in East Indonesia declared martial law in the territory over which he had authority and asserted that he would not respond to the government in Jakarta until power imbalances between the central and regional authorities were addressed. On March 14 the cabinet under Ali Sastroamidjojo resigned and Sukarno declared martial law across Indonesia. He then appointed what he called a "working cabinet" (*kabinet karya*) composed of nonparty politicians such as Djuanda Kartawidjaja, known for being a conservative, and several leftists, but no PKI leaders. He also took steps to work closely during the rebellion crisis with General Abdul Haris Nasution, the army Chief of Staff, and all of these steps both consolidated his new position of authority and reassured the military and conservative groups that his *konsepsi* was not simply a ruse to give the state over to the PKI or the left more broadly. The first six months of 1957 provided the events that made it possible for Sukarno to acquire significantly greater power in Indonesian politics. The second half of the year saw the newly powerful PKI rise to a position of equal prominence in national politics. '

In addition to its accomplishments in elections, the PKI began in late 1957 to raise fears about its ability to mobilize urban workers and peasants and its willingness and determination to confront private sector capitalists. In December, trade unions affiliated with the PKI and the PNI "seized control of Dutch-owned enterprises in Indonesia" (Cribb and Brown 1995, 79). In addition, the PKI accelerated its efforts to organize and mobilize small farmers (Kartodirdjo 1977). In a detailed study of the politics of land reform and peasant politics in Klaten, a regency in the province of Central Java, Padmo notes that a trend began during this period of the use of property destruction and arson to protest land tenure. Party affiliation trends among peasant farmers who had never before used this particular approach suggest that, even though many had once belonged to "banned parties," meaning the PKI, the use of new and more aggressive tactics suggested that "an outside group had organized the destruction" (2000, 113). Newly aggressive mobilizing efforts of this kind raised considerable alarm, especially given their concentration on Java, which was the social base not only for Muslim organizations like NU but also for the Indonesian military elite: indeed, Suharto, soon to be president, was born and raised in central Java.

In February 1958, regional dissent and increasing tension between pro-West and anti-Communist political parties (the PSI and Masjumi, predominantly) culminated in the declaration of the Revolutionary Government of Indonesia (Pemerintah Revolusioner Republic Indonesia, PRRI) by a group of army officers and party leaders from PSI and Masjumi in Bukittingi, on the island of Sumatra. The United States provided covert support for this rebellion as a counterweight to Sukarno and the PKI.

The eventual end of the PRRI rebellion gave Sukarno the political capital with which to implement his *konsepsi* much more aggressively. In July 1959 he dissolved the Constituent Assembly that had been meeting to draft a new constitution, and he decreed the reintroduction of the 1945 Constitution. Not coincidentally, this constitution heavily emphasized executive authority, making cabinet ministers responsible to the president rather than to parliament and giving the president wide latitude to rule by decree. Not satisfied with these new powers, Sukarno began to refer to himself as the "Great Leader of the Revolution and Mouthpiece of the Indonesian People" (Cribb and Brown 1995, 83). In 1963 he was able to institutionalize these claims by pressuring the parliament to name him "president for life."

Throughout 1964 the PKI engaged in what it called *aksi sepihak* (unilateral action) against rural landowners on Java, Bali, and North Sumatra. In most cases, these landowners were conservative local elites with ties either to the PNI or to NU, and the actions taken by local PKI affiliate groups ranged from petitions to forceful land seizure and sometimes violent confrontation. The pattern of newly politicized and violent confrontation that Padmo (2000) documents having evolved in the regency of Klaten took place across nearly all of Indonesia's most populated provinces.

Sukarno's position, as mentioned above, depended to a degree on balancing army-PKI antagonism. In the early 1960s he attempted to bolster his own authority by engaging in two major military conflicts. First, throughout 1961 he threatened to pursue a military solution to the conflict with the Dutch over the western half of the island of Guinea (Irian). When United Nations mediation failed to produce an agreement, in January 1962 the Mandala command of the army, supervised by Nasution but field-led by Major General Suharto, formally began fighting for the "total liberation of Western Irian." In this case the Kennedy administration pressured the Dutch government to transfer authority to the UN, which it did in October 1962. Early the next year western Guinea—Irian Jaya—was officially transferred from UN to Indonesian authority. Second, only a few months after the resolution of the Irian confrontation, Sukarno engaged Britain, Australia, and the new federation of Malaysia in his *konfrontasi* campaign, which he claimed was intended to prevent Britain from establishing a "neo-colony" in Southeast Asia.

So economic policy in the years before Guided Democracy could be described as nationalist but in actuality was simply adrift. Once the constraints posed by parliamentary dynamics vanished, however, so did the veto points that could restrain policy. Included in Sukarno's Guided Democracy was the "Guided Economy," centered on "setting the right political climate within which the economy was expected to operate" (Cribb and Brown 1995, 90). In other words, the right ideological backdrop would produce a genuinely Indonesian economy, run by Indonesians and relatively free of the domination of "Nekolim"—an acronym of sorts drawn from "neo-colonialists, colonialists, and imperialists." Toward that end, political goals—such as the indigenization of businesses within Indonesia—drove economic policies such as the expropriations of the early Guided Democracy period. The military conflicts also contributed to the economic deterioration. Inflation ran at nearly 100 percent annually during the West Irian campaign. Finally, as the government's ability to respond effectively to economic crises eroded, the inflation that it had been able to manage in 1963 and early 1964 began to spiral out of control. So incapacitated was the government by this point that no state budget was even produced in 1965 (Cribb and Brown 1995, 90).

Despite his new powers, therefore, Sukarno's position became tenuous because of the dual economic and military crises that had emerged by late 1964. As they did, his ability to balance the army against the PKI declined, to the point that the PKI was considerably freer in late 1964 and 1965 to move to expand its organizational and social power. The party used the ideological mantle of *konfrontasi,* a trumped-up conflict with Malaysia, as a justification for the seizure of British plantations and for attacks on United States Information Service offices in Jakarta and other cities. Indonesia's withdrawal from the UN in January 1965, the apparent turn to China as the only major power willing to endorse Indonesian foreign policy, and attacks on western business—all of this served to bolster the PKI's domestic position, which it used to confront its internal rivals for power.

Sukarno's economic policies and his unwillingness to take state building seriously—preferring to force the creation of a "nation" instead—placed even greater strain on the Indonesian state apparatus than the dramatic drop in revenues from import taxes alone. Inflation, regional dissent, and a lack of priority by Sukarno's government in Jakarta meant that the 1950s battle for a unitary state came to naught in lieu of "de facto federalism" (Malley 1999, 115–19).

By the fall of 1965, then, the political climate that had emerged from the collapse of parliamentary democracy had set the stage for a major confrontation. The economy was in a state of meltdown in 1965, with inflation running at 600 percent, and the army, NU, and the PNI were all engaged in their own rivalries with the PKI. Abroad, the United States and Britain were increasingly unwilling to tolerate Sukarno's excesses in the interest of avoiding a Communist alternative: CIA, State Department, and other government documents from late 1964 through mid-1965 (NSA 2002a, documents 89, 99, and 103) reveal a clear consensus on the need to do something to secure American interests in the face of a perceived imminent threat of Communist takeover. Sukarno's collapse during a speech in August 1965 only served to confirm for many that he was on his way out and that something had to be done.

Parliamentary Fragmentation and the Rise of Mass Politics in Iran

The forced abdication of Reza Shah Pahlavi by the United Kingdom and the Soviet Union in 1941 left a huge hole in the Iranian polity, which parties, tribal leaders, professional organizations, aristocratic families, and the new Shah, Mohammad Reza Pahlavi, all moved to fill. The political arena was constrained by the British and Soviet occupation of Iran, whose only formal commitments were to try to protect the Iranian economy from the harshest effects of the war, which they failed to do, and to withdraw from Iran within six months of the war's end, a promise the Soviet Union broke (Keddie 1981, 113). Nonetheless, even under occupation, politics came alive in a way not seen since before Reza Shah's ascent to power. During the 1940s in Iran, as in 1950s Indonesia, economic upheaval provided the base from which new political organizations could mobilize supporters and use their social bases to contest elections. Four major parties were influential during this decade: the Tudeh Party, formed in 1942; the Iran Party, formed in 1941; the Justice Party, formed as a counter to Tudeh; and the Fatherland Party (which became the National Will Party shortly afterwards), formed in late 1943.

In June 1950 the pro-Shah government submitted its proposal to begin negotiations with the Anglo-Iranian Oil Company over revision of the 1933 concession. By this point renegotiation was no longer the viable option that it had been under previous governments. The National Front, supported by the officially illegal but still active and organized Tudeh, demanded the nationalization of the AIOC and accused the company of economic imperialism. During the ensuing public demonstrations, a pro-British member of the Majles (parliament) was assassinated. Prime Minister Ali Mansour resigned rather than try to force the bill through parliament. His successor, General Haj Ali Razmara, was loyal enough to the Shah to push the oil issue despite significant personal risk; indeed, he was assassinated in March 1951 by a member of the Feda'iyan-e Islam, a militant Islamist organization. The killing was celebrated in the streets of Tehran and "scared the deputies into reasserting their parliamentary rights" (Abrahamian 1982, 266). Razmara's successor, Hossein Ala', represented a resurgence of parliamentary assertiveness over the interests of the court and reflected the power of popular mobilization. Ala' was regarded as a conservative landowner, but one acceptable to the National Front. He consulted closely with Mossadegh in selecting his cabinet and stood by while Mossadegh introduced an oil nationalization bill that frightened deputies, but still passed out of committee, through the Majles, and even through the Senate. This crucial vote, which led to the first oil nationalization effort anywhere in the developing world, marked the first time that a party in Iran with such a small minority had managed to succeed legislatively by virtue of a direct appeal to the people.

The sudden parliamentary power of Mossadegh's National Front was matched by the resurgence of the Tudeh in street politics. In May 1951, the party organized a general strike in Khuzestan (the most oil-rich province in Iran, located in the southwest, on the border with Iraq) and mobilized demonstrations calling for the government to stop procrastinating on oil nationalization. Police in Khuzestan's capital city of Abadan fired on protesters, killing six of them. In response, the Tudeh organized "sympathy protests" in Tehran and Isfahan. Even though his supporters held a majority in the Majles and even though he had often spoken out against class-driven politics, the Shah took no action against the election of Mossadegh to replace Ala' as prime minister in May.

Given his small minority in parliament and his preferences for extra-parliamentary politics, Mossadegh's political strategies leaned heavily toward organizing mass demonstrations in the streets when Majles deputies (members of parliament) would not vote his way. Oil nationalization unsurprisingly took first priority on his agenda: in June 1951 he formed a committee of National Front deputies and sent them to Khuzestan to take over the AIOC's oil installations, refusing to negotiate with the company. The British closed down the installations and made a formal complaint before the UN Security Council and later began an embargo of Iranian oil joined by most other western nations.

New Majles elections were held in January 1952. By stopping the voting once a quorum of seventy-nine had been elected, Mossadegh emerged with a majority for the first time—most of the quorum members were from cities, where the National Front had done very well, preventing the majority of seats being in provincial districts, where his opponents had fared well, from being filled. His conservative opponents engaged in "side skirmishes," refusing to debate his economic policies, which were designed to mitigate the effects of the western oil embargo, making regional issues a part of the agenda, and other stalling strategies. The National Front responded by starting a public campaign against the aristocracy; ultimately, Mossadegh brought the conflict to the court as well by insisting on his constitutional prerogative to name the minister of war—for the first time directly threatening to take away the Shah's control of the military (Abrahamian 1982, 270).

The Shah refused to allow this. In what by now was a typical move for him, Mossadegh threatened to resign. Conservatives in parliament responded by selecting Ahmad Ghavam again as prime minister (he had also held the position from 1946 to 1947), a choice to which the Shah was amenable but to which Mossadegh and his supporters were immediately hostile. In response, protesters packed the streets of Tehran for five days, ultimately forcing the Shah to ask Mossadegh once again to form a government. During this five-day show of support for Mossadegh, bazaar merchants, guild leaders, Tudeh unions, and university students, among many others, all collaborated to give the National Front and, increasingly its partner in popular politics, the Tudeh a significant victory against the Shah.

Mossadegh almost immediately began a series of reforms aimed at consolidating his own power and diluting that of both landed conservatives and the court. He banned royalists from the cabinet, named himself minister of war, transferred Reza Shah's land holdings back to the state, and cut the court's budget. Moreover, he "forbade the Shah to communicate directly with foreign diplomats" and "forced Princess Ashraf to leave the country" (Abrahamian 1982, 272). In foreign policy, he declared a principle of "negative equilibrium," or reliance on the support of neither superpower.

He also took steps to increase his own power extensively, pushing through a vote in the Majles to give him emergency powers for six months to decree laws. After six months, he had the powers extended to conclude in August 1953. His decrees included land reform, upper-class tax increases, and a weakening of the Senate's power. Eventually, what was left of his opposition in the parliament resisted; in response the entire National Front caucus resigned, bringing the Majles below quorum and forcing an election. Mossadegh called for a referendum in July 1953 to approve the dissolution of the parliament. As he did so, the National Front split over the issue of extending Mossadegh's emergency powers. In the meantime, the United States, through the CIA and in collaboration with British intelligence, the court (somewhat reluctantly), and several army officers, had begun planning a coup against Mossadegh.[3] They carried out the coup between August 14 and 19, 1953. On the latter date, the Shah returned from a short trip abroad (part of the plan) to preside over Mossadegh's arrest and forced resignation as prime minister.

---

[3] As with the coup attempt in Indonesia, I do not intend to present the Iranian coup in any detail. See Gasiorowski (1987) and National Security Archives (2002b) for the most detailed accounts available of the coup itself.

The 1953 coup establishing the Shah as the central political authority in Iran began a period of consolidation. During the 1950s, the regime's political efforts were largely directed at dismantling the Tudeh and the National Front, which had been the two strongest political forces in Iran in the preceding decade. During this period, however, the regime's social base—an essentially conservative one made up of wealthy landowners, *bazaaris* (bazaar workers), and the *ulemā* (Islamic educated elite led by the Ayatollah Boroujerdi—remained intact. It was not until 1960, during an economic recession and under great pressure from the American government to reform, that the third period of Mohammed Reza Shah's rule began, in which rapid development directed by the state became the primary goal of the regime.

The Shah's first years were characterized by a serious economic crisis, which raises the important question of why the Shah did not have to make the decision to embark on sweeping economic policy changes during this period. When the regime was facing fiscal scarcity and the need to purge its most organized opposition, the theoretical argument advanced in chapter 1 would have predicted that decision. However, immediately after the coup, the Eisenhower administration stepped in to make good on the commitment to Iran's stability that it had assumed by organizing the coup against Mossadegh. In the first two years after the coup, the United States largely bankrolled the Iranian government, pouring capital not just into state expenditure accounts but into the economy as well, in effect sanitizing the crisis and making it possible for the Shah to concentrate only on tackling the opposition.

During the five years following the coup—until about the end of 1957—the Shah's government, helped by American military and intelligence assistance and extensive foreign aid, carried out a purge of the leaderships of both the Tudeh and the National Front. With extensive logistical support from the United States (specifically the CIA), the Shah built the Sazman-e Amniyat Va Ettela'at-e Keshvar (Organization for Information and State Security, SAVAK) into an agency for monitoring potential opposition groups and particularly aimed at preventing the revival of either the Tudeh or the National Front after the coup.[4] Thus, even the challenge of purging the opposition was made considerably easier by extensive American and British military and intelligence aid, especially in helping to build SAVAK.

Conservative landlords, those in the bazaar who had not been supporters of Mossadegh, tribal leaders from the provinces, and the *ulemā* under

---

[4] As will become clear in the chapters that follow, this focus on bureaucratic or formally organized political movements diverted the government's attention away from the many mobilizing resources within preexisting social groups. For a discussion of how these social institutions could become political on short notice, see Smith (2003a).

the leadership of the Ayatollah Boroujerdi became the primary support base for the Shah's government. His policies reflected this loose conservative coalition, and in political terms the priority was simply eliminating the organizational power of the National Front and the Tudeh. In stark contrast to his policies in the next decade, the Shah went to considerable lengths to maintain the acquiescence of these groups, for the most part giving them substantial autonomy. By 1957, 3,500 National Front and Tudeh members had been exiled or executed, and an unsteady stasis had emerged in which the government distributed oil and aid revenues as a substitute for economic planning.

Historical Antecedents to a Structured Comparison: The Case for Pairing Iran and Indonesia

In both Iran and Indonesia, policy fragmentation, the deterioration of democratic politics, and the rise of a left-nationalist coalition created fears among conservative domestic groups and western leaders alike that both of these countries were vulnerable to Communist takeover. Ultimately, that fear led to a coup in both countries, and the assumption of power by leaders with the assistance of foreign supporters. Moreover, economic crisis made significant structural changes a necessity, especially given the already heavy emphasis on reform by international lending institutions. In causal terms, the confluence of economic crisis, political instability, and expanding left-nationalist coalition provided the sufficient but not necessary conditions to catalyze decision on the part of the Shah's and Suharto's regimes to embark on rapid state-led development. As I discussed at the beginning of this chapter, the experiences of Iran and Indonesia make it far from clear that these conditions alone accounted for this kind of development program. What these cases do clearly illustrate is the one common set of conditions antecedent to rapid development that left the two regimes with similar institutional starting points.

In Iran in 1953, as in Indonesia in 1965, anti-Communist governments came to power under the specter of economic collapse. The states over which they gradually consolidated their control had deteriorated considerably. First, the capacity to collect revenues domestically had declined in both countries, albeit more drastically in Indonesia. Second, what Malley somewhat euphemistically referred to in Indonesia as "de facto federalism" was actually an erosion of central state authority over the provinces. While the rhetoric by both Sukarno and Mossadegh touted the power of the state to unify the nation and to assure its sovereignty from neo-imperialism, in both cases regional governors, local military commanders, and tribal strongmen all maintained significant power as the Shah and Suharto began to consolidate their own.

In short, the impressive array of common features shared by these two states makes it possible to be reasonably sure that those factors are not behind the variance in outcomes. Ethnic diversity, a past history of political instability, superpower intervention in domestic affairs, authoritarian polities, and common exposure to the oil boom of 1973–74 are potentially destabilizing factors shared by Iran and Indonesia, factors that cross-national analyses reveal as important determinants of regime viability. Yet here they fail to explain why it was that Suharto and the Shah fared so differently as they both confronted political protests in 1977 and 1978 and, all other things being equal, increase our confidence that key differences in the circumstances of late development offer the best explanation.

Another analytical advantage of pairing these two states is that they have been studied singly in depth, allowing for the assessment of the theory presented here against an array of case-specific, in addition to broader, explanations. For instance, two major hypotheses to explain variations in regime durability across the two states might be extrapolated from their sociocultural and geographical features. As a nation whose population is spread over an archipelago with more than 13,000 islands and several hundred distinct ethnic groups and languages, we might expect the social potential for collective action against the New Order state to have been too small to pose a challenge. That possibility might be suggested in both microeconomic terms—as a question of the potential for mass-based collective action requiring the strategic coordination of many different social groups—and in cultural ones—"primordial" cleavages that make impossible any sustained challenge to regimes that can skillfully manage communal tensions. However, Iran's population is as ethnically and linguistically diverse as Indonesia's in terms of ethnic and linguistic diversity (see Taylor and Hudson 1972, table 4.15; and Roeder 2001). Its geography—high mountains, often impassable during the winter, and vast salt deserts, impassable in summer—also creates a physical separation of regions that parallels the division of Indonesia's population across islands. Moreover, during the period of this study, the population of the island of Java alone, home to the capital city of Jakarta and 60 percent of the national population, was twice that of all of Iran and arguably much more homogeneous.[5]

One further cultural explanation is possible. It is one that highlights the Javanese, or more broadly Indonesian, culture of deference, which should

---

[5] Moreover, trade throughout the Indonesian archipelago for several centuries before independence meant frequent contact with the inhabitants of other islands, to some degree mitigating what are often characterized as sharp and untraveled ethnic divides. I am grateful to Lance Castles for bringing this to my attention.

make widespread protests against political authorities unlikely by social-
izing individuals to accept leaders as "natural." A predictive theory extrapolated from this analysis has trouble explaining the many instances of
protest in recent decades, beginning with the war of independence itself and
including the several million members of the PKI—especially on Java—in
the early 1960s and the massive "Malari riots" in January 1974 and later
student protests in 1977 (Liddle 1996). What distinguishes recent Indonesian politics is not the lack of protest against state authorities but rather,
until 1998, its lack of success. In short, we must look beyond static ethnic/
cultural explanations to assess the potential for these two societies to press
for political change.

One more theory advanced to explain the longevity of the New Order
regime is that it was simply too heavy-handed for its domestic enemies to
mount a sustained challenge to Suharto's rule. If this were true, it would
suggest a more general theory that coercion alone can sustain authoritarian rule or at least that coercion is the central means by which autocrats
stay in power. Again, though, the very coercion in 1977–78 that should
have kept the Shah in power is held up as a major reason for his overthrow,
because it brought even more Iranians to the streets against him (Kurzman
1994, 1996; Rasler 1996). It is also often argued that it was not the capacity of the Iranian state to repress that eroded during the revolutionary crisis but rather the will and that this erosion of the will to use violence led
to the Shah's overthrow (Bellin 2004). In chapter 4 I address this proposition in detail, but here it is important simply to note that the Shah's army,
SAVAK, and the police continued to use force—including firing into stationary crowds and the use of helicopter gunships and tanks—until very
late in the revolutionary crisis.

Nor, even in January 1979, were army desertions a debilitating problem. During the week of the Shah's departure, desertions still amounted to
fewer than one thousand per day out of several hundred thousand troops.
Throughout the crisis, the army and the police continued to follow orders
to use force, and during the martial law period in late 1978 they began to
exercise autonomous authority to use force. In short, the regime's "will to
repress" never collapsed at all: "fear of state reprisal lasted through the final hours of the old regime" (Kurzman 1992, 176). The problem was that
repression never succeeded in Iran; the ranks of protesters swelled so un-
controllably that, in the Shah's own words, "you can't crack down on one
block and expect people on the next block to behave" (quoted in Kurzman
2004, 114). Beyond the cases of Iran and Indonesia, cross-national research
has established that repression does not necessarily enhance regime longevity. And, although the research summarized in chapter 1 suggests that
repression is associated with regime survival, it does not appear to be a

mechanism linking oil wealth to regime survival. The effects of state violence are simply too varied to make any overarching claims (Opp and Roehl 1990; Lichbach 1987; Francisco 2002; and Karklins and Petersen 1993).

Iran and Indonesia form a nearly ideal most-similar pair for comparison. They evince broad similarities across many of the measures that scholars in comparative politics have concluded are crucial to the survival or failure of authoritarian regimes. Iran and Indonesia also share a history of ethnic or regional separatist movements. They experienced several unique historical periods together, from brief constitutional democracy after World War II to the rise and subsequent collapse of anti-Western nationalism to the initiation of rapid development and the oil booms of the 1970s. However, they differ on two crucial measures, the onset of rapid development and their subsequent ability to weather political crises.

Sequences and Institutions as Cases: Beyond Simply Looking at "Countries"

What constitutes a case in social research is theoretically determined by the questions at hand and by the argument tested against the cases (Ragin and Becker 1992). In comparative politics, countries remain the dominant units of analysis, despite predictions of the "eclipse of the state" (Evans 1997) and warnings that supranational integration has made comparative historical scholars "prisoners of the state" (Tilly 1992). In the analysis that follows, I focus primarily on the experiences of two countries but, methodologically speaking, there is more going on than two cases being analyzed. In particular, I pursue two strategies that increase the number of discrete units of analysis in this study: periodization (the study of distinct sequences or time periods) and a focus on individual institutions within national states.

The structure within which I pursue this study is an analysis of three sets of institutions (tax agencies, official parties, and local government) across these two states during two distinct time periods (see Haydu 1998 for a discussion of time periods as cases). By comparing pre- and post-development institutions at the juncture of late development as well as their initial trajectories before the 1973–74 oil boom and their longer-term trajectories after the boom, I follow two strategies suggested by Lieberman (2001). First, I take an approach to institutional origins across the two cases that highlights the importance of antecedent conditions to their creation: fiscal and political challenges at the onset of late development. Close attention to these broad social, political, and economic factors make it possible to do what Waldner has referred to as "recovering the macro-analytics

of state building" (2002). Second, by focusing on exogenous shocks well after the critical juncture, I show how, despite the magnitude of the first oil
boom as a shock to the political economies of these two states, this powerful "cause" common to both was filtered through preexisting institutions
to produce quite different effects. Focusing explicitly on the oil boom of
1973–74 makes it possible to assess its independent effects as an alternative juncture explanation to my own, which is concentrated on late development. Geddes notes that it can be difficult to distinguish between rival
critical juncture explanations: "I do not see how such disagreements can
be resolved without the development of measures of legacies (that is, the
interests or institutions created by the earlier choice), a theorization of the
effect of these legacies on later choices, and then a test of the theorization
on additional cases" (2003, 140–41). I address precisely these requirements
and attempt to cope with this problem by making the implications of my
own juncture argument, as well as the alternatives to it, explicit, as well as
developing a set of ways to "measure" the effect of legacies on distinct state
institutions, political organizations, and patterns of state-society relations.
I then show in chapter 4 that the boom itself did not create the dramatically different outcomes in Iran and Indonesia, questioning the implications of theories that posit a uniform, or nearly uniform, effect of the oil
windfall of the 1970s on exporting states.

In short, rather than present two countries over twenty years as whole
units, I in effect analyze six cases in each of two chronological chapters,
testing the logic of the argument against twelve separate groups of data
points. These "sub-case cases" are clearly not independent of one another,
so it is imprecise to talk here about greater or fewer degrees of freedom.
What I am suggesting is that by constructing historical comparisons this
way, it is possible to test independently the components of sometimes
lengthy causal chains, producing a more compelling causal sequence argument than would be possible by including many more countries in much
less detail (see Haydu 1998 and Rueschemeyer and Stephens 1997 for discussions of constructing this sort of historical-causal comparison). In Geddes's (2003, 117) words, these are twelve "nonquantitative collections of
time series data." To my mind, this approach is a crucial first step in establishing the validity of a theoretical argument and of an explanation of
the very different fortunes of these two autocrats. Once assured of the initial validity of the argument in this structured comparative setting, expanding the scope of cases against which it may be assessed ought to be
more fruitful. I move in this direction in chapter 5 by testing the broad implications of the argument against all of the highly oil export-dependent
states in the developing world. I also select two additional cases from the
sample and conduct another structured comparison to test the sub-hy-

potheses regarding party formation, taxation, and local institutional development against a new set of cases.

Iran and Indonesia entered the global economy as late developers during roughly the same period (Gerschenkron 1962; Chaudhry 1992). In these two countries the state, as in other developing countries, played a formative role during the 1960s and 1970s not just in channeling social demands but also in shaping both society and the burden it placed on political institutions (Migdal 1988, 1997; Migdal, Kohli, and Shue 1994; Evans, Rueschemeyer, and Skocpol 1985). To a large extent, these are both stories about the social strains induced by the politics of late development. Yet the plots diverged dramatically after the first oil boom. In Iran, the social protests culminated in a violent social revolution that overturned a monarchy with an army of 700,000, sending the Shah into exile, where he died in 1981. In Indonesia, Suharto remained in power for another nineteen years.

Why such drastically different outcomes from such similar starting points? Why was it that the Shah's opponents grew in number and became bolder and bolder in the late 1970s, while Suharto's opposition during the same period was unable to mount much challenge to his government?[6] To bring the discussion back to oil, why is it that externally derived revenues are put to such varying uses, sometimes strengthening the state and sometimes apparently causing it to deteriorate? I search for answers to these questions in the following chapters by studying the development of these two states through three institutional lenses.

On the eve of the initiation of late development, those three institutions were in disarray in both Iran and Indonesia. Nationalist economic policy-making deemphasized tax extraction in Iran and Indonesia prior to 1961 and 1966, respectively. Sukarno's and Mossadegh's preferences for nationalist politics over administrative penetration of local settings—again, common to both countries—led to de facto federalism with dramatically weakened central authority outside of Tehran or Jakarta. Finally, as the Shah and Suharto began to think about the political underpinnings of their development programs, neither had any kind of powerful political organization at hand that could easily be retooled to provide a base of political support or a means to mobilize supporters. Thus, on the eve of late development, Indonesia and Iran had not only recent political histories in common but also weak state institutions and political organizations.

---

[6] I realize that this question assumes that both periods of protest could have ended similarly, which in turn assumes that either the Indonesian protesters in early 1974 and 1977–78 might have had revolution on their minds or at least that the Iranian ones in early 1978 might not have. There is evidence to suggest that both are true, and in particular I would refer to the early and even later statements by protesters and opposition groups in Iran in 1978, few of whom (excepting Khomeini) claimed to be trying to bring down the monarchy. This is to say that there is nothing inevitable about protests leading to revolution, even if we know retrospectively of cases where it in fact happened.

Having confronted a number of major political and economic challenges at nearly the same time, Suharto's Indonesia and the Shah's Iran embarked on late development within a few years of one another. Those common challenges, however, overshadowed some powerful domestic differences in the challenges that confronted the two autocrats. In the next chapter I turn to the constraints on, and the strategies crafted by, these governments to direct the state's new role in the economy, focusing specifically on the timing of political and fiscal challenges relative to rapid development.

CHAPTER 3

The Impact and Legacies of Oil and Late Development

Coalitions and State Building before the Boom

In chapter 2 we discussed the political and economic crises that Iran and Indonesia shared and that made state-led development the likely economic strategy. This chapter explains the extraordinary differences between the two states that emerged from the genesis of this common strategy. That variation, I argue, resulted from the timing of late development. To reiterate, the key timing factors are when each regime confronted its opposition and when it gained access to substantial oil revenues in relation to its initiation of late development projects. To illustrate the causal importance of timing, I first present the period in which these regimes adopted development programs and, second, outline the political trajectories that emerged as a result. I trace the processes of political and economic development to the eve of the first oil boom, consciously addressing a central rival hypothesis. That is, I challenge the argument that the boom was *the* critical juncture in the political development of these and other exporting states.

I maintain, by contrast, that it was late development and its timing relative to oil wealth and to the confrontation with the organized political opposition that shaped the institutions and ties to society that each leader had at hand when the serious protests emerged. I intend to show that in fact the trajectories were already in place several years before the boom of 1973–74 and that, despite some skepticism (Geddes 2003, 140–41), it is possible to evaluate the merits of rival critical juncture explanations by tracing the processes by which legacies to specific junctures emerged. In the remainder of the chapter I show how those trajectories took different shape in the two countries in the wake of adopting rapid late development as a direct result of its timing relative to the political and fiscal challenges associated with opposition groups and oil revenues.

Indonesia: Rent Scarcity, Political Crisis, and Late Development

By nearly all counts, the first years of Suharto's New Order were ones of serious desperation. The economy was in a state of meltdown, with factory production, oil output, imports, and state revenues all having seriously deteriorated in the early 1960s from an already precarious economic footing dating back to the Great Depression (Glassburner 1978b, 137). A World Bank consulting team that surveyed Indonesia's economy in early 1966 found that, with the exceptions of cement and urea production, the industrial sector was running at no more than 20 percent of capacity (World Bank 1966, 15, cited in Winters 1996, 50). Oil exports in 1965 amounted to less than half their value in 1960 (Glassburner 1976, 1101). Inflation ran at 600 percent during 1965 as a result of the growing crisis and Sukarno's willingness to print money without regard for its economic effects. In a signal that it would not be easy to restore Indonesia's perceived creditworthiness on international markets, in October 1965 the Indonesian Central Bank reported for the first time that it would be unable to pay on letters of credit. Japan's Ministry of International Trade and Investments took the first step in underscoring the seriousness of the crisis by refusing to insure shipments to Indonesia (Mas'oed 1983, 66–67).

All of these private sector problems paled in comparison to what Winters has described as the "fiscal breakdown of the state" (Winters 1996, 50). Government receipts amounted to only one-fifth of routine expenditures, and in 1965 the budget deficit was three times total government revenues (51). The state was not only unable to extract sufficient revenues to sustain its payments but, more broadly, was also unable to perform most of its routine duties.[1] Finally, the instability created in part by the economic crisis of the late Sukarno years led to the flight of most mobile foreign and domestic capital, leaving the country with no means of creating jobs or of pulling itself out of a deep economic disaster. Ultimately, the survival of the new regime depended on whether it could craft an effective economic

[1] Brown argues that the bureaucracy under Sukarno ran relatively efficiently relative to its capability under Suharto's leadership (2001, 84), so my assertion here is not a completely unquestioned one. His detailed account of rent-seeking and -seizing in the regulation of the Indonesian timber industry, however, does not provide Sukarno-era data with which to compare relative capabilities and is ultimately dependent on the assumption that rent-seeking varies inversely with institutional capacity. Also, his argument runs counter to nearly every other account of governance under Sukarno; institutional collapse is an almost unanimous description of the Guided Democracy period. Rent-seeking under Sukarno exerted centrifugal pressure on political authority, whereas under Suharto its effects were largely centripetal. Moreover, I argue below that the volume of demonstrable rent-seeking by itself is not a satisfactory measure of institutional capacity; when centralized it can under certain circumstances actually strengthen institutions. For a general argument in this vein see Kang (2002); for very specific accounts of how rent-seeking actually strengthened the capacity of institutions in Indonesia, see MacIntyre (2000 and 2001) and Amal (1992).

response and whether it could build a coalition that could maintain it through considerable political turmoil until economic recovery began to manifest itself.

Political Challenges

The economic crisis during which the New Order regime came to power was not the only test that its leadership faced. In contrast with the Shah's Iran, the onset of late development coincided with severe economic catastrophe and with the persistence of a powerfully organized opposition movement—the PKI—and sizable pockets of support for Sukarno in the bureaucracy, military, and many social organizations. From the point of view of Suharto and other anti-Communist army officers, the PKI's success not just at mobilizing within Indonesian society but also at creating divisions within the ranks of the military was cause for great alarm. That a number of armed forces units had declared their loyalty to the officers who had led the attempted coup suggested to the Suharto group that the PKI's mobilizing prowess extended deep into the military, before 1965 the one institution in society whose coherence and organizational clout rivaled the PKI. It took several years to unify the military and to purge it of PKI and Sukarno supporters. Of concern, too, was the persistence of the PKI for two to three years after the 1965–66 rampage against it: guerrilla-style attacks by former party militias in central and eastern Java continued against landowners and military installations until late 1968.

Finally, Sukarno himself refused to bow out quietly. In August 1966, he defended his ideology of "Nasakom" (*Nasionalisme, Agama, Komunisme*—Nationalism, Religion, and Communism) and called for the formation of a "Sukarno Front." On September 1, following the early failure of Suharto's government to obtain loans from the West and Japan, he gave a speech lambasting the new government's economic policy, claiming that it did nothing but promote Indonesia's foreign dependency. This speech took direct aim at the regime's plans for late development. On September 6, he claimed that Marxism was "in his blood" forever. In October 1966 PNI members in east and central Java issued declarations of support for Sukarno; pro-PNI and pro-Sukarno army units fought with units loyal to Suharto throughout late 1966 (Mas'oed 1983, 101–5). All of these uprisings suggest a considerably different and more challenging consolidation of Suharto's authority than the portrayal of "quick and dirty" mass killings as the endpoint. Rather, they point to a much lengthier and more difficult period of dealing with political opposition and one that extends much further into the period in which the regime was simultaneously trying to paint a picture of political stability in order to attract foreign investors (Winters 1996, 48–49).

In addition to its opposition, the Suharto regime in its first months had to contend with an equally well-organized coalition of more ideologically compatible social forces who were nonetheless intent on pressuring any new government to pursue policies favorable to their own interests. Muslim and Christian organizations that had been facing ideological and sometimes physical attack by PKI cadres or affiliated groups demanded the banning and destruction of the party and, in the case of Muslim organizations, demanded a greater say in government policy (Bresnan 1993, 36–37; Bachtiar 1968, 190–91). Student organizations, many of which strongly supported anti-Communist trends among the Indonesian intellectual community, demanded for their part a rapid effort to revive the economy: after all, student protests over rising bus fares in Jakarta had been one of the crucial episodes of contention that began Sukarno's fall. During the first three months of 1966, the ability of KAMI and other university groups to mobilize thousands of students for anti-Sukarno and anti-Communist demonstrations were crucial in Suharto's effort to compel Sukarno to sign the famous Letter of Instruction of March 11, which transferred sweeping powers to Suharto. Even though the strongest of the student organizations, KAMI, was actually created with the assistance of an army general,[2] it quickly took on a position of real political power, and its leaders were able to extract significant concessions from the military (Bresnan 1993, 37–38; Bachtiar 1968, 195–97) in return for their support in the purge of the PKI. Furthermore, they demanded a stake in policymaking for the pragmatic intellectuals that they supported, pushing Suharto and his advisors hard to grant broad economic authority to professional economists. Finally, landowners, who included not just rural elites but Islamic foundations and, increasingly, army officers, had dramatically increased their national political power by collaborating with the army's "shock troops" during the killings of 1965 and 1966 (Wertheim 1966, 123–24).

In brief, the New Order regime, when it began to mull strategies for economic recovery, faced grave economic circumstances, a seriously weakened state, and a powerful array of organized social forces across the political spectrum. Moreover, the early exigencies of dealing with the PKI compelled close relationships with student and Islamic groups and with rural elites, all of which actively participated in the killing of Communist sympathizers but many of which, by the mid-1970s, had themselves turned into opposition groups. As I argued in chapter 1, it is not by contingent event or by the flukes of personality that leaders like Suharto make decisions about development and coalitions: they, like the Shah, would rather

---

[2] KAMI stands for *Kesatuan Aksi Mahasiswa Indonesia* (Indonesian Student Action Union); it also is the inclusive word for "we," or "all of us," in Indonesian. KAMI was created in late October 1965 at the home of General Sjarif Thajeb (who was also minister of higher education) during a meeting of students and anti-Communist military leaders.

have made low-cost decisions to maximize their political autonomy. When circumstances do not permit, however, then high-cost concessions become the only alternative. This was the case for Suharto's new regime.

Coalitions and Social Forces

A primary demand of the Indonesian student movement was that any new government give greater authority in economic policy to professionals—in this case academically trained economists rather than the politicians who directed policy in the "Old Order" of the Sukarno era. To this end, KAMI endorsed a group of Berkeley-trained economists at the University of Indonesia (UI) that came to be known as the "Berkeley Mafia." Because they were trained in the United States, they were intellectually amenable to both market-driven development and foreign investment. However, they also remained politically sensitive to normative issues of social equity after years of exposure to Indonesia's post-independence attempts at solidarity building. These economists, collectively hired as a "change team,"[3] were simultaneously confident that capitalism could propel the country forward and committed to a strong role for the state as guarantor of some form of social justice (Bresnan 1993, 72–85).

The UI group had published a book, edited by economics professor Widjojo Nitisastro, in November 1965 that argued for a complete overhaul of Sukarno's economic policy (Nitisastro 1965). KAMI invited the members of the group to a seminar in January 1966 to present their plan for action; future New Order leaders Nasution and Adam Malik also participated. In an attempt to signal not only to KAMI but to domestic and foreign investors as well that the new regime was prepared to listen to expertise, the new cabinet adopted most of the group's proposals and hired many of them into the government's new economic policy team (Mas'oed 1983, 84–95).[4] As a result, the student movement could point to real authority in the new government during this period by virtue of the economists for whose jobs they had lobbied so hard. By the early 1970s, the same students were protesting the New Order's heavy reliance on foreign capital and lack of attention to indigenous capitalists. However, by then the same network of ties to stu-

---

[3] Waterbury coined this term to describe politically insulated economic reform teams brought in to direct import-substitution industrialization and, later, the privatization of state-owned enterprises (1993).

[4] They did so shortly after a seminar sponsored by the University of Indonesia's economics department entitled "Resurrection of the Soul of '66: Charting a New Path" (UI 1966). A perusal of the list of speakers and participants at various panels of the student seminar reveals a mix of senior professors, religious leaders, and, interestingly, pro-Suharto military officers. See the section entitled "Chusus Bidang Ideologi" (Special Section on Ideology) in UI (1966, 1).

dent groups that developed during the first years of the New Order enabled the regime to monitor and coopt them.

Religious political parties and other organizations also took a central position in the immediate post-coup period. On October 1, 1965, Subchan Z. E., the vice chairman of Nahdlatul Ulama (NU); Harry Tjan, the general secretary of the Catholic Party; and Mar'ie Muhammad, the general secretary of the Himpunan Mahasiswa Islam (Islamic Students' Association, HMI) met to discuss a coalition aimed at countering the student and youth organizations of the PKI. Seven days later, they met directly with Suharto to make requests directed at expediting their ability to mobilize students and others—permission to travel at night despite the curfew, funding for and permission to hold demonstrations, and the provision of small arms by the army. Subchan, Mar'ie, and Harry were in contact almost every day with generals close to Suharto after that, primarily Generals Ahmed Kemal Idris, Sarwo Edhie Wibowo, and Ali Moertopo. NU, HMI, and the Catholic Party played a central role not only in the street demonstrations in late 1965 and early 1966 but also in the killings in central and east Java. They became an important part of the coalition.

During the last years of Sukarno's rule, land reform was formally adopted, in 1959, but only enacted in a few areas; the lack of implementation was a primary motivation for the rural poor in joining or supporting the PKI. While Suharto's government may have not been predisposed to land reform in any case, the support that it needed from NU and other large landowners in rural Java compelled a much stronger anti–land reform policy. Far beyond merely excluding land reform from their economic policy package, New Order policymakers explicitly called land reform "PKI propaganda." This was a major act of support for rural elites and especially for the NU, which relied heavily on their support and which owned a great deal of agricultural land itself. As Lev notes, "The Nahdatul Ulama has been frank in its joy that without the PKI the land reform and similar efforts may now be ignored altogether" (1966, 110). By taking such a strong anti-reform stand, the Suharto government managed to bring NU and Javanese rural landowners into the ruling coalition, even though these groups were uneasy about opening the economy so thoroughly to foreign investment.

By early 1967, the New Order regime had taken strong steps toward consolidating a coalition around late development. Inside the government, the regime took initial steps, despite its self-imposed austerity mandate, to gain the loyalty of the bureaucracy in January 1966 by enacting a 500 percent raise in civil servants' salaries. The government doubled salaries in January 1967 and raised them by 50 percent in April 1967. In effect, the New Order had shown a key support group that (1) it was willing to help individuals by mitigating the costs of residual inflation from the Sukarno years, (2) its declarations about improving bureaucratic efficiency were based not on contempt for civil servants but rather on its recognition of their centrality in the New Order stabilization project, and (3) the New Order would place first priority on keeping the "Grand Coalition" happy rather than placating international capital at any cost, even in the face of so many demands for austerity by foreign creditors (Winters 1996, 52).[5] By declaring its support for the bureaucracy as a set of institutions rather than as a collection of party-dependent individuals, the regime also made an important change in the state of job security for civil servants. During the period of parliamentary democracy and even under Guided Democracy, party affiliation was crucial to job security since so many ministries were divided up according to the makeup of the ruling coalition at any given time. In the pre–New Order era, individuals had had to rely on increasingly fickle balances of party power for career advancement (Malley 1999, 123–25).

In addition to the bureaucracy and the army, which served as the primary institutional bases of the regime, the major student organizations, religious parties and organizations, and rural elites on Java all coalesced around the exigencies of order and development. While it was building the coalition, however, the regime had to deal with the institutional needs of development. As we shall see, the desperate times in which the regime began to restructure the economy had powerful effects on its decisions about institution building.

Politics and Parties

Whereas by 1967 the New Order had largely succeeded in purging supporters of Sukarno and the PKI from the military and from the bureaucracy and had begun to see the results of its carefully crafted development strategy, Suharto and his closest advisors remained concerned with legitimizing the regime. More important, it is clear that he and the other generals in the government wanted to construct a political organization that could reflect, represent, and provide support for government policy.[6] Given Suharto's ap-

---

[5] There was some attention paid to austerity. The need for cuts was reflected in widespread dismissals of civil servants who were known to have been PKI supporters; the logic in these cases, borne out by the lack of outcry, was that firing suspected Communists would generate little or no sympathy for them among their former colleagues.

[6] I focus almost exclusively in this section on the institution building aspects of the rise of Golkar. There is another side to the party's success in the 1971 elections and beyond—intimidation and other strategies designed to weaken rival parties. It is not my intention to brush off those efforts; rather, since they were also part and parcel of the Shah's repertoire of rule, I intend to focus on the significant differences in how these two governments built their respective parties. My lack of emphasis on heavy-handed strategies or "dirty tricks" simply reflects a conviction that it is not what accounts for the variation in outcomes.

parent concern for consolidating his political authority "by the book," a strong performance in the first elections of the New Order were given especially high priority in the late 1960s.[7] Moreover, the Consultative Assembly's confirmation of his executive authority in July 1966 was conditional and temporary, pending elections in 1968 in which his government would be required to demonstrate its popular support. Thus, even in his position of power Suharto faced considerable institutional uncertainty and a probable challenge in the pending elections.[8]

After the experience of the 1955 elections, which led to more, rather than less, political turmoil, the prospect of another multiparty electoral campaign was at best an unattractive option for the government. The political parties were weaker as a result of Sukarno's campaign to "bury" them. Nonetheless, the remaining parties after the decimation of the PKI—especially Masjumi, the National Party, and NU—held enough political support to make it impossible for Suharto to simply declare himself president or to dissolve the parliament. As a result, in July 1967 Suharto and his more moderate supporters in the regime negotiated a compromise electoral reform bill with the major parties that called for the government to appoint one third of the Consultative Assembly, which elected the president, and twenty-two percent of the parliament (Bresnan 1993, 89–91). The compromise shook out this way in the face of opposition within the regime itself: Nasution, Kemal Idris, and particularly General H. R. Dharsono, three prominent New Order radicals, opposed the deal. Dharsono actually tried to install forcibly a two-party balance in Bandung, where the Siliwangi Division of the army that he commanded was based. Suharto ultimately named Dharsono ambassador to Thailand and assigned Kemal Idris to be head of the East Indonesia Division, based in Makassar, Sulawesi.

Once the rules of the game, in which any official party of the regime would compete, were established, the focus shifted to what kind of political organization would become the new public face of the New Order. Three basic options were available: throw in the New Order's lot with an existing party (the PNI, the Indonesian National Party, was the rumored favorite); create an independent group of New Order intellectuals who as a

---

[7] Despite the violence with which the New Order regime and its allies pursued, arrested, or killed PKI members and supporters, this facet of Suharto's consolidation is often overlooked. His hesitance to confront Sukarno directly and his insistence on waiting until he could maneuver Sukarno into signing authority over to him in an official manner both provoked serious tension between Suharto and his moderate supporters and what were effectively the "New Order radicals," who wanted an immediate confrontation with Sukarno to push him out of the presidency by any means necessary.

[8] It was through lobbying by NU members in the parliament that the bill affirming his authority was passed. The early date scheduled for the elections may well have been an attempt by the NU leadership, as one of the best-organized political organizations at the time, to maximize its position as a "first comer" to the new electoral game.

proto-party would be the cornerstone of the government's electoral campaign;[9] or rely on some other organization to mobilize supporters to cast their votes for the New Order's economic development program. The first choice would have left the regime at least partially dependent on existent party elites and subject to the same potentially centrifugal politicking that had undercut previous governments. The second would have thrown a new and untested group of politicians with no organizational base up against a seasoned, if somewhat chaotic, array of existing parties, with the additional disadvantage of favoring the radicals among the New Order governing group. The third option—taking an organization outside the "old" elite of the party system but with accessible institutional and social roots and giving it a new ideological face—seemed the best option. Suharto and the New Order moderates turned to the army's Sekretariat Bersama Golongan Karya (also known as Sekber Golkar, the Joint Secretariat of Functional Groups, hereafter Golkar) for the answer. Golkar had its origins in a series of social organizations established by anti-Communist army officers in late 1964 to compete with the mobilizing efforts of the PKI (Suryadinata 1989, 10–13).[10]

Before 1967, however, Golkar had not yet achieved much in the way of institutionalization or capacity to mobilize and recruit: "Its organization and sphere of influence was largely limited to Jakarta [and] from its inception was forced to rely on the support of the army. The result was that it was largely a paper organization" (Boileau 1983, 46). During the early New Order years, Golkar was badly in need of resources, making it difficult to serve as a real electoral vehicle. Given the scheduled date for elections in 1968, the chances were slim that it could be rebuilt in time to guarantee that the "Panca Sila forces be victorious," as the army was hoping (quoted in Crouch 1978, 248). Suharto thus announced in January 1968 that Indonesia's political conditions were not conducive to productive elections and postponed them due to "technical problems" involving voter registration. More important, he also used the economic crisis as a justification for putting the elections off until 1971. His explicit hope was that the first Five-Year Plan (*Rencana Pembangunan Lima Tahun,* or Repelita) would provide a boost to Golkar's electoral chances by getting the economy back on its feet (Boileau 1983, 49). Suharto and his advisors then set about building an organization in Golkar that could deliver the election for them.[11]

---

[9] Note the similarities of this option—pushed by the New Order radicals and dismissed by Suharto—to the Shah's choice of the Progressive Circle in 1963 to spearhead his vision of a new official party.

[10] Note that there existed an organization called Golongan Karya from the 1940s as well, which became part of the new Golkar. I use *Golkar* here to refer to Sekber Golkar rather than its predecessor.

[11] It is worthwhile to note here that the regime claimed throughout this period that Golkar was not a party at all but rather merely an organization to represent the functional

Like Iran Novin in its early years, which I discuss later in this chapter, Golkar in 1967 was essentially an undeveloped central organization with more than 200 affiliate groups that agreed on little and had questionable ties to the central leadership. Whereas in Iran there was little incentive to move quickly in drawing those groups closer to the regime through a central party apparatus, however, in Indonesia the still-recent memory of the PKI's mobilizational power and the organizational clout of the remaining parties left the government with little choice but to try to mobilize its own base of support and impose some discipline on an unruly conglomeration of social organizations. Thus, the Golkar leadership dramatically cut the number of organizations and replaced many of their leaders with men it knew it could count on to provide loyal leadership. Second, it created a much smaller group of four coordinating bodies called *Kelompok Induk Organisasi* (basic organizational units) to simplify the process of directing the affiliate organizations: one each for functional groups related to material development, spiritual development, religion, and the armed forces. The spiritual development group was primarily made up of cultural organizations representing writers, artists, teachers, young people, women, and ethnic groups. Within each of these subgroups was another secretariat. While the whole organization remained somewhat unwieldy, the new hierarchical arrangements made it possible to coordinate the incorporation of the groups into something resembling a single political movement. Despite beginning with a somewhat chaotic structure similar to that of Iran Novin, by 1970 Golkar was, by most accounts, operating with impressive coordination.

The same process of "Golkarization" took place at the local government level. The threat of coercion that hung over the heads of former leftists and the social mobility offered those willing to demonstrate loyalty to Golkar and Korps Pegawai Republik Indonesia (Indonesian Civil Servants' Corps, or Korpri) led to the deterioration and eventual political death of three of the four main opposition parties by 1971 (Schiller 1996, 73–74). The PKI and Masjumi parties were outlawed, leaving only the NU as a potent political force. With the PKI destroyed, the major remaining obstacles to Golkar's electoral effort were PNI support in the civil service and the autonomous institutions of the Islamic movement. NU, the Partai Muslimin Indonesia (Parmusi), Muhammadiyah, and various other national bodies in addition to local and mosque-level organizations all presented alternatives

---

groups. This distinction allowed the regime to ban civil servants, for instance, from party membership while encouraging their active participation in Golkar. I refer to the restructuring of Golkar as "party building" consciously; the regime's rhetoric aside, Golkar was a political party in all but name.

to the regime's Golkar. The regime first pursued strategies directed at diluting and, where possible, coopting these organizations.

The PNI, in the view of the regime, had the potential to perform very strongly in the elections for two reasons. First, its major base of support had always lay in the Javanese-dominated civil service: most of its supporters had been in their jobs since the late 1960s. Second, the absence of the PKI left few ideologically palatable alternatives to its former supporters, and the PNI leadership had always professed loyalty to Sukarno's conception of "Indonesian socialism." In the first years of the Golkar party-building period, therefore, recruitment of government employees was a top priority for the regime. Alongside the purges of Sukarno supporters in the bureaucracy, political recruitment served to build and cement loyalty to the new leadership. Under Sekber Golkar, newly appointed high-level bureaucrats and military officers spread the ideological word to their staffs, encouraging and pressuring them to join the party and to bring out the vote (Mackie and MacIntyre 1994, 12–13).

This less formal recruitment was later augmented by a formal socialization and recruitment program for all civil servants called the "P4" (*Pedoman Penghayatan dan Pengamalan Pancasila*, "guidance in the comprehension and implementation of Pancasila"[12]), courses intended to embed new bureaucrats in Golkar as they entered the government workforce (Mackie and MacIntyre 1994, 27). By 1970 this was institutionalized among other organizations in the Korps Karyawan Departemen Dalam Negeri (Kokarmendagri), the civil servants' corps for the Department of Home Affairs (Reeve 1985, 287). In addition to Golkarizing the bureaucracy, these strategies gave the regime a new and powerful source of patronage to substitute for its lack of ready oil rent payoffs and took that same source of patronage away from one of its most powerful political rivals. By 1970, nearly all of the PNI's members had abandoned it for Golkar.

The regime also made concerted efforts to capture a portion of the Islamic vote by setting out to coopt as many leaders and groups as it could. Suharto invited over 800 Islamic leaders to Jakarta, for instance, for an all-expenses-paid conference in which the primary goal was to establish patronage relationships with as many local leaders as possible. Efforts to establish these sorts of individual relationships to the New Order were directed through Golkar mostly by means of providing funds through Gabuhan Usaha Perbaikan Pendidikan Islam (Union of Efforts to Improve Islamic Education) for individual kiayis (Islamic teachers), to establish

---

[12] "Pancasila" is Sanskrit for "five principles," which the regime used as a broad legitimizing ideology. The principles are: belief in only one god, just and civilized humanity, Indonesian unity, democracy based on mutual consultation, and social justice for all of Indonesia's people.

schools or mosques. An Islamic newspaper wrote, "Religious leaders were lured to the conference by promises of grand material profits" (quoted in Boileau 1983, 53).

Another social group initially outside the purview of Golkar was the Indonesian student movement. The party also took steps to coopt this powerful group, via the Komite Nasional Pemuda Indonesia (National Committee of Indonesian Youth, or KNPI), the student organ of Golkar. As a result, by 1971 the leadership of the KNPI was composed almost entirely of former anti-Sukarno student opposition leaders from the mid-1960s (Reeve 1985, 329–30). In addition to incorporating the leaders of movements like KAMI when it could, the Suharto regime gave blocs of seats in the parliament to groups like HMI as a way of integrating them into governing and into Golkar. By the mid-1970s, as with KAMI, much of the HMI leadership from a decade before had taken up careers made possible through membership in Golkar.[13]

By the mid-1970s, the combination of pressure and patronage resulted in the incorporation or dissolution of most of the oppositional political organizations from the 1960s. Those that remained outside the official Golkar apparatus, such as the NU, largely took on the role of loyal opposition, buying into the official state ideology of Pancasila in return for material and political incentives. NU, for instance, received significant policy authority in matters of religion, personal status law, and other social issues; it gained this authority after leaving the United Development Party (Partai Persatuan Pembangunan—PPP in 1975 and essentially negotiating its own deal with the government (Suryadinata 1989, 128–29). It is true that, in absolute terms, Islamic social groups in general lost influence during this period. Lev's (1972) study of Islamic courts charts a broad trend in New Order Indonesia in which religious courts came to serve, albeit subtly, the interests of the state. Nonetheless, one episode nicely illustrates how lightly the New Order regime had to tread when it came to confronting Islam. A 1973 draft law giving authority over marriage law to the government met with serious protest in parliament and in the streets, much of which was organized by NU and other Islamic groups. On September 27, 1973, when the minister of religion spoke before the parliament to endorse the bill, HMI protesters stormed the building and occupied it. The law was passed

---

[13] The role of former student leaders continues today. The recently departed head of the post–New Order Golkar, Akbar Tandjung, a former HMI leader, was until 2004 head of the House of Representatives and one of the four or five most powerful politicians in the country, despite a criminal conviction for illegally using state funds to support the 1999 Golkar election campaign. In fact, lobbying by his fellow Golkar MPs succeeded in convincing members from the Partai Demokrasi Indonesia—Perjuangan (Indonesian Democratic Struggle Party) to stall parliamentary investigation of his actions in 1999. See, for instance, Jakarta Post, July 1, 2002.

anyway in January 1974, and it is with its passage that most accounts stop, attributing great power to the government to bulldoze social opposition. However, a close reading of the debate over the law—which in its original form would have subsumed marriage in all of Indonesia's religious communities under one secular law administered by the Department of Justice—suggests a more nuanced reality.[14] Emmerson outlines in careful detail the actual process by which Islamic opposition to this bill was overcome. It was not by force but rather by changing the law to include most of the Islamic community's demands that the law came to a vote and was passed (1976, 228–35). In fact, the law increased the authority of religious communities and left decisions related to marriage under the authority of the Department of Religion, which was still dominated by NU. In short, selective cooptation and substantive concessions during challenges such as this made it possible to manage the Islamic and other movements sufficiently to prevent a serious challenge to the government. Moreover, this incident reflects the regime's ability to "reach into" the opposition, as a result of its contacts with powerful groups like NU, to prevent open confrontations from emerging or spreading.

Early patterns of interaction between the regime and social groups such as Islamists and student organizations go far to explain why Suharto's government was able to consolidate its power as successfully as it did. Close ties to NU and to KAMI, among others, made it possible for the regime to foresee potential conflicts, to manage them when they did emerge, and, above all, to bring on board leaders from various social groups. Thus, although KAMI and other early regime allies turned against it as they realized that democratic governance was unlikely to arise under the New Order's military rule, by the early 1970s most of the important actors from the 1965–66 period fell into three categories: part of the regime's coalition, fragmented by cooptation of individual group leaders, or marginalized.

Under Suharto, the treatment of political parties reflected a sense of urgency born of the dislocation of 1965–66. From 1966 to the late 1970s, using Golkar to reshape the political party landscape was of the highest priority, and how the party system was used to build the regime's capacity to mobilize support indicates again a focus on institution building rather than on the centralization of authority in Suharto personally. The evidence suggests that this was a product both of the uncertainty of Suharto's political authority and of a conscious strategy to strengthen the regime as much as the state. Golkar party recruitment, fragmentation via cooptation, and marginalization strategies aimed at social forces all worked to create a solid

---

[14] Prior to this, marriage law was the prerogative of each religious community. For a discussion of its general importance in social control, see Woods (2004).

network of patronage and ideological support linking state and society that considerably helped the government to weather the uprisings of the late 1970s.

The 1971 elections were the first official and perhaps the most important test of the extent to which Golkar had succeeded in transforming itself into a viable official party, and the results exceeded even what the government had expected. Forecasting a victory that would give Golkar perhaps one third of the elected seats and therefore a ruling majority coalition (with the appointed members), the party actually won 63 percent of the votes cast nationwide. Of the other parties contesting the election, NU was the only major party to win more of the vote than it had in 1955, moving from 18 to almost 19 percent of the vote. Both the PNI and Parmusi lost ground dramatically, largely as a result of Golkar's efforts to pull away their bases of support. As New Order Indonesia moved toward the 1973–74 oil boom, then, the regime had succeeded in building Golkar into the most powerful political organization in the country. And, despite its heavy-handed approach to politics, it had become one that attracted significant support and that could both mobilize and provide patronage to millions of supporters.

The other side of the expansion of Golkar's organizational capacity was government policy toward other political parties and organizations, a policy best characterized as fragmentation and cooptation. During the two years after the 1971 elections, which were to be the test of the new Golkar electoral machine, the nine other existing political organizations were lumped together into two, the PPP (Islamic) grouping and the PDI, a combination of nationalist and Christian parties. The reorganization was intended to produce sufficient factionalism within the two new groups to prevent any serious political challenge to Golkar. The NU, one of the only strong political forces remaining by the mid-1970s, broke with the PPP because of this factionalism and reached its own accommodation with the Suharto government, one that included control over many educational institutions and the Ministry of Religion (Suryadinata 1989, 128–29).

Oil, Taxes, and the Political Economy

In large part because of the political turmoil of the Guided Democracy period (especially 1963–66), Indonesia's oil revenues came to a halt as western fears of the spread of communism to the Sukarno regime led to a halt in oil purchases. Oil revenues began to accrue again after 1966 but did not become a major portion of total government revenues until 1970–71 and only passed 40 percent of revenues after the oil boom in 1973–74. In terms of Indonesia's political economy, this left the Suharto government with nearly seven years of post-upheaval state and coalition building to accomplish without access to the patronage resources that a vibrant oil sector would have made possible.

During the first two years after the 1953 coup, the Shah also faced a major government revenue crisis. However, the United States provided massive grant aid to fill the financial gap until 1955, when oil revenues returned to their previous levels. In Indonesia, no such external aid was forthcoming. Because investors and foreign creditors had become so wary of Indonesia's market worthiness during the late Sukarno years and because State Department officials were cautioning the Johnson administration to take a "low-key" approach to aid for the nascent New Order government,[15] the latter had some difficulty convincing western governments to resume loans to Indonesia. While the government's many missions abroad in search of loans eventually generated tens of millions of dollars (for detailed discussions of these missions, see Mas'oed 1983, 98–114; Winters 1996, 53–76) in new credits, the foreign aid would not cover all of the costs of development expenditures, routine expenditures, and Indonesia's massive debts.[16] Finally, given the lack of ready export revenues from oil, domestic extraction too looked to be a necessity if the New Order were to fund its first few years of recovery and state building. Moreover, the full resumption of loans and investment from the West would depend on putting the institutions of state back in order. One product of the augmented capacities of the government was increased tax-extraction capacity, which would not be joined by oil revenues until the end of the 1960s.

There is little question that solvency and, beyond that, sufficient revenues to fund economic recovery and development drove much of the regime's early decisionmaking about reforming the extractive institutions of the Indonesian state. During the first year of Suharto's New Order, national tax revenues increased 600 percent and by as much as 1700 percent in resource-poor former Communist strongholds such the Special District of Yogyakarta in central Java (Biro Pusat Statistik Indonesia, 1963–68; Pusat Data Propinsi DIY 1980). That non-oil tax revenues remained a larger portion of Indonesian state income than oil revenues until 1974 reveals a

---

[15] While it does not come up explicitly in documents from the period (at least those available to the public) or in scholarly accounts, it is in my view a plausible argument that the experience of high-profile intervention in Iran a decade earlier may have made policymakers more cautious about putting a blatantly American stamp on the anti-Communist turn in Indonesian politics. A learning effect among American policymakers, therefore, might account for some of the difference.

[16] In addition to the fact that aid revenues were highly conditional at the outset—in contrast to oil revenues, which were almost completely discretionary—foreign aid, significant though it was, was nowhere near enough in the 1966–69 period to lift the Indonesian government out of its economic hole. See Palmer for a detailed discussion of the weight of foreign aid relative to Indonesia's debts and expenditure needs (1978, 26–30).

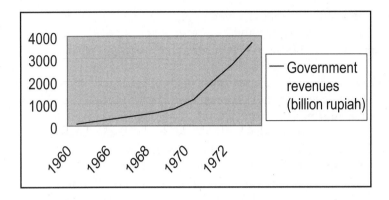

Figure 3.1. Indonesian government revenues, 1960–76

marked contrast with the ideal-type rentier state behavior of the Pahlavi state in Iran. The aggregate figures for government revenues provide a striking first cut at the speed with which the Suharto government worked to put the state's fiscal affairs back in order.

Two things must be said about taxation and state capacity under Suharto. First, a look at total government revenues between 1965 and 1968

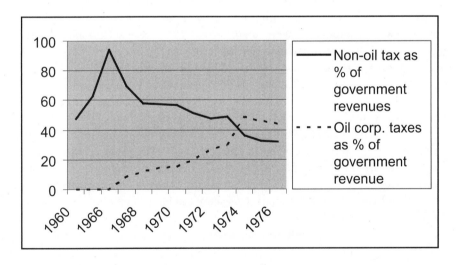

Figure 3.2. Oil and taxation in Indonesia, 1960–76

Source: Central Bureau of Statistics, Indonesia, *Monthly Statistical Bulletins* and Bank of Indonesia, *Yearly Reports,* cited in Uppal (1986, 53).

reveals an immense spike in revenues, of *2000 percent*. Even when we discount that increase to account for the substantial inflows of international aid starting in 1967, the rise is remarkable, speaking strongly to the immediate efforts of the New Order regime to rebuild the state's extractive capacity. Second, generally speaking, non-oil taxes remained a significant share of total government revenues. As I discuss in the next chapter, they even did so during the first oil boom, when by all theoretical predictions they should have seen a sharp drop. This extractive capacity stands in contrast to that of Iran and several other oil states during the same period. In addition, despite the observations made by a number of scholars that the Indonesian tax bureaucracy operated throughout the 1970s at considerably below its revenue potential (for instance, see Uppal 1986, 15–21), personal income tax collection rose at a consistent rate each year during the decade, though it remained a small percentage of total collection (12, 24).

The overall figures for tax revenues speak strongly to the continued national importance of Indonesia's extractive institutions, a conclusion that is supported by case studies of local tax collection. Schiller notes, for instance, a marked increase in local revenues to the Jepara district government: "Between 1969–70 and 1980–81 Jepara local[ly derived] government revenues grew from Rp.49.7 million to Rp.574.9 million—an eleven-fold increase in 11 years" (1996, 83).[17] During the same period, the total staff of the Jepara government rose from 722 to only 1150 employees, suggesting not just an increase in the number of tax collectors but also a real increase in the state's collection efficiency. Most important, this period encompassed both oil booms, in which extractive apparatuses in Iran and Saudi Arabia deteriorated and were dismantled, respectively. Indonesia illustrates a very different institutional trajectory. In Jepara and, as I discuss below, in most of the country, institutional capacity grew with the economy.

The capacity to extract taxes has been associated with the more general capacity of states to exercise social control, especially through the acquisition of information about citizens and businesses (Chaudhry 1997; Levi 1988; Lieberman 2003). This generalization from tax collection efficiency to state capacity finds support in the Jepara district government: "all respondents in Pemda [*pemerintah daerah*, local government] believed that more information is more accurately collected than at any time in their careers" (Schiller 1996, 90). In part, this seems to have been a result of the influx of oil-generated central government subsidies to districts. In sum, in contrast to Iran and Saudi Arabia, where extractive capacity and oil rev-

---

[17] Jepara is a city on the north coast of central Java, for decades the center of Indonesia's teak furniture industry. It has also been a local government unit that retained more autonomy than did most under the New Order, making Schiller's conclusions about its integration into central authority all the more noteworthy.

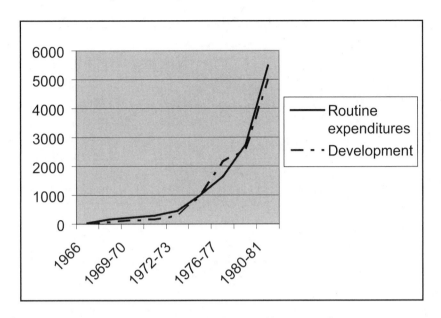

Figure 3.3. Indonesian government expenditures, 1966–81 (billion rupiah)

Source: 1968–1969 Statistical Pocketbook: Indonesia Development News; quoted in Dapice (1980, 21).

enues were inversely correlated, in Indonesia oil income seems to have been generally used to *enhance* the state's capacity to collect taxes rather than to supplant it (97–98). The steady increase in tax revenues, along with total government revenues in the five years following Suharto's rise to power, suggest a concerted effort to build state capacity across Indonesia.

Another marked difference worth noting is the change in routine (administrative and state-related) and development (for state industries and the encouragement of private investment) expenditures. As discussed below, expenditure patterns in 1960s Iran seem to reflect a low priority for state building, if budget allocations are representative. Patterns of budget allocation for Indonesia during the same period—from the beginning of rapid development to the late 1970s—reveal an interesting and telling contrast. Figure 3.3 provides year-to-year figures for routine and development expenditures from 1966 to 1981; they suggest that, throughout this period, investing in the state and its institutions took as high a priority as development projects did. This macro-trend affords a useful context in which to place the analysis of political party and local institution building.

By the early 1970s, when oil revenues again became available to the

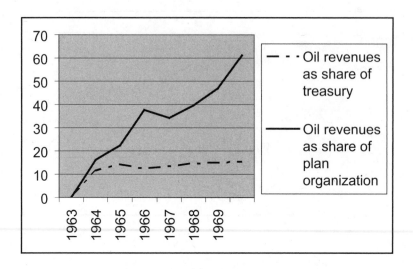

Figure 3.4. Allocation of Iran's oil revenues, 1963–69

Source: Bank Markazi Iran (1969,86); Amuzegar and Fekrat (1971, 37).

regime and when the government had finally succeeded in wresting control over state oil corporation taxes from Pertamina head General Ibnu Sutowo, the revenues generated by taxes were less crucial than the information generated simply by continuing to send out collectors. Thinking about the practice of institutions, rather than their strict duties, it makes more sense that a regime like Suharto's, which had turned to rapid state-led development under such trying conditions, would continue to emphasize the process of tax collection—which provides valuable information—over their ostensible goal of collecting revenues. In the section on local government below I discuss how, despite a dramatic decline in the *need* to tax, the regime employed strategies to maintain revenue collection, especially at the local level.

Local Government

The extension of central authority and policy direction into local government must be counted among the most important aspects of the consolidation of the New Order polity. Under Suharto, "Jakarta's control over the 27 provincial and numerous 'second level' municipal and *kabupaten* [regency] governments increased to a degree that would have been barely imaginable in Sukarno's time" (Mackie and MacIntyre 1994, 22). What is remarkable about this transformation, as I discuss below, is that it was accomplished not by weakening provincial government relative to the center but by significantly strengthening local institutions while simultaneously tying them more closely to central authority. This absolute increase in authority contrasted starkly with the zero-sum approach to local politics in Iran. Moreover, provincial institutions were given much of the responsibility for promoting development, which as in Iran was the primary legitimizing principle of the New Order government in Indonesia.

Local government, as Jim Schiller notes, was greatly strengthened after 1966 "by the increased financial resources that flowed from Jakarta. The rapid growth of the state seems likely to have made it a more formidable force in local society" (Schiller 1996, 34). Moreover, as discussed above, those financial resources were directed not only toward industrial production but also toward strengthening the local agencies themselves. The chaos of 1965 and early 1966, Schiller argues, "probably made it easier for district government to ensure obedience by its local employees and by the public" (34). Not only administrative but also fiscal duties were increasingly shifted to provincial and local institutions in the late 1960s and early 1970s, while the central government was steadily reducing their political authority. Thus, in contrast to Iran, in which local government gained in administrative responsibility but lost both political and fiscal authority— resulting in weak local agencies that could not implement central goals— Indonesian local institutions received increasingly larger proportions of their revenues from the central government and became able to accomplish more and more even as they were incorporated more tightly into the lines of authority emanating from Jakarta.

Aside from income and corporate taxation, much of Indonesia's tax revenue was collected at the local level; thus, while I treat taxation and local governance separately here, they were functionally intertwined. What is important is the degree to which the New Order regime in its early years placed a strong emphasis on the *process* of revenue collection and continued to do so well after the revenues extracted ceased to be of much significance in the grand scheme of government revenues. In other words, well into the first oil boom, when the government no longer needed to collect taxes effectively at the local level, it continued to invest in local extraction by heavily subsidizing the salaries of tax officials in order to maintain institutional capacity and to continue the collection of information.

Economic studies of center-local relations in the early New Order years bear out these claims. In the late 1960s, local tax offices were given significantly increased responsibility for revenue collection. At the same time, their staff operations were funded almost completely by revenue transfers from the center (Devas 1989, 81–83; Buwazier 1988, 2). Whereas provincial-level agencies had long relied on grants from the central government, under the New Order regency and municipality (Dati II—*Daerah Tingkat II* or Local Level II) agencies also became progressively more dependent on central grants.[18] This increased dependence coincided with an absolute increase in the revenues collected by local government; thus, central grants did not replace local extraction but rather appear to have made it possible for local collectors to do their jobs more efficiently. Recalling Schiller's observation above (1996, 90) that his interviews revealed that information was more effectively gathered under the 1970s New Order than at any time in their careers, a broad trend is recognizable in which provincial, municipal, and city agencies grew in size and greatly expanded their capacities.

In the Special Capital Region of Jakarta and elsewhere, for instance, a dense system of neighborhood organization also took shape as a result of the regime's state-building strategies. Jakarta and other major cities were divided into neighborhoods of about forty households, each of which made up a *rukun tetangga* (literally "neighborly harmony," RT) unit. A *rukun warga* ("harmonious association," RW) was a group of several RTs. Local neighborhood leaders, who were not paid or officially employed by the government, were chosen to help the local government implement decisions made at the national or provincial level, to chair neighborhood meetings (which, in addition to serving as a forum for local decisions, served to transmit societal demands upward to provincial and district leaders), and to "give advice, reprimands, and reminders to members who violate the decisions of the RT" (quoted in Logsdon 1974, 53). In essence, the social control function of local government was augmented by the creation of unpaid positions whose responsibilities consisted largely of holding neighborhood meetings that seemed at first glance designed to provide a mechanism for collective local decisionmaking.

To tie local government offices more closely to the military leadership under Suharto, military officers replaced many of the local officials purged during the sweep of government agencies to remove Sukarno supporters. In Central Java, for instance, where support for Sukarno and the PKI had been strongest, the number of military officers named to head individual districts tripled between 1965 and 1968 (Schiller 1996, 34–35). However, alongside military officers in district leadership positions in the late 1960s came an unprecedented number of native residents as senior appointees in the provincial governments. In regions in which the opposition had not been so strong or the political dynamics were different, the Suharto regime appointed local political leaders to governorships, figuring that in such ar-

[18] In Indonesia's system of government, municipality and regency are horizontally equivalent units but refer to urban and rural units, respectively.

eas loyalty would be best accomplished through cooptation rather than re-placement. Amal, for instance, noted a consistent pattern of appointing na-tive sons to the governorships of both West Sumatra and South Sulawesi. As he observed, whether the regime chose to install one of its own or to ap-point a *putra daerah* ("son of the region") depended heavily on the dy-namics of a given province (1992, 138–84).

These two aims of local government appointment—to strengthen ties to Jakarta and to give powerful local social forces a stake in the New Order polity—helped to consolidate the Suharto regime during its early years, when its hold on power was less secure. In addition to the widespread use of political and economic patronage and corporatization via Golkar, the first five years after Suharto's rise to leadership saw genuine attempts to embed the New Order regime in Indonesian society. It was not a democratic embeddedness, to be sure, but one born of political necessity and one that proved durable and of considerable capacity.

As with the Golkar party-building effort, the Suharto regime made sig-nificant efforts at the local levels of government to depoliticize politics. To this end, all political parties were barred from mobilizing supporters below the *kabupaten* level. Army officers in the regime, most of whom main-tained a serious distrust of party politicians (Amal 1992, 125; Crouch 1978, 271–72), conceptualized a "floating mass" (*massa mengambang*) of citi-zens who would remain apolitical between elections. The exception was of course Golkar, which was designated as a secretariat of functional groups rather than as a political party and thus allowed to maintain offices at every level. The prevalence of Golkar offices at each level of government, from provincial to village, along with increasingly powerful local agencies meant that as the regime grew more powerful, so did the state, to the point that "through [local] officials, institutions and programmes, the Indonesian state is present in most spheres of people's lives" (Antlöv 1995, 57).

The White Revolution in Iran: Rentierism, Social Forces, and Late Development

By 1957, the Shah's government had managed to decimate the leadership of the National Front and Tudeh, exiling or executing most of their leaders and purging their supporters from the military. By 1960, there existed nei-ther any broad coalition in Iranian society nor any political organization outside the regime with access to newspapers or radio. What opposition the Shah might have confronted at this point was limited to sporadic cross-class protests and otherwise group-specific one-shot demonstrations. The confrontation with, and purge of, the two movements that could have formed a serious opposition coincided neatly with the reemergence of oil revenues as the major source of state revenues. Indeed, the Seven-Year Plan for 1955–62 relied on oil revenues for 64.5 percent of its funding.[19] By the time that overspending made the need for an overhaul of economic policy more compelling, the Shah's regime faced no further organized opposition and, even with its spendthrift approach to allocation, had ample oil revenues that amounted to more than 40 percent of the state's annual income.

Moreover, the economic problems that had confronted the Shah in 1953–54 had largely been sanitized by the willingness of the United States government under Eisenhower to step in and fund the government with few conditions until oil revenues came back on line two years later. In effect, American aid filled in the budget gaps during this brief period. This aid took the air of fiscal necessity out of the immediate post-1953 coup period and removed any incentive for the Shah to move toward sweeping industrial transformation at the same time that he was consolidating his rule and reviving the oil industry (Ramazani 1974, 129–32).[20] As I discuss below, this American policy stood in marked contrast to that used in Indonesia twelve years later, in which Washington placed much more stringent conditions on Suharto's government as a first step toward attaining western economic aid. It also, however, meant that by the time Iran embarked on full-scale industrial transformation in 1963, the Shah's regime confronted neither fiscal scarcity nor an opposition that could mobilize a broad movement against the regime.[21]

Social Forces and the Dismantling of a Ruling Coalition

In the late 1950s, Iran's agricultural production remained essentially feudal, with a small number of families each owning thousands of villages. These rural elites, who had been wary of Mossadegh because his coalition too strongly reflected the interests of the Tudeh, were a major part of the ruling coalition from the coup until the onset of late development, the oth-

---

[19] Author's calculations based on data from Amuzegar and Fekrat (1971, 43).

[20] Counterfactually, it is quite plausible that, had the conditions of aid been as stringent as they were for Suharto, the Shah may have begun late development much earlier. Had that happened, he may well have had to make the same sorts of tough decisions and concrete concessions to social groups, thus leading to the same kind of robust coalition and institutional capacity that emerged under Suharto.

[21] Gasiorowski (1993a) details an alleged coup plot against the Shah by General Vali-ollah Qarani in 1957 and 1958 and argues that it reflected broad dissatisfaction with the Shah's rule. I do not mean to assert that the Shah had no detractors during this period or any other period. Where Gasiorowski and others focus on diffuse dissent, however, my interest is in the presence or absence of organized political groups that can mobilize effectively to challenge a regime or to constitute a viable alternative to the authority of current rulers.

ers being the bazaar and the highest echelons of the *ulemā*. For landowners and the *ulemā*, the Shah's regime was socially far preferable to the Front-Tudeh coalition: its early stance was essentially conservative. Moreover, the "semi-liberal" economic policies of the government during the 1953–60 period were very good for the bazaar, as the economy came to be characterized by heavy foreign capital inflows (from oil and aid) and by equally heavy government spending and, subsequently, by a marked increase in private consumption, much of which came in the form of purchases in the bazaar (Karshenas 1990, 112–31). Notwithstanding their support of the Shah's newfound political authority, however, landlords, bazaar merchants, and the *ulemā* were still a political force in the 1950s and exercised sufficient political influence that the Shah became wary of the rural gentry as a potential threat to his centralizing ambitions (Katouzian 1981, 192–98; Majd 2000a). By 1960, this perceived threat from conservative social groups coincided with the Shah's own plans for development and with pressure from the incoming Kennedy administration on the Shah's government (Katouzian 1974; Goode 1991; Saikal 1980, 82; Najmabadi 1987b, 9–11).

Together with the economic recession of 1957–60, these pressures compelled the Shah to move toward limited land reform and political liberalization (Parsa 1994, 138; Katouzian 1981, 229). One such measure was to allow independent candidates to campaign for the 1960 Majles elections. The Shah's hope was that candidates in the two official government parties would dominate the elections. When candidates from the Second National Front began to make strong efforts in the campaigning, however, the Shah ordered measures to prevent their election and to assure friendly representatives in the Majles. The rigged elections sparked protests in August 1960. In response, the Shah canceled the election results and dismissed the new parliament, announced new elections for early 1961, and reached a compromise with the representatives already in place (Parsa 1994, 139). As a result, only one candidate from the Front was elected in the January 1961 elections, which led to more protests, this time by a collection of university students, bazaar merchants, and teachers in addition to the Second National Front. The compromise reached called for the removal of Prime Minister Sharif Emami and his replacement by the "radicals' choice," Ali Amini, a strong supporter of land reform who was also the preferred choice of the Kennedy administration. Finally, in May 1961, Amini was named prime minister.

By appointing Amini, the Shah apparently hoped to end American pressure on his regime. Domestically, he also intended to out-radical the radicals of the National Front by exceeding their demands for land reform, by establishing the monarchy's political centrality among the peasantry and securing the latter as a base of social support, and by weakening landowners as a force of political opposition. Thus, there were certainly political incentives for the Shah to move on land reform. They were not the only reasons, however. Land reform was a necessary component of an expanded, accelerated focus on industrial transformation.

Najmabadi (1987b) in particular maintains that pressure from the United States and a desire to liquidate the power of landowners explains only the timing of land reform rather than the fact of land reform itself. She posits that land reform had to be a constituent part of any development program as a mechanism for providing a new domestic market for manufactured goods and a commodity surplus base from which to springboard into industrial transformation. In short, she argues that land reform was a means to the end of industrialization rather than simply a political strategy.[22] Thus, while land reform became a charged issue because of its longterm presence on the political agenda, it was actually implemented to serve the government's broader economic priorities.[23]

A crucial fact overlooked by scholars of Iran's land reform is the transformation that took place among the landowning class. It is true that many of them lost land to the state, which then sold it to peasant farmers who already had legal rights, or *nasaq*, to cultivate land. Land reform, however, took place at the same time as extensive privatization of state-owned enterprises: the government explicitly encouraged former landowners to use the proceeds from the state's purchase of their lands to become industrialists, and many did. Some of the landowners who might have been predisposed to oppose the reforms actively desisted because they stood to gain in the "new" economy. While it was not the case that rural elites moved wholesale into industry, enough of them did so, which created a split in a class that might have been able to resist the reforms had it remained united. Thus, the regime was able to coopt some landowning elites at a time when class unity was critical to any resistance to the Shah. Opposition to land reform had little success in preventing its implementation, largely because it was so disorganized. First, landowners possessed no means for coordinating their opposition to the Shah and, given widespread public support for land reform among most of the population, they would have had to present any serious challenge to the Shah as one that went against the domi-

---

[22] Whether land reform was in fact necessary for industrial transformation is a matter of debate: see for instance Ashraf (1996, 21–24) for a counterargument to Najmabadi's case. The important point is that the Shah was convinced of its necessity, as were his American supporters. For a discussion of the latter, see Latham (2000, chaps. 3 and 4).

[23] Similarly, Tabari (Parsa and Tabari 1983) notes that a number of less sweeping strategies could also have accomplished the same goal of taking political power from landed families: outright military conquest or individual seizure of land would both have carried smaller infrastructural costs.

nant political grain. As mentioned above, the lack of coordination increased as some landowners found themselves in a position to gain as first comers in the new state emphasis on industrial transformation.

Second, the *ulemā*—who through extensive holdings of their own in *awqaf*, or foundations, had a strong interest at stake in land ownership and opposed redistribution—coincidentally lost their leadership at the moment at which it would have been most needed. The Ayatollah Boroujerdi, a strong opponent of land reform, died in March 1961. In addition, he maintained a close working relationship with the Shah's regime even when its interests diverged from those of the Shi'a hierocracy under his authority.[24] Once Boroujerdi died, the authority behind the bargain did as well; further, he was the one figure who could hope to challenge the Shah. Conservative opponents of land reform, in short, were too disorganized and too marginalized in Iranian society by their anti-reform stance to mount any serious challenge to the Shah.

Despite some real progress toward reform as a result of Amini's persistence, the Second National Front remained divided on whether to support him. The National Front was internally divided between its older members, who had been active in the original National Front, and its younger, more radical members, who wanted no part of any policy adopted by the Shah's government. Furthermore, the new National Front had no political program, other than "change," around which it hoped to build a coalition. The radicals hoped they could strengthen Amini enough to challenge the Shah, and the moderates were simply trying to force him to hold general elections, which, as Parsa notes, "were not in Amini's power to guarantee" (1994, 144). As Amini pushed against the Shah to expand the land reforms, the National Front moderates attacked him as "America's prime minister." The Shah responded with force in mid-1962 by sending in troops to break up National Front demonstrations and student protests in support of the Front. After only fourteen months in office, Amini resigned, leaving the Shah's radical but disorganized opponents without an ally in the government. In effect, the progressive opposition to land reform directed by the monarchy focused its early energies on defeating Amini. When it succeeded in bringing the issue to a head, it gave the Shah an excuse to dispense with conciliatory appointments and to restructure the cabinet to suit himself. The limited opposition that the Shah's opponents could offer in 1962 was largely a result of (1) the lack of any remaining organizations that could serve as a cross-class, cross-group mobilizing resource and (2) their conflicting interests, which would have made any broad coalition difficult at best. By introducing land reform himself, the Shah made it nearly impos-

[24] Mottahedeh describes their accommodation as a "bargain" (1985, 236–40).

sible for conservative and progressive social groups to cooperate in the face of his new assertiveness in challenging them. In short, the timing of late development policies geared towards industrialization in Iran took place at a moment when the regime's opposition was neutralized and in disarray.

The end of financial scarcity by the early 1960s and the subsequent increase in the Shah's patronage capacities strongly influenced the evolution of relations between the regime and the most important social groups in Iran, including industrialists, *bazaaris*, the *ulemā*, and intellectuals. After naming his close friend Asadollah Alam to the prime ministership, the Shah modified the land reform program to limit its scope and effects. He also announced additional policies: forest nationalization, public sale of state-owned factories, profit-sharing in industry, enfranchisement of women, and the establishment of a literacy corps (Pahlavi 1967; Ashraf 1996). He called this sweeping social change program the "White Revolution." The title was intended to reflect its peaceful initiation and to stand in contrast to potential "red" or "black" revolutions carried out by Communists or what he thought of as religious fanatics. All of these reforms were part of a broad effort to prepare Iranian society for accelerated industrialization.

The Shah's White Revolution came to include, crucially, a major new focus on industrial transformation under the new Ministry of Economy and Industry. Whereas the Second Plan had been little more than a catalogue of where the government's money had gone, the Third Plan, scheduled to begin in 1963, was a highly coordinated effort to direct the state's involvement in and encouragement of industry, in an effort involving both the private and public sectors. After officials at the Plan Organization (the agency created in 1949 to administer Development Plans) got into a dispute with the Ministry of Agriculture over how much autonomy to grant the former, the Shah decided in favor of broad autonomy. Hassan Arsanjani, the agriculture minister, had come into the government under Amini as an ally against the Shah. By deciding against him, the Shah not only took sides in a horizontal conflict between institutions but also in effect significantly shielded development policy from political lobbying (Nasr 2000, 98–102). The pattern was clear: the Shah wished to remain in control of any reforms and, further, sought to use them to prepare Iranian society to move toward what he called the "Great Civilization" (Pahlavi 1977). The peasantry were to become one pillar in this plan, as were industrialists and their workers, through land reforms, economic development, and worker profit-sharing, respectively.

While the state took an unequivocal stand on landowners and the *ulemā* by attacking them and on peasants and industrialists by courting them, several other important social groups remained on uncertain terms with the state in the aftermath of the 1961–63 period. *Bazaaris* and intellectuals, who would form a major part of the urban opposition to the Shah in the late 1970s, were ringleaders of the early 1960s protests, yet in the interim they mostly faded from the political scene. In order to answer the question of how the bazaar and university communities came to their uneasy accommodation with the Shah's regime, it is important to recall the emergence of oil in about 1955 as the major source of revenue for the state (Mahdavy 1970; Karshenas 1990, 82) as well as the initiation of the White Revolution, which resulted in a major change in the regime's approach to its relationship with both groups. A referendum was held on January 21, 1963, to approve the White Revolution, to which *bazaaris*, the *ulemā*, university students and professors, and the National Front responded by organizing protests.

The protests also marked the emergence of a central opposition figure: the Ayatollah Ruhollah Khomeini, whom the West would come to know very well in the decades to come. Khomeini used the occasion of the "public" endorsement of the White Revolution as well as a pending bill in the Majles that would give diplomatic immunity to all American personnel working in Iran to release a public letter condemning what he depicted as total surrender of the country's sovereignty to the United States. Despite widespread support for him, however, by June the government had succeeded in crushing the protests and forcibly restoring order. Khomeini was arrested after delivering a speech against the monarchy. He was released, arrested again soon afterwards, and exiled to Najaf, Iraq, in 1964. The outcome of these events was the restructuring of the social balance of power in Iran. As mentioned above, landowners virtually disappeared as a political force, while the state's acceleration of industry created a small group of industrialists who "became the beneficiary and basis of support for the state" (Parsa 1994, 155). The peasantry both came under increased state authority and, in some areas, became another base of support for the state.[25] It is important to note here that the dislocation effected by the Shah's reforms here uprooted exclusively rural social institutions, while leaving urban ones largely intact; the distinction became a crucial one in the political crisis of the late 1970s.

---

[25] Support for the Shah among the peasantry was in places quite strong well into the revolutionary crisis. Jane Bestor, an anthropologist who has conducted field research in Iranian Kurdistan and Baluchistan, observed Baluch villagers in Zahedan province fighting Khomeini's supporters as they tried to knock down a statue of the Shah in late 1978 (cited in Beck 1990). Ramazani's reporting of informal interviews across various strata of Iranian society indicates that support for the Shah and his policies was strongest among peasants (1974, 133–35).

Politics and Parties

As of 1960, notwithstanding the brief exceptions for the National Front, only two political parties were allowed to compete in Majles elections. The Melli (National) and Mardom (People's) parties were formed in 1957. Melli represented the regime and Mardom the "loyal opposition." These remained the only two sanctioned parties until 1963, when the Melli party was replaced by Iran Novin (New Iran) as the official party of the government. These parties by no means represented a democratic political system, but neither did they demand political participation in support of the regime. Rather, as one Iranian intellectual active in student circles in the early 1970s characterized it, "Melli and Mardom were a working facade of democratic politics."[26] This two-party facade reflected an accommodation of mutual autonomy between the Pahlavi state and Iranian urban society, in which the state made few political demands and the majority of Iranians made no demands on the state for political representation.

It also reflected a fundamental weakness in the desire and ability of the regime to mobilize supporters in any organized way. As discussed in chapter 2, political party building, like taxation or administration at the local level, is institution building. The major reason that the Tudeh seemed so politically threatening during the late 1940s and early 1950s was precisely that, like the PKI in Indonesia, it had built strong organizational foundations on which to base its ideological program. Party cadres, affiliated unions and trade groups, and other organizations made possible the effective delivery, in Olson's (1965) words, of "selective incentives" to hundreds of thousands of members. The same logic of collective action applies to parties that represent the interests of a regime. Regardless of their ideological bent, strong party institutions serve to keep individual members—and thus societal groups—in touch with the government and vice versa. These ties are particularly important, in my view, to regimes that base their legitimacy on economic performance. Without a means such as an institutionalized ruling party to maintain a coalition through tough economic times, leaders face a much greater risk of defection during those periods.

The Melli and Mardom parties were created by the Shah in 1957 after he lifted martial law. Rather than campaigning on a respective party platform (of which there were none), elected deputies were invited to choose a party and to join it. Since nearly all of the deputies were hand-picked for loyalty to the Shah, few had any incentive to build their parties into real political organizations. Nor did the Shah himself envision the parties as entities that might mobilize resources in a serious fashion. Rather, they were a way to

[26] Personal communication with Ahmad Karimi-Hakkak, February 1997.

impose some neatness on parliamentary politics while ensuring that his policies moved smoothly through the legislative process. Ultimately, the parties' origins showed in their lack of development, as "neither party took seriously or fully comprehended the task of organization building" (Weinbaum 1973, 441). By the time of the 1960 election, when politics had seemingly become stable enough that the Shah felt comfortable allowing candidates from outside the two official parties to stand for office, neither one had yet built any kind of social constituency. The vibrancy with which former National Front candidates campaigned stood in stark contrast to those from Melli and Mardom. The first real election in which they would have competed essentially killed the parties, and they served no role during the 1960–62 hiatus in electoral politics. Thus, when the Shah called for elections to be held in late 1963 in search of a "mandate" for the reforms of the White Revolution, the option of reviving his nominal two-party system was not a viable one. Neither was the no-party option—it would have required the flagrant use of the police and other measures to rig the elections and would have left no means in the Majles for pro-Shah "partisan zeal" on behalf of the reforms (Weinbaum 1973, 443). Allowing the campaigning of all parties except the Tudeh raised the specter of the same partisan chaos that paralyzed policy in the 1950s. Of the four options, creating a new party, particularly one that would seem to have been created for and by the White Revolution, presented the best prospect. It could also put a new face on what in many respects was a genuinely new government with a dramatically different conception of its role in Iranian society.

Iran Novin was created in late 1963. It emerged from an active *dowreh* (regular discussion group) called the Progressive Circle and composed of nine[27] liberals, royal court members, and reformed Communists.[28] Several of these young Iranians were officials of the National Iranian Oil Corporation (NIOC), and all were intellectually committed to the idea that Iran's economic future was to be found in rapid economic development spearheaded by a strong state role in planning and investment (Weinbaum 1973, 443). Despite the small size of the Progressive Circle, its members formed a natural constituency for the Shah. He turned to them in the summer of 1963 to convene a Congress of Free Men and Women that would select candidates for the Majles elections in September. This move by the Shah, in addition to an unusual public declaration that the Progressive Circle had

[27] My discussion of Novin's early years draws heavily from Milani (2000) and Weinbaum (1973). Weinbaum numbers the Progressive Center's founders at eight.

[28] *Dowreh* means "circle" in Persian, and came to signify in twentieth-century Iran a discussion group of regular membership, usually no more than fifteen individuals, who met weekly or biweekly to discuss political, social, and other issues.

his support (Milani 2000, 154), made it clear that the group was moving up in Iranian politics.

The founding members of the Progressive Circle created Iran Novin in December 1963 and received the Shah's blessing to spearhead the public presentation of the White Revolution. Like the Ministry of Economy, the expanded Plan Organization, and numerous other institutions created to enact industrial transformation and land reform, Novin was to be the ideological standard-bearer for the White Revolution. Just four months after the Majles elections of September 1963, Hassan Ali Mansour, a founder of the Progressive Circle and then of Novin, became prime minister and was handed a majority in the Majles for his new party. Mansour appointed only Novin deputies to his cabinet. He also became the party's general secretary. With the appointment of Mansour and his Novin colleagues in the new cabinet, a change team of western-educated technocrats that came to be called the "Harvard Mafia" took over the direction of economic policy, much in the same way that, as we saw earlier, the "Berkeley Mafia" controlled government economic planning during the early Suharto years in Indonesia. In both Iran and Indonesia, these young professionals had close ties to foreign economic and political advisors and, more important, were not established political figures with constituencies other than the bureaucracies from which they emerged. Because in both cases they shared the regime's commitment to economic development, an alliance grew around that goal that overshadowed what in both cases seems to have been a real allegiance to democratic rule by the young professionals.

The new leaders of Novin were mostly civil servants, and the party itself was very small, numbering only 350 when it took over the government, of which 140 were its Majles deputies (Weinbaum 1973, 444–45). Given the Shah's desire for the party to represent his regime and its policies, it would have been reasonable to expect him to order an early effort at institution building by the party leadership. Instead, Mansour seemed to have operated without much direction either from the royal court or from the party itself. During the remainder of 1964, he used the party largely as a tool to advance his own interests, rewarding civil servants who were young and inexperienced but loyal to him with promotions that created great resentment among more senior employees. Mansour commandeered the state radio and news outlets to make party statements over the objections of other members of the party elite. During its first year, Novin saw little in the way of institutional development.

In January 1965, in large part because of his heavy-handed approach to steering through the Majles a bill granting diplomatic immunity to all Americans in Iran, Mansour was assassinated by Mohammed Bokhara'i, a seventeen-year-old high school student who was later found to have been working closely with the Feda'iyan-e Islam.[29] The Feda'iyan were a militant group that in the 1940s and early 1950s killed two prime ministers, one education minister, and a prominent secular intellectual; earlier the group had tried to kill the Shah and several other government officials.[30] Mansour's close friend Amir Abbas Hoveyda, a founder of the Progressive Circle serving as minister of finance, replaced him as prime minister, but the Shah named one of his own loyalists, Ata'ollah Khosravani, to the post of party general secretary.[31]

Hoveyda was warned by a friend not to accept the leadership of the government under such circumstances (Milani 2000, 177). In terms of the party's condition, this was good advice. Despite Mansour's claims of 9,000 regular members and 400,000 affiliated members (in workers' syndicates, guilds, rural cooperatives, and other social organizations), the majority of Novin's limited membership was in the bureaucracy. Weinbaum estimates that perhaps half of the 111 official party cells in Tehran were active (1973, 445). Given about twenty members in each cell, the numbers for Tehran looked to be roughly 2,000. Moreover, the provincial offices touted in party pamphlets usually did not exist in any real form, and by late 1965, a split had emerged within Novin's Majles faction over the party's direction in its brief history. In addition to running the government for the Shah, Hoveyda had to contend with a near-total lack of party support.

Perhaps in response to the party's weakness and perhaps because he was more focused on preventing the emergence of what Iranians referred to in the late 1960s as "super ministers" who could challenge Hoveyda's preeminence, he gave relatively little attention to Novin during his first four years as prime minister. Instead, Hoveyda spent this period consolidating his authority over the cabinet, particularly on winning a battle for the Shah's ear with the young economist, Alinaghi Alikhani, who served as minister of economy from 1963 to 1969 (Nasr 2000). By 1969, Hoveyda's position in government was secure, so, apparently eager to avail himself of the party as well, he pushed Khosravani out of the party during a conflict

---

[29] Milani documents closely Mansour's efforts to mislead the Majles and the public about the extent of the immunity law (2000). The Ayatollah Khomeini led the opposition to this law; it was this incident that spurred the Shah to exile him to Iraq.

[30] After the revolution it became clear that a number of Khomeini's closest advisors, including former President Ali Rafsanjani, were active members of the Feda'iyan. Rafsanjani in fact claimed to have provided the gun that killed Mansour; see Milani (2000, 172).

[31] There is some debate over the intent of Khosravani's appointment. Weinbaum (1973) maintains that Hoveyda modestly would not accept appointment to the party leadership while serving as prime minister; Milani names Khosravani as the Shah's hand-picked candidate based on reports from the U.S. Embassy in Tehran (2000, 274). Given Hoveyda's consistent strategy of accumulating personal power, Milani's account fits the evidence better.

over Khosravani's attempts to force the appointment of his party loyalists to high positions in various ministries (Weinbaum 1973, 446). When he did take over the party, it was no more capable of mobilizing support for the Shah's government than it had been four years earlier: Novin had "not yet been able to overcome public apathy in order to enlist mass support, nor [had] it been able to gain the loyalty of important segments of the intellectuals, bureaucracy and business community," which were its crucial center (Miller 1969b, 349).

Hoveyda became the chairman of Novin's executive committee and transferred most of the power of the general secretary to this new post. He gave a close friend and co-founder of the Progressive Circle, Manuchehr Kalali, the position of general secretary (Milani 2000). From Hoveyda's accession to the party's leadership until the mid-1970s, Novin came closer to becoming a truly capable political organization than any other party had under the Shah. The motives behind Hoveyda's efforts to revamp the party are a matter of debate. Abbas Milani, a scholar and former political prisoner under Hoveyda's government whose self-declared goal at the outset had been to discredit him, characterizes Novin as Hoveyda's best effort at injecting a modicum of representation into an otherwise autocratic polity: "He was a liberal at heart who served an illiberal master" (2000, x). Others (Nasr 2000; Alam 1991) portray him as a Machiavellian politician whose political instincts drove him to increase his power ceaselessly. The accuracy of these characterizations is less important than—once he decided to serve the Shah as party leader—Hoveyda's desire to turn Novin into a party with real organizational teeth.

Whereas Mansour and Khosravani had both been satisfied to make broad claims about the institutional and social foundations of Novin, Hoveyda worked to turn many of their "fanciful" descriptions into reality across much of the country in only a few years. By 1971 nearly 90 percent of Iran's rural cooperatives and most of the trade unions and guilds in larger cities were affiliated with the party. Perhaps most important of all, the vast majority of provincial, district, and city officials had entered politics as Novin candidates, reflecting at least some effort to recruit individuals. Standing for office as a candidate of the party meant no ideological commitment other than to economic development and to the White Revolution (Weinbaum 1973, 447). Moreover, it had been the case until 1969 that candidates for all local office were vetted by the Ministry of the Interior, SAVAK, and the royal court. Under Hoveyda's leadership the executive committee of Novin took on this responsibility so that, increasingly, successful candidates owed their positions to him rather than to the Shah. And during election campaigns, the party platform, positions on crucial issues, and even funding was highly centralized, which made "rogue" candidates largely a thing of the past. Even the threats of politics by mass demonstration or by foreign embassy intervention vanished as a means of political mobility during the early 1970s.

Despite its institutional development during Hoveyda's leadership, however, Novin was not a mass party with a cross-cutting base of support. Local meetings were often sparsely attended, affiliated groups participated in pro-regime activities only irregularly, and over time the party's membership actually declined. Thus, while Hoveyda was able to consolidate a limited constituency for the regime through the party, it did not become broadly popular or powerful enough to be an organization on which the regime could ride through a major crisis. Rather, Novin became a major base of support for Hoveyda against his rivals in the government: his "control over the party apparatus was a key element of this institutionalized power" (Milani 2000, 275). On the eve of the 1973–74 oil boom, the Shah's official party stood at a kind of crossroads—from which it could continue to grow into a vehicle for political mobilization or deteriorate altogether.

Oil, Taxes, and the Political Economy

I hypothesized in chapter 2 that plentiful oil rents at the onset of late development would allow politicians to engage their first preference of not focusing on tax collection. When oil revenues can substitute for domestic extraction, leaders can take this route. In the years after the Shah's government began to pursue industrial transformation, the Pahlavi regime's capacity to collect taxes effectively seems to have corresponded closely to this argument. By the early 1960s the regime had been heavily reliant on oil revenues for nearly a decade, a dependence that would have noticeable effects on the shape of state economic institutions.

First, the state's fiscal base changed significantly. The state-building efforts of the Shah's father, Reza Shah Pahlavi, centered largely on two institutions—the army and the tax bureaucracy. The first was instrumental in securing Iran's borders and in fighting off domestic political challenges and the second in bankrolling state expansion and, equally important, in weakening social challengers. Thus, when Reza Shah was deposed in 1941, the constitutional monarchy his son inherited had reasonably strong state institutional capacity (Cronin 1997; Banani 1961). The policy drift inherent in the fragmented politics of the 1940s weakened the state somewhat, but the 1950s—when economic crisis and the government's campaign against the Tudeh and the National Front might otherwise have spurred earnest state building—actually saw the state's extractive and administrative capacity decline further. Likewise, what could have been a strong state ready to engage in effective industrial transformation instead became, in Delacroix's words, a "distributive state," prepared mostly to allocate oil revenues (1980). Scholars in successive generations noted the disorganized manner in which industrial transformation was inaugurated and the regime's own lack of knowledge about what was required for the kind of economic revolution the Shah intended to accomplish (Ramazani 1974, 131–32; Nasr 2000, 100).

Jahangir Amuzegar, an economist who served as minister of both commerce and finance and as head of the Iranian Economic Mission to the United States under the Shah, noted the seriousness of this problem in a book otherwise entirely laudatory of the Shah's economic policies. "The obvious danger," he wrote, "is the incongruity that may emerge in the long run between *the feeble capability of the fiscal apparatus to generate sufficient revenues* and the mounting requirements of a developing economy for such public income" (Amuzegar and Fekrat 1971, 57, emphasis added).

The allocation of oil revenues in Iran in the pre-boom years is an excellent illustration of the rentier pattern theorized in so much of the literature on exporting states. During every year between the creation of the Plan Organization in 1949 and the merging of the Development (Plan Organization) and Current (State Operating) budgets in 1973—the government issued two budgets to reflect its investments in development versus in the state itself. The two budgets were allocated, respectively, to the Plan Organization, in which nearly all development expenditures were located, and to the Treasury, which operated the government's day-to-day budgets and apportioned what were essentially the regime's investments in the state.

As oil revenues steadily increased during this period, there was almost no increase in the amount allocated to the Treasury, in which all funds earmarked for government agencies were deposited. By marked contrast, oil revenues accounted for only 10 percent of the Plan Organization's budget in 1963 but skyrocketed to nearly 60 percent by 1969 (see figure 3.4). These broad statistical indicators suggest that nearly all of the incoming oil wealth was channeled out to industrial projects and to various incentives for private investment.

Iranian state data for oil and direct taxation revenues tells a similar story. Figure 3.5 shows oil revenues, non-oil revenues, and direct taxes (most of which came from income and corporate taxes) as shares of state income between 1963 and 1969. It is worth clarifying two things before moving forward. First, oil and non-oil revenues seem to rise almost in tandem. This reflects (1) a sizable investment in public (state-owned) enterprises, especially heavy manufacturing and (2) the accrual of revenues from those enterprises directly to the state. Thus, late development took off dramatically

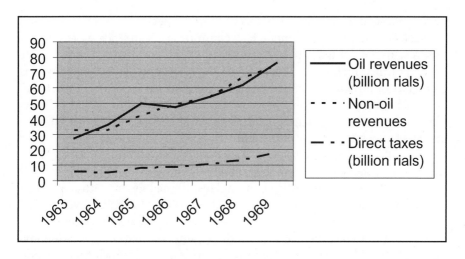

Figure 3.5. Oil revenues in Iran's state revenues, 1963–69

Source: Bank Markazi Iran (1969, 99); Amuzegar and Fekrat (1971, 37).

during this period and did so in close correlation to income from the sale of oil. Second, between 1963 and 1969, when the economy was expanding so impressively, direct tax revenues rose hardly at all, much less kept up with the expansion of potential revenues. Had the extractive capabilities of the state merely remained static, we should have at least seen those figures keep up with the economy. Combined with the apparent lack of budgetary interest in institutional upgrading, these figures suggest not just a stagnation in extractive capabilities but also an actual decline in the ability of the Pahlavi state to gather accurate information about economic activity outside the public sector.

Taxation during this period reflected a lack of fiscal necessity and a tendency to use taxes punitively to sanction merchants. One episode in business-state relations in the early 1960s illustrates the trends reflected in the macroeconomic data in figure 3.1. During the protests against the cancellation of the 1960 elections, pro–National Front *bazaaris* in Tehran closed their shops in solidarity. In response, the regime levied taxes against only those merchants that it suspected of supporting the Front (Parsa 1994, 147–48). Of all of the economic activity in Iran, bazaar commerce is arguably among the most easily located and taxed. Nearly all bazaar trade in this period took place within the confines of a centrally located and spatially distinct market area comprised of dozens of *rastih* (walkways).[32] So we would expect that if the government had committed to and possessed the resources to collect taxes from bazaaris, it would have done so. But despite their political inefficacy, Tehran's bazaaris refused to pay the new taxes as a matter of principle, complaining that the state, in its obsession with industrial growth, was doing nothing to promote commerce. Three years later, a state-run newspaper reported that more than 300,000 bazaar merchants had yet to pay any of the punitive taxes; in the end, the government never collected these taxes at all (*Ettela'at*, May 21, 1963).

This episode reflects more than merely the state's lack of capacity or will to collect taxes. It also confirms the collapse of the loose coalition of which the bazaar had been a part between 1953 and 1960. Until late development began in earnest, the conservative coalition on which the Shah's regime rested did not coalesce just around the regime's active confrontation and defeat of the left and nationalist movements but also around economic policy that was favorable toward commerce rather than toward manufacturing. Once it changed, those conservative groups—which might have been willing to surrender some political clout if their material interests had not simultaneously come under attack—had nothing to gain and everything to lose by remaining in the coalition. Ten years earlier, the Shah might have been able to keep them in the coalition *and* begin his development program by giving them a genuine stake in an anti-Communist ruling coalition and offering them a choice of his regime or a possible leftist takeover.

Coming as it did several years after there was any organized opposition to the Shah's development program, the moment at which a coalition might have been built presented no incentives for conservatives to compromise. Moreover, the regime's immediate access to external revenues while it confronted the National Front and the Tudeh and while it began to restructure the economy made possible the first choice of strategies: give no concrete concessions to build a coalition, and pay for development with oil revenues rather than with domestic extraction. Under these conditions, oil revenues and a late start to development allowed the coalition to take a much more shallow and fragile shape, one that was dependent on stable economic performance and on continued oil wealth.

---

[32] By the mid-1970s many *bazaaris* had moved outward from the bazaar itself and also owned businesses in other parts of their home cities. For instance, northern Tehran in the vicinity of Tajrish Square grew into an upscale shopping district, and *bazaaris* owned a number of carpet stores there in addition to their more "traditional" shops in the bazaar in the center of town. Author interviews, Tehran, Iran, summer 1998.

Local Government

In addition to taxation, I hypothesize that both early reliance on oil revenues and a lack of organized opposition were likely to have an effect at the local level of government as well. As resources are increasingly invested in centrally directed development projects and in the agencies to run those projects, they tend to be invested less and less in more mundane agencies such as those of provincial governments. More specifically, there are two reasons that "easy" consolidations of state-led development like the one that the Shah enjoyed are likely to lead to low investment of attention and resources in local institutions. First, regimes that have been able to consolidate late development at relatively low political cost are less likely to fear the emergence of a challenge to their rule, making local institutions—some of the most important eyes and ears of government—seem less valuable. Second, development that can be sustained through the allocation of oil or other external revenues does not need a significant tax base. The information on which tax assessments are made is ultimately collected locally, so when taxes take low priority, the agencies that generate them do as well.

In Iran, data on the governance in many provinces is hard to come by, given the Islamic Republic's unwillingness to disseminate much in the way of information about the workings of the Pahlavi state and the scarcity of research conducted on local institutions in Pahlavi Iran. While the evidence I present below about Iranian local government must be taken as suggestive rather than conclusive, it does provide support for the above hypotheses. Moreover, it was possible to find data on what might be considered a crucial case for local government capacity building (Eckstein 1975, 113–20), namely the municipality of Qazvin.[33] Qazvin is a medium-sized provincial city[34] in Zanjan province[35] about 150 kilometers west of Tehran. It is situated on the major highway connecting Tehran to Rasht, the largest Iranian city on the Caspian coast and alongside the one railway running across Iran from east to west. As a city that is close to the capital, heavily focused on commerce and industry, and located along major transport routes, Qazvin has most of the important features that ought to compel any government to invest in administrative capacity: sizable merchant and industrial working classes (both of which were central to the political movements of the 1940s and 1950s and to the National Front and the Tudeh),

[33] Qazvin in the Iranian system of government in the 1960s and 1970s was a *shahrestan*, which is usually translated as "municipality." It is roughly equivalent to either a city or county government level in the United States.

[34] In 1970 the population was approximately 100,000.

[35] Qazvin was located in Zanjan province until Qazvin was granted provincial status under the Islamic Republic.

proximity to political currents and to the central government in Tehran, and significant economic importance in the context of broader developmental goals. Given the mountains on all sides but to the west, the expansion of industrial production in the greater Tehran area during the 1960s was most prominently a westward one, and Qazvin's location helped to ensure that it would become a major beneficiary of national industrial policy through domestic and foreign investment (Rotblat 1972, 40–44). In short, Qazvin plausibly seems like a city in which the regime should have invested heavily in institutional capability, even if it may have chosen not to in other regions.

In Qazvin, as in other regional cities, social and economic life was regulated by both municipal and national government agencies. At the first, local, level, administrative responsibility was increased during the 1960s, so that municipalities like Qazvin's became responsible for significantly greater economic regulation as a result of land reform and the commercialization of agriculture more broadly. Setting prices, issuing merchant permits, and assessing tax obligations were just a few of the duties handed to local government as part of the White Revolution. The *fiscal* and *political* responsibilities of the Qazvin municipality, however, actually declined over the course of the 1960s. Functionally, city officials were asked to do more but given less funding and leeway with which to do it. To take one important example, a survey of the Commerce Office—which was accountable for bazaar trade, commercial agriculture, and the issuance of business permits and tax assessment—found that only 17 percent of its staff had "formal employment." The rest—83 percent of an agency with administrative authority over nearly the entire economic life in the city—were essentially temporary employees with no benefits or job security (Palangi n.d., 36).

The Commerce Office was also responsible for all state interaction with the bazaar of Qazvin. In Qazvin, as in most urban areas in Iran during the 1960s and 1970s, the bazaar accounted for up to 60 percent of economic activity; the Iranian government estimated that, as of the mid-1970s, one-third of all Iranians depended in one way or another on the bazaar for their livelihoods (Denoeux 1993, 139). However, as Rotblat notes, "the Office [was] understaffed and the functionaries underpaid" (1972, 224). One reason for this was the strategic approach employed by the agency.

Because merchant guilds had been so important for bazaar involvement in Iranian politics—from the Tobacco Rebellion and the Constitutional Revolution of the late nineteenth and early twentieth centuries to the uprisings surrounding the overthrow of Mossadegh in 1953—the orders from Tehran were to desist from adopting policies that could encourage the establishment of autonomous merchant organizations. To avoid having to deal with the representatives of what could potentially have become strong corporate bodies, the municipal government chose as often as possible to deal with individual merchants. Given the lack of funding and staff and the monumentally greater administrative costs of dealing with hundreds of individuals rather than a single guild representative, it is unsurprising that merchants were "only minimally affected by the rules of the local government" (Rotblat 1972, 224). Business permits, which were another responsibility of the Commerce Office and one that produced information valuable to more than simply tax assessors, were collected with no greater success. An interview that Rotblat conducted with a clerk in the Commerce Office centered on the presence of only four coppersmiths on the previous year's (1348/1969) permit ledger; Rotblat's own calculations based on fieldwork turned up at least twenty-two. Asked about the discrepancy, the clerk replied, "Don't worry. They will come in little by little" (69, 224).

During the same period, the national government had enacted economic policies that had a powerful impact on the structure of the economy in cities like Qazvin. Land reform and the policies designed to encourage domestic investment in industry—tariffs on foreign manufactured goods, the distribution of land to hundreds of thousands of new farmers, and the establishment of rural cooperatives in villages—simultaneously increased the pace of work for urban merchants and the volume and variety of goods available to them. They also introduced late competition through the new subsidized cooperatives and shifted the balance of market power in favor of the newly landed farmers by giving them a constant source of income as opposed to an income in surplus only a few times a year (Rotblat 1972, 240–50). All of these changes magnified the need for government agencies that could administer and regulate the changing economy. With few exceptions, however, the Shah's government did not invest in such agencies as it had in development projects. Whether these phenomena specific to Qazvin may be generalized to the Pahlavi tax bureaucracy at large is uncertain, but they are broadly consistent with macroeconomic and fiscal data for the national government. Moreover, it seems safe to say that the state's monitoring capacity declined during the 1960s and early 1970s even as its ability to transform social economic relationships increased.

Field research by other scholars in the early 1970s also turns up evidence of limited state capacity. From anthropologists concerned with the maintenance of cultural traditions among nomadic tribes to political scientists committed to testing Huntington's (1968) theory of institutionalization, there emerged a consensus that local authority in Iran by the early 1970s was better equipped to accomplish social change than social control. Beck (1991) notes throughout an ethnographic study of one Qashqa'i tribal leader in 1970–71 that despite the transformation of rural life and economics through the White Revolution, her primary informant, Borzu Qermezi, and many other tribal figures continued to turn to khans and other traditional village authorities rather than to agencies of the central government because they could better enforce their decisions and made more reliable mediators. Focusing on Novin's lack of institutionalization, Weinbaum notes that much of the state's rhetoric of having replaced all local authority with its own remained "fanciful claims," since provincial government remained so characterized by "moribund units" (1973, 450).

In short, by focusing so much of the government's physical and financial resources on industrial production, the drive toward economic prosperity in 1960s Iran actually made the state weaker across numerous fields of authority. By the early 1970s, it was less capable of extracting revenues domestically and of regulating and administering social life in the provinces and in the cities outside of Tehran despite its impressive abilities to enact policy autonomously. In the one institutional venue in which the Shah's regime made headway—party building—the progress was provisional and depended on the Shah's continued perception that Hoveyda's authority was a smaller danger than that posed by the lack of a viable official party. Finally, other than the loyalty displayed by the small number of bureaucrats whose careers depended on party membership, the lack of an organized opposition to the Shah's government between 1962 and 1964 provided few incentives to build a broad or deep ruling coalition. What opposition there had been consisted largely of sporadic street demonstrations, one coup plot in 1958–59, and the assassination of Mansour in 1965. As a result, the answer looked to be in playing rival groups off against one another. This strategy, then, rather than institution building, became the primary strategy of survival for the Shah, and the implications of that choice would carry deep into the boom years.

Conclusion

In the last chapter, I traced the remarkably similar trajectories of the political economies of Iran and Indonesia before late development, seeking to show how (1) the events and processes the countries had in common made it likely that a right-leaning regime determined to pursue late development would emerge and (2) since the events leading up to the onset of late development varied little across the cases, one can be confident that they do not account for the variation in the later abilities of the Pahlavi and Suharto regimes to manage economic and political crises. This chapter aimed to highlight the crucial role of the sequencing of late development relative to purging the opposition and to becoming dependent on oil revenues. In both states, it marked a crucial turning point in their trajectories and powerfully shaped their relations with their respective societies and the institutional capacities into the oil boom years.

In Iran, the Shah's regime began its push toward industrial transformation in the absence of any organized opposition movement capable of mass mobilization nearly a decade after it had come to rely heavily on oil revenues for both development and routine expenditures. The government, subsequently, had few incentives to make politically costly decisions to focus on domestic extraction or to make concrete concessions to social groups to build a coalition. As a result, little attention was given to institution or coalition building other than in the allocation of resources for industrial development. Both domestic extractive capacity and local government capacity declined throughout the 1960s and early 1970s, by which time the central government had much less ability to collect taxes domestically or to enact policies effectively through local institutions. Moreover, the relatively low level of opposition organization at the onset of Iran's late development provided an atmosphere of little challenge, and there existed little motivation to invest in a strong party apparatus that could have mobilized supporters behind the development program. In short, by the eve of the first oil boom, the weak institutions that many scholars have attributed to the boom were already manifest.

In Indonesia, where the government adopted a similar development program of late development, the trajectory diverged sharply from the Iranian one. The persistent strength of the PKI and of Sukarno loyalists in the military and bureaucracy provided a powerful obstacle to the consolidation of Suharto's young regime around late development. As a result, this regime made concessions to student organizations and to Islamic parties and groups that meant giving up real power over significant areas of policy. Moreover, the regime went to great lengths to incorporate civil servants into the coalition and to restore unity in the military. In the process of building this coalition, Suharto and his advisors developed close ties with the leaderships of these groups, interacting with them often, even daily, as regime consolidation proceeded. From this early coalition-building period came the ability not just to receive demands from these groups but to monitor them as well. When, for instance, students began to protest New Order economic policy for depending too heavily on foreign capital in 1970, the early relationships made it possible for the regime to isolate the students, preventing the spread of dissent. When necessary, too, the regime used these close ties to back out of potentially dangerous conflicts with ambivalent coalition members through bargaining, such as in the marriage law dispute in 1973.

The combination of a powerfully organized opposition and the scarcity of flexible revenues also accorded much greater priority to institution building in early New Order Indonesia. Substantial investment in domestic tax collection in its first years combined with much closer attention to provincial and local institutions of the government made it possible both to weather revenue shortfalls by extracting domestic revenues and to monitor the population at the local level, augmenting the regime's ability to keep an eye on potential dissent by tying officials on the ground much more closely to the central government. Finally, the resources and effort expended to build Golkar into a powerful mobilizing vehicle through exclusivity in the bureaucracy, through career advancement, and through side payments to over 200 social groups gave the regime a strong social base, which only fortified the efforts it had made in other areas. It was with these institutional trajectories already in place, then, that Indonesia and Iran faced the first oil boom in 1973–74.

CHAPTER 4

The Oil Booms and Beyond

Two Exporting States Confront Crisis

In October 1973, American support to Israel during the Yom Kippur War provoked the Arab nations of the Organization of Petroleum Exporting Countries (OPEC) to collaborate in quintupling the price of oil. Iran and Indonesia, like many other developing countries, experienced massive revenue windfalls in late 1973, in a single year almost quadrupling the discretionary revenues available to state leaders. And these revenue windfalls *were* almost entirely discretionary: as one scholar notes, the differences between exporters in the developing world were overshadowed in influence by the centrality of the state in "ownership, acquisition, and disposition of oil revenues" (Amuzegar 1999, 1). That is, the nearly exclusive control of oil revenues by rulers in exporting countries gave them the same authority and incentives to make use of boom windfalls.

It is no longer counterintuitive to claim that those windfalls had a negative effect on exporters' domestic economies. In most oil-exporting countries, the late 1970s and early 1980s were marked by a decline in the size and competitiveness of non-oil traded goods and exports, inflation spurred by a huge increase in public sector spending, income maldistribution caused by skewed government allocation of revenues, and the advent of unbridled rent-seeking as a result of patronage spending. These economic effects of the booms led to antistate protests in many exporting states, well before the bust of the 1980s spurred yet another wave of economic and political instability.

Despite these commonalities, the end of the boom decade witnessed a striking divergence in the abilities of the (mostly) authoritarian regimes in exporting states to cope with economic and political crises. Analysis of this period across oil-exporting states affords the opportunity to assess the success—and failure—of state leaders to build support structures for themselves during the preceding decades. As Gourevitch observes, "Hard times expose strengths and weaknesses to scrutiny, allowing observers to see relationships that are often blurred in prosperous periods, when good times slake the propensity to contest and challenge. The lean years are times when old relationships crumble and new ones have to be constructed. It is then that institutions and patterns are built which will persist long into the next cycle" (1986, 9). That hard times offer a unique opportunity to look inside the politics of coalitions and state capacity is no less true for developing or authoritarian governments than it is for advanced industrial democracies. If anything, increased vulnerability to global shocks and a lack of democratic institutions through which to restructure ruling coalitions make hard times even more trying for autocrats in developing countries—all the more so for those in oil-exporting states. During these hard times, we can look at ruling coalitions to see the degree to which mechanisms other than patronage existed to hold together disparate political interests when oil rents dropped dramatically.

In this chapter, I seek to shed light on the effects of adopting late development in the 1960s by tracing the attempts of two regimes to cope with the tumultuous oil boom years of the late 1970s. Previous studies have characterized the behavior of state leaders during booms as "petro-mania" or some other form of action generated by the booms themselves. In contrast to that line of argument, I posit that Suharto, the Shah, and many other leaders incorporated their windfalls into pre-established institutions and patterns of decisionmaking. In short, boom-era patterns of state-society relations and institutional change tended to be very similar to those in place before the booms—in other words, the windfall revenues merely magnified existing patterns.

In both Iran and Indonesia, the first boom reinforced prior patterns of institutional change. In Iran, distribution remained the major priority of state policy, and investment in urban industrial projects accelerated while local government continued to deteriorate. In Indonesia, by contrast, the 1973–74 boom was followed quite quickly by a major new program of central investment in local political institutions, which tied them closely both to late development and to the Golkar party apparatus. When protests against both of these governments' heavy-handed policies flared up in 1977 and 1978, the political trajectories each regime followed during the previous fifteen years left them with very different options for dealing with the crises.

OPEC's Overdue Collective Action and the First Boom: The Global Politics of Oil Prices

The first oil boom of the 1970s did not take place strictly as a result of the Arab oil embargo of October 16, 1973. It had its roots in a series of structural and institutional changes in the international oil market that took place after World War II. First, the shift from a wartime to a peacetime footing in Western Europe and the United States greatly boosted the demand for petroleum products throughout the 1950s and 1960s, so that by the late 1960s world demand for oil rose by an average of 7 percent each year. In the first six months of 1970 alone, the global demand for oil rose 9 percent. In addition, a series of exogenous events in the decade before the boom intensified the growth in demand. Supply disruptions caused by the closure of the Suez canal in 1967, damage to the Syrian pipeline from Saudi Arabia to the Mediterranean coast in 1970, Libyan production cutbacks in 1971, and growing demand among industrialized countries caused the oil market to swing in favor of sellers.

The late 1960s and early 1970s were also years in which OPEC began to act more like a cartel and less like a loose grouping of self-interested states. An OPEC declaration in 1968 in Caracas asserted the "permanent sovereignty" of oil-producing countries over their oil reserves. The 1971 Tehran Agreement by OPEC nations enacted the cartel's first price fixing policy, and in 1972 new concessions forced on foreign oil companies gave producers the right to make yearly adjustments to royalties and taxes against depreciation of the dollar and, for the first time, participation in running the oil companies themselves. As a result of these sweeping changes in the balance of power between producers and oil companies, in mid-1973 the price of a barrel of oil rose from $2.18 to $2.90, a 33 percent increase.

These events were all important in setting the stage for OPEC domination of the oil market. However, the Yom Kippur war between Israel, on the one hand, and Syria and Egypt, on the other, provided the catalyst for a much more powerful display of the exporters' new clout.[1] After the Arab members of OPEC imposed an embargo on oil sales to much of the West, the cartel at large on October 16, 1973, raised its selling price to $5.12 per barrel. Because nearly all of the world's non-OPEC producers were at or close to 100 percent production capacity, the embargo and price increase sent the market price even higher. In December 1973, another agreement in Tehran raised the price again. Realizing that short-term spot sales at as much as $17.04 per barrel could not be sustained, cartel members sought to stabilize the price somewhat, albeit at a level nearly five times that of a

---

[1] For a detailed account of the boom period, see Yergin (1991, 588–632).

year earlier. Calculating the cost of an alternative "barrel" of energy from other sources and figuring a share of each barrel of $7 for producers, OPEC members reached a decision to set the price of oil at $10.74 starting January 1, 1974. The announcement of OPEC's decision caused yet another spike in market prices, so that between early 1970 and late 1973 the price of oil rose more than sixfold, from $1.80 to $11.65. For nearly all exporting countries and for Iran and Indonesia in particular, the new revenues accrued directly to the state and thus to a small group of political leaders.[2] Regimes suddenly had access to anywhere from three to six times the discretionary revenues that they had had just a few years before. As it was for other exporting states, the effect of that windfall on the political economies of Indonesia and Iran was immense.

Oil and Accelerated State Building: Indonesia during the First Boom

The Economic Response

In 1974, the first year of the oil boom, the Indonesian government was forced to divert nearly 40 percent of its windfall revenues to paying off the debts of Pertamina, the state-run oil company. As a result of the New Order regime's success in restoring and expanding oil production, by the first oil boom Pertamina's available capital had reached nearly half that of the government's (Bresnan 1993, 164). Under General Ibnu Sutowo's direction and flush with revenues, Pertamina in the late 1960s and early 1970s had diversified far beyond its economic and organizational capacities into shipping, pipeline construction, telecommunications projects, and fertilizer, among other sectors. Having headed Pertamina since its inception in 1957, Sutowo operated the company with considerable autonomy from the government until 1974. By then, his extracurricular investments, which Mining Minister and Pertamina Chairman Mohammed Sadli described as "not economical and lack[ing] any direct relation with the basic function of Pertamina," had accrued a debt of $10.5 billion (quoted in Bresnan 1993, 167).

These questionable investments and the huge debts that came with them came to a head in 1974, and the Indonesian government was forced to assume Pertamina's multi-billion dollar debts to retain its own credibility. In addition to thoroughly restructuring the company and removing Sutowo from leadership, the government was obligated to assume responsibility for Pertamina debts and to use a sizable portion of the first year's revenues to restore the company's, and the country's, credibility with international lenders.

---

[2] This structure of ownership is a crucial variable linking resource wealth to its political effects. See, for example, Jones Luong and Weinthal (2001).

Despite this significant economic setback, Suharto's government managed to turn the first boom in its favor. Where the pre-boom period had been characterized by government encouragement of light manufacturing—as per the recommendations of the IMF and its cabinet allies in the "Berkeley Mafia"—the first boom saw an increased emphasis on import substitution industrial investment (Amuzegar 1999, 63). The government invested particularly in the production and development of liquid natural gas, basic metals, fertilizer, cement, paper, and hydrocarbons. In addition to their perceived long-term comparative advantage for Indonesia,[3] these projects served a powerful political purpose: many of them went to military leaders and helped to cement the army's unity after the scare of the January 1974 protests, discussed below. Many of these projects were also labor-intensive and added many jobs to the economy and reduced the chances that unemployment would produce protesters.

In an effort to make social and economic use of the windfalls, the government also allocated funding to telecommunications, banking, and insurance, as well as investing heavily in human capital (primarily education) and infrastructure in the form of roads, telephone and electrical lines. As a result of this last set of boom-funded expenditures, which made regions more and more profitable, private sector investment rose severalfold between 1973 and 1978, with a noteworthy focus on manufacturing. Finally, the regime continued to emphasize agriculture and significantly raised its investment in rice production, again increasingly banking on a viable rural economy to prevent the kind of peasant farmer mobilization that the New Order had feared during its early years.

The State and Social Forces: Dealing with Dissent before and during the Boom

Just as Suharto's government was beginning to feel the effects of the first oil boom—before the Pertamina crisis—a political crisis erupted that by most accounts provoked serious fear among the New Order leadership. As a result of a drought season and the low rice harvest that followed, inflation rose from 6.5 percent in 1972 to 31 percent in 1973. By December 1972, the New Order leadership watched as the same student organizations that had been instrumental in bringing it to power six years earlier now took to the streets to condemn its handling of economic affairs, which from the beginning had been the regime's raison d'être. Intermittent student protests

---

[3] Like many import substitution projects in other developing countries, many of these firms did not prove to be profitable. As much as oil revenues permitted, however, the regime subsidized them to maintain their political value. Many of these state enterprises were privatized during the reforms of the late 1980s.

in late 1973 were cause for some concern, but in January 1974 they reached a level that forced the regime to take notice.

The student protests of January 1974—which came to be called the "Malari" riots in Indonesian, short for *Malapetaka Lima Belas Januari*, the "January 15 Disaster"—had their roots in the foreign-oriented direction of New Order economic policy, in the students' unrealized hopes for a democratic polity, and, most proximately, in the drought of 1972. The last of these came after several consecutive years of increased rice harvests, and after the Badan Urusan Logistik (National Logistics Agency, or Bulog) held off on announcing the state's purchase price for rice until well into the 1972 spring harvest. Bulog had sole authority over most of Indonesia's rice production by 1972, and its volume and pricing were a major determinant of output. The production increases each year since 1969 apparently made Bulog's management overconfident, and, rather than announce the price at the beginning of the year, they waited until May, creating uncertainty among rice farmers across Indonesia. The combination of drought and uncertain profits led to a total procurement of rice that amounted to only one-third of the 1971 harvest. And, because the drought was a region-wide problem throughout Southeast Asia, Bulog faced a serious shortage and ultimately was forced to pay four times the 1971 rate for importing over a million tons of rice to meet needs in 1972 and 1973. The increased price was also reflected in domestic pricing and, as a major staple, it pulled other consumer prices upward, leading to a rise in the rate of inflation from 6 to 40 percent by early 1974 (World Bank 2001).

With inflation came increased social tension and protest. In August 1973, a Chinese driver in Bandung, the capital city of West Java province, hit an Indonesian pedicab driver with his car. False rumors that the pedicab driver had been killed spread quickly, and thousands of student rioters stormed through Bandung destroying Chinese-owned businesses. Among those arrested were nineteen officers and enlisted soldiers in the army. Student demonstrators also picketed periodically throughout late 1973, spurring Suharto to ask Soemitro, the head of the state public security agency, to begin a series of meetings with student organizations (Ramadhan 1996, 371–76). Although he declared the beginning of a "new style of leadership," Soemitro's overtures were "received with criticism" (Bresnan 1993, 139).

In early December, the government announced a visit to Jakarta by Prime Minister Kakuei Tanaka of Japan. Since Japanese investors were the largest group of foreign investors, the general opposition to dependence on foreign capital took on a more specific anti-Japanese tone. In response to the pending visit, student groups, already mobilized by the inflationary crisis, began to picket the Japanese embassy and, on December 31, held a "night of concern" at major universities in Jakarta, Bandung, and Bogor. In early January, amid rumors that Soemitro might have begun working with student organizations in secret, Suharto summoned him to a meeting also attended by Suharto's political advisor, Ali Moertopo. Soemitro delivered a public address immediately afterward in which he declared that his remarks about the need for reform indicated no ambition to higher office. Shortly after this incident, student organizations in Jakarta issued the "Three Demands of the People," which included Suharto's dismissal of his key advisors, an end to corruption, and a decrease in the rate of inflation. The title of the document was a symbolic reference to the "Tritora," which KAMI had issued in 1965 calling for the banning of the PKI, an overhaul of Sukarno's entire cabinet, and decreased inflation. The "Three Demands" brought together a set of concerns shared by student organizations that had been growing for months and were frequent topics in Indonesian newspapers (see, for example, *Harian Kami* and *Indonesia Raya* throughout November 1973). At the same time, prominent critics of the New Order's open economy policies, such as former vice president Mohammed Hatta, became more vocal, going so far as to question whether the regime's coziness with foreign investors violated the spirit of the Constitution (*Indonesia Raya*, December 5, 1973).

Neither the symbolism of the "Three Demands" nor the recent political potency of Indonesia's student movement escaped Suharto. Within a week he acceded to their requests for an audience and met with student representatives from thirty-one universities around the country. Several of his advisors also spoke in public about the need to combat corruption and to consider the scope of foreign investment in Indonesia (*Sinar Harapan*, January 8, 10, 11, 1974). While Suharto made no concrete concessions at the meeting, he did promise to keep the channels of communication open. The scope of the riots two days later, however, raised fears of other, more alarming, channels of communication between the military and student organizations.

When Prime Minister Tanaka arrived on the evening of January 14, eight hundred students were waiting for his plane; they fought police and army troops; some managed to enter the airfield before his plane landed. The next morning students from three Jakarta universities held a protest march in the center of the capital. While they marched, bands of young people around the city began to stop the drivers of Japanese-made vehicles, deflate the tires, and set the cars ablaze. They also attacked dealers of Japanese-made automobiles and other Japanese-owned businesses (*Suara Muhammadiyah*, February 1974; see also Bresnan 1993, 136).

The protests drew in other groups as well: one group of nearly 500 arrested for demonstrating included almost 300 "laborers and peddlers." Although the regime succeeded in putting an end to the protests by January 17, there is no doubt that "the government had been shocked to its very roots" (Bresnan 1993, 137). Heavy-handed tactics from military force to newspaper closures and questionable arrests were a central component of the regime's response. Equally important, however, was Suharto's other courses of action. In line with student demands, by the end of January 1974 he had "abolished the posts held by four senior army officers in his personal staff; announced a series of measures to protect indigenous enterprise; and issued orders designed to moderate the extravagant life-styles of senior military officers and civil servants. He also removed General Soemitro from his post and dismissed General Sutopo Juwono as head of central intelligence" (Bresnan 1993, 137).

For their part, the student protesters—some of them, at least—apparently thought that they had the active support of certain members of the government; their beliefs seem to have had some support in the inaction of army troops during the first day's protests, when soldiers literally stood by and watched rioters engage in the destruction of property. Some of the students also believed that they had an opportunity to bring down the government (Bresnan 1993, 142). In any event, they did not; in addition to cracking down on the protesters, Suharto's regime made a series of strategic concessions in the weeks following the protests. Whereas the ultimate enactment of those concessions—most notably the measures to protect indigenous entrepreneurs—is open to question, the regime's immediate steps to allay the students' primary concerns went further to consolidate the regime's hold on power than the bare use of force would have.

The regime's standing contacts with student leaders, even while they could not ultimately put off the protests, "had been a valuable source of information that helped the government to track the outcomes of its policies and to know when and where correctives were needed" (Bresnan 1993, 163). Numerous leaders from among the student organizations that mobilized against the regime were also incorporated into Golkar in the following three years and emerged as important figures in the 1977 elections (Suryadinata 1989, 76). The New Order regime, authoritarian though it was, managed in large part to move beyond the protests of early 1974 by virtue of its contacts with, and earlier cooptation of, parts of the student movement and its willingness to act on information provided via those contacts to reach a "settlement" with protest leaders.

Boom–Era State Building and Provincial Government: Law No. 5 of 1974

In chapter 3, I outlined New Order strategies for building local government that would be capable of spearheading development projects rather than passively receiving them from the center and of acting as a viable arm of central authority in regional locales. Given the scarcity of external revenues during its early years, the regime's focus on local state building is somewhat unsurprising. During a period of resource abundance, however, we might expect regimes, as Chaudhry (1997) theorized from the case of Saudi Arabia, to "let up" their state-building efforts and to rely on windfall patronage as a substitute for domestic statecraft. I hypothesized in chapter 2, in contrast to Chaudhry's proposition, that rulers who come to power facing the dual challenges of political opposition and revenue scarcity are likely to use later windfall revenues to continue their state-building projects.

Indonesia provides strong support for this proposition. On April 30, 1974, just as the likely revenue effects of the boom were becoming clear and after the Malari riots had emphasized the need to continue the regime consolidation project, the government submitted to the parliament a bill— Law No. 5—that would powerfully reshape provincial and district governments in their roles, capabilities, and relations to the center. On May 19, the government presented its explanation of the bill's purpose and of the regime's vision for restructuring central-local relations (Sujanto 1991, 3– 19). The bill laid out the concept of *daerah otonom* (autonomous regions) as government units responsible for carrying out the development plans of the central government. The effect of the bill was to clarify less the rights than the duties of newly defined provincial, district, and sub-district units (Morfit 1986, 57–58). The language of the bill makes this clear: "The region has the right, the authority, and the obligation to organize and manage its own affairs in accordance with prevailing government regulations" (Republic of Indonesia 1974, Article 7).

Law No. 5 was a central mechanism through which the regime sought to structure its plans to invest a sizable share of the oil windfalls in development projects. More important, it reflected a strategy to involve locales more actively in national development and simultaneously to tie them more closely to the authority of the central government. According to the law, provincial governments, most of whose powers were held by the governors, gained administrative responsibility for tasks that had been the sole domain of the center for all of Indonesia's post-independence history (MacAndrews 1986b, 16). Governors gained the duty of levying and collecting provincial taxes, of exercising authority over all locally appointed civil servants, of establishing local enterprises and, with the authorization of the Ministry of Home Affairs, of borrowing money.

From the immediate post-Sukarno period, during which Indonesia's provinces were so out of Jakarta's control that center-province relations amounted to de facto federalism (Malley 1999), to the end of the 1970s, a sea change took place at the local level of government in Indonesia. The goals of moving development down to the local level and of cementing central control over local politics lay behind this change. To an impressive degree, the restructuring of center-province relations managed to achieve these goals by increasing the quality of local knowledge available to central planners. Anne Booth shows a strong correlation between investment project types and the available infrastructure in specific regions to absorb them (1986, 86–87). Further, she shows how development projects were outlined in coordination with new province-level agencies—the *Badan-Badan Perancanaan Pembangunan Daerah* (Regional Development Planning Bodies, or Bappeda)—both to account for, and to make the most of, what a region had to offer. Provincial Bappeda units grew out of an initiative adopted by the government in 1976 to complement the new organization of local government. Thus, the government generally avoided throwing good money after bad by, first, building institutions that could collect information effectively about infrastructure and the structure of capital in a given region and, second, by directing development aid (funded largely by the oil boom) to where it could be best utilized.[4]

Accurate information is not merely useful for productive public sector investment: it is also a means for exercising social control at a much lower political cost than would be required by the constant use of coercion. Thus, newly bulked-up local government institutions served to cement the regime's longevity as much as they enabled sensible and locally viable development projects. Antlöv's long-term ethnographic study of the village of "Sariendah" in West Java highlights the changes accomplished in a very short time by the implementation of Law No. 5 of 1974 and by Law No. 5

[4] The New Order regime in Indonesia, unlike the Pahlavi regime in Iran, survived the crises of 1977–78 to receive another oil boom windfall in 1979–80. Building on what they had accomplished in 1974 with the reorganization and consolidation of government from the province to the city level, New Order political planners took advantage of the incoming revenue surplus to extend institution building down to the village level with Law No. 5 of 1979. Political life in Indonesian villages took on much the same organizational structure as that of the cities. The *kepala desa* (village head) stood at the top of the village hierarchy with two centrally appointed but locally born officers to aid him, one each from the army and national police. By appointing members of the army and national police who were almost always natives of a village, the regime ensured both loyalty and a modicum of local legitimacy (Antlöv 1995, 52–53). As with higher levels of government, the new and newly responsive offices of village politics served to implement national development strategies at the same time they served as the eyes and ears of the regime in villages.

of 1979, which achieved for village government what the 1974 Law had for province and district-level institutions. In addition to the simple presence of so much new state "machinery" in village life, the everyday activities of the various organs of village government injected the state into the village on a level never before seen in Indonesia. Myriad new official rituals and social-political obligations (Antlöv 1995, 58–67) only added to the ubiquitous presence of state offices, creating by the end of the 1970s something close to congruence between what Migdal terms the "image of the state" and its actual practices (2001a, 15–16). In short, the first oil boom made it possible for the New Order regime to invest in institutions that could ensure its longevity on a scale that could not have been possible without the windfall. Moreover, this persistent strategy of sinking surplus revenues into institution building stood the received wisdom regarding commodity booms and state capacity on its head. Rent-seeking increased with the boom in Indonesia, to be sure; the strictly hierarchical nature of rent allocation, however, in concert with what MacIntyre (1994, 2000) has described as highly centralized and disciplined corruption, actually contributed to the social control capacities of the Indonesian state.[5]

As crucial to the New Order state building project as the two boom-era local government programs were, the regime did not rely solely on the "mono-loyalty" that it demanded from local officials.[6] In addition to investing locally through the institutions it had created during the 1970s, the government also invested directly in regional development through what it called *Instruksi Presiden* (Presidential Instruction, or Inpres) grants. These grants were paid directly by the central government to regions for specific projects. At their inception in 1969, Inpres grants were allocated only for village-level projects; by the eve of the first boom in 1973, they had expanded also to go straight into province- and district-level funding and to schools. In the first year of the oil boom, these grants doubled from 62.9 billion rupiah to 126.3 billion, or from roughly $152 million to $304 million (Indonesian Ministry of Finance, cited in Davey 1989, 177).[7] By 1977, health development and "greening" projects were added to the list, and in 1979, road construction too came to be funded through the Inpres program. In the early 1980s, at the height of the second oil boom, Inpres funding to local government amounted to nearly 70 percent of the total amount allotted to the regions in routine expenditures. Whereas routine budget ex-

---

[5] Kang (2003) argues along a similar line that certain structures of corruption not only do not hinder growth but also foster stronger state authority.

[6] "Mono-loyalty"—*monoloyalitas* in Indonesian—was the buzzword of civil servant training programs during this period.

[7] Conversion data from World Bank is available at lnweb18.worldbank.org/eap/eap.nsf/ by the search terms "Indonesian rupiah exchange rate 1973." This version was accessed on August 22, 2006.

penditures were somewhat more tightly defined in scope and purpose, Inpres funding was apparently constructed with the idea of giving some authority over allocation back to local officials who, for the most part, followed orders from the top (Davey 1989, 180–81).

In sum, Indonesia's experience with local government institutions does not square well with the received wisdom about the effects of oil booms on state capacity; indeed, it is directly in conflict with that wisdom. Rather than allowing local government to deteriorate during the boom years, the New Order regime used the windfalls precisely to bolster this key component of the state, strengthening regional institutions using boom revenues. The evidence suggests that the regime did so because of its own legacy of consolidating itself and its development plans. Fiscal scarcity and stiff opposition in its early years provided a strong historical incentive to use a fortuitous revenue boon for expansion of the capabilities of state agencies.

Politics and Parties: Golkar, the Oil Boom, and Hegemony

As Suharto's quasi-official party approached the peak of the first oil boom and the 1977 elections,[8] a number of crises and setbacks appeared, again, to represent a threat to the regime's viability. The Malari riots of January 1974; the Pertamina debt crisis of 1975; a "phantom coup" orchestrated by Sawito, a former official at the Ministry of Agriculture; and the debacle that emerged from Indonesia's annexation of East Timor in 1976—all taxed the regime's legitimacy. More general but no less pressing issues such as official corruption, foreign economic dependence, and distributional inequity added to the problems facing Suharto's New Order. Finally, the "absence of any protective philosophical covering by nongovernment intellectuals and students and the increased prominence of Islam as the principal opposition force," when combined with so many other problems, weighed heavily on Golkar's ability to orchestrate another election victory (Liddle 1978b, 179).

Despite these obstacles, the regime's party won by only a fraction of one percentage point less than its 1971 vote total, taking in 62.11 percent in 1977 as opposed to 62.8. In this second New Order election, Golkar and its institutional constituents in the bureaucracy and military made less prevalent (and blatant) use of heavy-handed tactics in turning out the vote. In addition, the regime in many regions was much less concerned about restricting the ability of the two remaining opposition parties to campaign, since its institution-building project and increased access to bureaucratic

---

[8] The elections were originally scheduled for 1976, five years after the previous round, but were postponed for reasons discussed below.

patronage enabled it to offset the votes it might lose. Where the regime had been explicitly anti-Islamic in 1971, by 1977 it had developed intricate patronage ties to *kiai* (local religious leaders) across Indonesia, especially in Java. Religious leaders who tapped into these funding-for-votes networks came to be known in PPP as *kiai bayaran*, or "bought *kiai*." Derogatory labels or no, these leaders stood at the head of their own patron-client networks at the local level and helped to account for Golkar's electoral success even as it decreased its concerted action to obstruct the other parties.

The regime's access to boom-generated windfall revenues also made for good party building. At the village level, local leaders were for the most part left in place—in central Java, for instance, the *lurah* (village head) generally remained the inherited position that it had been for generations. What changed was the relationship of the *lurah* and other local leadership roles to the central government and, by association, to the ruling party. Inpres, Bappeda, and routine local development expenditures took on the part of inter-election public relations. By grafting massive development allocation onto preexisting and locally legitimate political structures, Golkar used its access to state funds both to strengthen local patterns of authority and to tie their maintenance more closely to the continuity of the regime. By the end of the 1970s, then, it was not uncommon to hear subjects in voting surveys make remarks such as, "Golkar likes development. We have a beautiful bridge, a smooth asphalt road because of development" instead of opposition parties (quoted in Gaffar 1992, 128). Although Golkar's local hegemony did face challenges from Islamic leaders (Gaffar 1992, 151–56), its leaders' ability to read local politics by virtue of careful institution building made the party into more than a mere shell for the regime's ideology of development and order.

In the capital district of Jakarta, Golkar actually lost the election to the PPP, the amalgam of Islamic parties from the 1971 elections that the regime had forcefully merged in 1973. It seems more likely that the PPP's strong vote in urban areas such as Jakarta—which were more secular in outlook—reflected a protest vote against Golkar rather than some expression of confidence in the PPP. Nonetheless, the very fact that an opposition party had done well despite its constraints raised concerns. The obvious signs of discontent among the regime's former coalition allies in the student movement and Islamic organizations suggested a need to strengthen the Golkar party apparatus as a way of compensating for the narrowing of the ruling coalition. In response, the regime began to restructure the party, and its internal structure came to reflect the social challenges it had faced (Bahasoan 1982, 55–56).

Before the 1977 elections, despite the first wave of party building, Golkar still looked rather like a loose secretariat of functional groups. Functional groups were but one way to rise within the party hierarchy: the active use of party cadres in the 1971–77 period was a key means by which former student leaders and other intellectuals were able to move upward through Golkar's ranks. In part to impose greater bureaucratic discipline on the party membership and probably in larger part to marginalize students who had been insufficiently loyal, the cadres were eliminated and individual membership ceased to be an option (Bahasoan 1982, 73–74). The reorganization forced membership through the functional groups, which in turn were brought much more tightly under the control of the central Guidance Council, now headed by Suharto himself, and the council then interacted directly with the groups. In the October 1978 the Golkar *Musyawarah Nasional* (national conference), the Suharto-led central Guidance Council eliminated the Kinos, coordinating bodies for functional groups (see chapter 3).[9]

Golkar's top echelons were also streamlined and progressively embedded "in the power structure" in order make the party even more "an extension of the government's authority" (Bahasoan 1982, 77). The government replaced the Kinos with national, provincial, and regency-level councils that received the institutional weight that they had lacked, and in most cases put political leaders at each level at the head of these councils. In addition to meshing the bureaucratic and party hierarchies, national Golkar leaders became full-time officers of the party, where before the 1977 elections they had also held permanent jobs in the military or bureaucracy (Dewan Pimpinan Pusat Golongan Karya 1978, 23–43).

During the boom years, in short, the New Order regime sunk significant resources into strengthening Golkar at a time when it could simply have chosen to dole out patronage in the form of payoffs. Again, it illustrates a pattern of investing the windfall revenues into institution building. Moreover, it reflects a strategy not of strengthening the political power of the regime vis-à-vis other power centers alone—such as the heads of Kinos within Golkar—but of doing so while simultaneously fortifying the institutions themselves. In other words, rather than pursue a lower-cost path and simply take down institutional structures, the New Order leadership for the most part managed to expand them and to bring them under its own authority without undermining their ability to mobilize supporters or monitor potential rivals.

---

[9] Three Kino leaders resisted this move. They had come into Golkar from leadership positions in preexisting social organizations and believed that the party's best hope was to maintain a grass-roots base and nonbureaucratic structure (see Bahasoan 1982, 78–79).

The Oil Boom and Taxation

The capacity of the Indonesian state to collect taxes has been a matter of some dispute among specialists in economics and political science. Winters (1996) and Uppal (1986) maintain that the state collected beneath its capacity throughout the 1970s. Hill (2000), Schiller (1996), and Gelb (1986b), on the other hand, argue that Indonesia did better than most oil exporters and better than many other developing states in general. As should be clear, my argument is closer to the latter group of scholars, albeit with some qualification. I do not claim against evidence to the contrary (see for instance Uppal 1986, appendix 15) that New Order Indonesia had a model tax structure among developing societies. What I do wish to suggest is that the Indonesian state under Suharto performed surprisingly well given the regime's enormous oil revenue base, the upheaval and economic chaos of the mid-1960s, and the politically costly task of making extractive bureaucracies function adequately.

Most specialists seeking to show the sorry state of taxation in Indonesia rely on a common measure: tax revenues as a portion of gross domestic product (GDP). In the case of countries that depend significantly on the export of a commodity whose price fluctuates as much as that of oil, however, this common measure means less than it does elsewhere. A glance at figure 4.1 illustrates why this is. Where oil revenues accrue directly to the state, as they do in almost every exporting country, a fourfold increase in the price of oil could increase government revenues by nearly the same amount, immediately shrinking the relative contribution of non-oil tax and other revenues. All of this is simply to say that, to get a clear idea of changes or trends in non-oil tax revenues, it is important not to measure them as a share of GDP but rather to measure them both absolutely and as a share of non-oil GDP, seeking to show how they track with economic growth.

Between 1975 and 1978, Indonesian government revenues more than tripled, largely as a product of the rise in oil prices. Oil corporation taxes grew by an average of 64 percent each year and their growth rate reached a high of 182 percent in 1974–75. During the 1970s, however, non-oil direct tax revenues grew at an average of 39 percent per year. More importantly, even the collection of personal and corporate income taxes—arguably the most difficult to collect, given the information required[10]—rose by an average of 34 percent per year despite easy access to oil windfall revenues (see

---

[10] Figures from the Biro Pusat Statistik in Indonesia treat private income taxes and civil servant taxes as separate categories; the latter are classified as "withholdings." It is useful that they do so: civil servants are much easier to find, and it requires much less information to locate them and withhold taxes, so their exclusion resolves the plausible question of whether income taxes might simply rise as a state hires more bureaucrats.

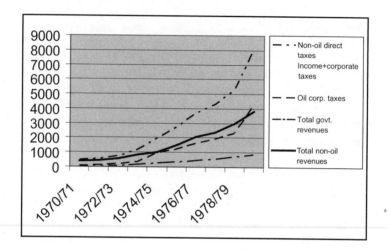

Figure 4.1. Indonesian state revenues during the boom

Source: World Bank (2001).

table 4.1). Given that the Indonesian economy grew during this period at an average of only 7.9 percent (World Bank 2001), these figures suggest that the government continued to emphasize domestic tax extraction even as it grew rich from oil.

In direct contradiction to what rentier state and resource curse theories would predict, the Indonesian state does not seem to have undergone the wholesale disintegration or dismantlement that Chaudhry (1997) and others have argued is likely during an oil boom; in fact, just the opposite happened. Gelb (1986b, 61) notes that across several large exporting countries, non-oil tax revenue remained fairly constant throughout the boom period: this suggests that the deterioration theory of oil's effects on domestic extraction may have limited scope.[11] Even Karl, whose central argument is that oil wealth, particularly in booms, creates weak institutions and especially weak extractive institutions, scales back her claim near the end of her book to note simply that non-oil taxation failed to increase much during the boom decade (1997, 200–201). The "puzzling" case of Indonesia hints at a dynamic within many exporting states that may account for the mismatch between theory and evidence. The infrastructural base of the New Order state took shape under conditions of political and economic desperation in which the lack of alternatives to "game-saving, last-resort

[11] Indonesia is included in Gelb's sample; Iran is not.

TABLE 4.1.
Relative growth in Indonesian state revenues, 1970–1980

Fiscal year	% Increase non-oil direct tax	% Increase income/ corporate taxes	% Increase oil corporate tax	% Increase total government revenues	% Increase total non-oil revenues
1970/71					
1971/72	0.3	0.26	0.63	0.21	0.14
1972/73	0.64	0.27	0.77	0.33	0.22
1973/74	0.55	0.45	0.73	0.57	0.51
1974/75	0.59	0.71	1.82	0.69	0.22
1975/76	0.34	0.41	0.28	0.38	0.47
1976/77	0.25	0.11	0.3	0.35	0.39
1977/78	0.32	0.3	0.2	0.17	0.14
1978/79	0.22	0.27	0.18	0.23	0.27
1979/80	0.26	0.28	0.85	0.52	0.28
Average yearly growth	0.39	0.34	0.64	0.38	0.29

strategies" precluded low-cost approaches to regime consolidation (Waldner 2002, 76). As a result, static typologies of the petro- or rentier state fail to capture the logic behind state and regime building in Indonesia and, as the next chapter suggests, for many other states.[12] In the next section, I outline a more commonly theorized boom trajectory and use the case of Iran to illustrate it. However, I posit that the dynamics of the late 1970s were a logical continuation of the previous fifteen years; they did not simply emerge in a couple of years because of the boom. It was during the decade before the first boom that the institutions and patterns of state-society relations emerged that would determine how the trajectory unfolded. Using an institutional approach to analyze Iran's boom-era political economy, I show in the remainder of this chapter how boom effects amplified traits that were already present as a result of the politics and policies of late development.

The Boom in a "Classic" Rentier State: Iran, 1973–79

State investment in Iran's fifth Five-Year Plan, covering the 1973–78 period, was already five times the amount invested in the fourth. However,

[12] Waldner (1999) makes this observation for Syria, noting that when oil revenues became available late in the game for the Ba'athist regime, they were put to institution-building uses aimed at solidifying the party's support base.

once the magnitude of the windfall became apparent, the regime nearly doubled its expenditure forecast in 1974 from $37 billion to almost $70 billion (Amuzegar 1999, 68). In the words of a former Iranian minister of finance and commerce and chief of the Iranian economic mission to the United States, the added expenditures were "revised with haste and in an atmosphere of unbridled euphoria" (Amuzegar 1999, 69).[13] Many of the revised-plan projects were in flashy sectors such as nuclear energy and satellite communication, in addition to more conventional ones, such as direct reduction steel and equity investment in foreign firms. For the most part, the government spent the windfalls domestically, relying on a capacity for capital absorption that did not currently exist. Little of the windfall revenues were invested in infrastructure either, so that within a few years it was common to see freight ships lined up at Iranian ports waiting weeks to unload their cargoes.

In terms of industrial investment, the Shah's regime focused mainly on capital-intensive projects that relied heavily on imported foreign technology, raw materials, semi-processed goods, and equipment; the effect was to deemphasize the creation of jobs by concentrating capital away from labor-intensive sectors. As had been the pattern since the 1960s, little attention was given in the fifth Five-Year Plan to agriculture. During the 1973–78 period, private consumption rose by 40 percent, gross domestic capital formation by 100 percent, and merchandise imports by 350 percent.

Politics and Parties

In the years before the oil boom of 1973–74, Amir Abbas Hoveyda, prime minister and (as of 1969) general secretary of Iran Novin, had some success in building the party. As I discussed in chapter 3, however, this success came more from patronage building by Hoveyda himself and less from institution building. The general secretary had substantial support among the party's membership and among the bureaucracy, but the party was highly dependent on him for its cohesion. Nonetheless, it was the party that the Shah had handpicked to mobilize support for the White Revolution and especially for state-led industrial transformation, and it had accomplished more in the way of institutionalization than previous official parties.

The oil boom apparently changed the Shah's perceived need for Iran

[13] It is interesting that Amuzegar in this quotation separates himself from the decisionmaking process of the time, qualifying the statement by saying that it was the case "by all indications." Having been at the center of economic decisionmaking himself, it is likely that Amuzegar as much as any other members of the Shah's economic team responded in this fashion.

Novin and for a nominal two-party system more generally. A well-attended annual meeting of the Iran Novin party, in which Hoveyda was given a reception of honor as general secretary, seems to have been important as well, as it signaled that the party had become a source of personal support for the prime minister.[14] In late 1974 the government announced that Majlis elections would be held the following spring, and the Shah apparently was confident enough of his political position to allow opposition parties to participate. The result was vibrant political participation in the election campaign, and the sanctioned opposition party, Mardom, won several by-elections before the main parliamentary balloting, throwing into doubt the national victory of Iran Novin and raising questions about the control commanded by the regime (Abrahamian 1989, 25).

This political setback took place against a backdrop of a state budget that had been hastily doubled once the magnitude of the oil windfall became apparent to economic planners. Given the ongoing economic plan based on the tripling of oil prices, the obstacle posed by a questionable electoral mandate[15] apparently spurred the Shah to announce the creation of the Rastakhiz (Resurgence) Party on March 2, 1975 (Kayhan, March 3, 1975; Milani 2000, 275; Alam 1991, 415–16; Abrahamian 1989, 22–28). In a day, the Shah undid what Hoveyda had spent six years building by abolishing Iran Novin and Iran's "two-party" system along with it.

The ostensible purpose of the new single-party system was to eliminate the friction caused by party politics and to support the Shah's visions for a "Great Civilization," spearheaded by a massive increase in state spending on industry and infrastructure (Pahlavi 1977, 183–226). Soon after the revision of the state budget to reflect the new price of oil, the Shah announced that by the year 2000, Iran would become the world's fifth largest industrial power and that its economy would exceed in size those of several European countries. The Rastakhiz Party apparently fit into the political

[14] The Shah himself maintained that he abolished Novin and Mardom in favor of single-party rule under the Rastakhiz Party to move Iran beyond mere party politics (see Pahlavi 1980b). Milani (2000), presenting Hoveyda's ideas, argues that the Shah was convinced by President Anwar Sadat of Egypt of the need for single-party rule during a visit to Cairo just before announcing the party's creation in March 1975. It is also interesting that, upon his return from signing a treaty in Algiers with Saddam Hussein, then vice president and Ba'ath party leader in Iraq, the Shah chose almost immediately to create a party with the same name in Persian as the Ba'ath: both mean "resurgence" or "renaissance" in English. In any case, the Shah's exact motive for creating the party when he did is a matter of debate.

[15] Note that in the months before this election, as in the months before the 1971 and 1977 elections in New Order Indonesia, rulers who could not by any measures be considered democratic still felt that they needed the show of support that would be conveyed in an election victory. A forthcoming study (Brownlee 2007) illustrates a supportive effect of "electoral authoritarianism" for incumbent rulers who can successfully manage periodic displays of limited pluralism.

picture as a means of coping with the still-present apathy among Iranians toward the Shah. Whatever its reasons, the party had the effect of destroying the equilibrium that had emerged in the years since the 1963 uprisings.

National politics had been the sole domain of the regime since 1963 but had been fairly non-intrusive for those who did not challenge the regime publicly. In other words, Iranian citizens were not forced to declare allegiance to the regime-loyal Iran Novin party or even to belong to any party. The regime made no concerted attempt to achieve social control outside of politics, and in response the vast majority of Iranians did not participate in public political life. The creation of the Rastakhiz Party changed this status quo completely, demanding that all Iranians become active members to retain full citizenship rights (*Kayhan International*, March 3, 1975).[16] The Shah, in fact, announced that Iranians who did not wish to become members of the party could leave the country.

In addition to the fact that the party became in its first months a vehicle through which the regime could harass various social groups for their lukewarm or nonexistent support, two trends in the party's development stand out. The first is its recruitment strategy. While the Shah demanded membership in the Rastakhiz Party from all Iranians, the means eventually pursued to gain such widespread membership belied the surface image of social mobilization and control. While recruiting Iranians into the party on an individual basis might well have provided a more solid basis of support, the new party was anxious to sign up 5 million members before the rescheduled elections in May 1975. Thus, Rastakhiz recruiters simply went into businesses, schools, and government agencies, extracted pledges of staff membership from managers, principles, or owners, and celebrated the party's rapidly expanding cadres.[17]

One Iranian American recounted to me his arrival at work in March 1975 and his discovery that he had been signed up for the party by his employer. From then on he was counted as a member with no further action.[18] Sattareh Farman Farmaian, a member of one of Iran's most prominent aristocratic families, had much the same experience with Rastakhiz recruiters who had come to the school of social work that she established. Farman

[16] See also remarks by the Shah in various editorials of *Rastakhiz*, the party's daily newspaper, for instance "Musharakat-i Siyasi: Vazifi-i Melli va Hizbi" [Political Participation: A National and Party Duty], May 24, 1975/3 Khordad 1354, p. 4, and Nabavi (1978).

[17] During the first weeks of the party's existence, dozens of corporations, factories, and state agencies all publicly pledged the support of their employees to the Rastakhiz Party. See the March 3–May 31 issues of *Kayhan* and *Ettela'at* and the May 1–May 31 issues of *Rastakhiz* for examples of the full-page advertisements.

[18] Author interview, Palo Alto, California, June 25, 1997. His recollections track closely to other interviews by the author in Iran, July and August 1998, and in Seattle and Los Angeles, 1997.

Farmaian, whose lineage gave her high-level access to the court, recalled being assured by Asadollah Alam, the Shah's close advisor, that "the old parties had never done anything; this one was really going to get things organized" (Farman Farmaian 1992, 279). Nonetheless, once she had filled out the "group membership application" for her school, no further action was required.

This pattern of recruitment was the norm, and it reflected a sense of little or no political urgency in the Shah's regime. It suggests that the party was not perceived to be necessary for the regime's continuity and political stability but was simply a means to prevent an official opposition party from embarrassing the state one. The result was uncertain and very likely noncommittal membership except among the highest echelons of the party. We see this in Prime Minister Amir Abbas Hoveyda's declaration shortly before the elections in May 1975 that the figure of five million members of the Rastakhiz Party was probably no more than an estimate of the total employment of organizations whose leaders had pledged support (see Afkhami 1985, 71–73). An active member of the party who also taught in the political science department at Tehran University noted that, a year after its establishment, the party secretariat still had yet to produce any reliable membership figures (Nabavi 1978, 9n6).

Another clear implication of this method of recruitment is a lack of commitment by individuals who may have officially been members. The channeling of social interests and demands through a state party to make it a two-way conduit for political demands is arguably a necessary condition for the success of that party. Individual recruitment, in which members are offered preferential job opportunities, state contracts, outright payoffs, and the like, are much more likely to build loyalty and organizational capacity than a party recruitment structure in which individuals are given no incentives to become members other than veiled threats if they fail to do so. The result in the case of the Rastakhiz Party was a new dynamic of state-society relations that may be characterized as (political) taxation without representation.

The second major trend in the development of the Rastakhiz Party was in institution building or, more accurately, the lack of it. Prime Minister Hoveyda did, however, apparently attempt at first to build the party into an institution with real power to mobilize, using recruitment offices left over from the defunct and underdeveloped Iran Novin apparatus.[19] He had been opposed to the creation of the party, committed as he was to Iran Novin but, when asked to direct it, took the Rastakhiz seriously. For his efforts, Hoveyda was removed after two years of trying to create organiza-

[19] I am grateful to Vali R. Nasr for bringing this to my attention.

tional structures for the party by the Shah, who appointed in his place Ja-hangir Amuzegar, an economist and technocrat with few political credentials. By the time the Shah took away Hoveyda's party leadership, little action had been taken to turn the many proposals from the party's first conference into reality. A plan to create groups to represent various groups in society—not unlike the function groups that made up Golkar—never came to fruition, as the existence of any of the twenty-one planned "organizational committees" was in question as late as 1977 (Nabavi 1978, 19). Amuzegar was a figure who could be counted on never to develop a political following independent of the Shah. Even if his tenure as party leader had not been cut short by the revolutionary crisis of 1977–78, it is doubtful that the party would have grown much, if at all. Hoveyda fell victim, it seems, to the same political impetus that allowed him to emerge victorious from his conflict with Alinaghi Alikhani, head of the Plan Organization, eight years earlier and, with his fall, so did the chances that the party could have become a political organization capable of maintaining a base of supporters.

In addition to its material capabilities—institutions, resources, and the capacity to manage side payments—the ideology of an official party may indicate the degree to which its leaders are committed to mobilizing large numbers of supporters and channeling social demands. If a party is to be a genuine pillar of support for the regime, it must have an ideology that serves to attract supporters or, at the very least, does not alienate them. In the case of the Rastakhiz Party, loyalty to the Shah as the leader of national development, to the 1906 Constitution, and to the White Revolution were the initial components of its ideology. Almost immediately, however, the failure of the party to draw much in the way of a following meant that its leadership's insistence that participation was a "national and party duty" was largely falling on deaf ears (*Rastakhiz*, May 24, 1975). Even the Shah's own much-feared SAVAK could find little positive to say about the party. In late 1977 SAVAK officials reported that "Rastakhiz is seen as dependent on the government, is not having much influence on people" and that "most Rastakhiz offices are hardly active" (Uyuzi 2001, 292–93).[20]

High levels of inflation and the Shah's persistent preference for government intervention over monetary solutions gave the party an excuse to blame the one business group not dependent on the regime—the bazaar. Firaydun Mahdavi, who served simultaneously as minister of commerce and as deputy general secretary of the Rastakhiz Party, found that his agency was not up to the task of generating effective tax collection to make up for government revenue shortfalls. Falling back on his position in the party,

---

[20] Thanks to Charles Kurzman for bringing these documents to my attention.

Mahdavi spearheaded an anti-profiteering campaign, using *Rastakhiz* youth groups to attack individual bazaar shops and arrest their owners. The party thus took on the public face of the Commerce Ministry's determination to control distribution through price controls (Afkhami 1985, 84).

For their continued apoliticism, Iranian intellectuals also became a target of the party. The Shah's wife, who had remained out of public politics, began to excoriate the Iranian intelligentsia for its apathy. In an article in *Kayhan*, she blasted the intellectuals for their continued inactivity: "There is no room for intellectual apathy. . . . Indifference among intellectuals toward problems of their own society is inexcusable . . . *it is the duty of intellectuals to create social cohesion* and sound ideas in future generations" (*Kayhan*, April 10, 1975, emphasis added). In short, attacks on intellectuals who refused to join the party and *bazaaris* identified the party's enemies in the first five months after its creation, overshadowing the first, more inclusive, ideological commitments and reducing the party to an instrument of invasion.

By promising to expand the profit-sharing plan for workers, the Shah and his advisers apparently hoped to mobilize them against *bazaaris* and intellectuals.[21] The profit-sharing plan failed to live up to its claims. Moreover, what might have been modest successes in party mobilization were cut short by the Shah himself, who came to see the Rastakhiz Party as a threat to his centralized authority and replaced general secretaries before they were able to consolidate their positions.[22] Despite the intentions of Hoveyda and others, the party was hamstrung by the Shah's unwillingness to see it reach its potential, demonstrating again his perception that a strong single party was ultimately a greater threat to his rule than the possibility of social resistance to the party's intrusions.

The short history of the Shah's single-party experiment with the Rastakhiz Party suggests two conclusions. First, the regime's lackluster attempts at recruitment through the party strongly support the argument that this arena of institution building, like others, carried a sense of little urgency. With no perceived threat to the Shah's rule, little effort was made to make the party into a genuine means of political mobility or even of patronage via jobs or state contracts. Second, the state-society legacy of the 1960s and early 1970s left the Pahlavi state with no solid ties to social groups on which it could build the party constituency needed to create a

---

[21] This inclination of the party's leadership may have arisen from the half led by "Imperial Marxists" such as Mohammed Baheri. Moreover, despite the many books and articles focused on the heroic role of the working class in the revolution, strikes did not become a major component of anti-regime protests until late August 1978, after nearly a year of serious uprisings led by other social groups.

[22] I am grateful to Vali Nasr for discussions of intraparty politics in the Rastakhiz Party.

real base of support. The depoliticization made possible by oil revenues left the state unable to channel or respond to social demands, so that when it began to make its own demands through the Rastakhiz Party, it was unable and unwilling to offer anything in return.

Oil and Taxation during the Boom

Since the Pahlavi regime lasted only five years into the boom era and during 1978 was preoccupied with the emerging revolutionary movement, it is difficult to make any definitive statements about the trends in tax extraction during the 1970s. A few points are clear, though. First, as figure 4.2 illustrates, both economic growth rates and income from the sale of oil were somewhat unstable after 1975, and the economy actually shrank slightly (by a single percentage point) in 1977. Second, as oil revenues declined after 1975, income and corporate taxes as a share of GNP rose slightly, although they did not increase in absolute terms and actually declined in real numbers over this period (Karshenas 1990, 188–93). In large part because by the mid-1970s the Iranian extractive bureaucracy was not able to raise sufficient revenues to compensate for the low oil receipts, the regime turned to foreign borrowing as a means of financing its budget deficit.

In addition to its economic effects, taxation took on the same political character that it had in the early 1960s during a bout of inflation in the three years after the 1973–74 oil boom. In August 1975, six months after the creation of the Rastakhiz Party, the Shah's government announced an "antiprofiteering" campaign aimed at the bazaar, again choosing interventionist rather than market measures to combat inflation. Without consulting any of Iran's commercial class (Nabavi 1978, 22), the regime implemented a sharp increase in taxes and a wide array of price controls on basic commodities, intervening directly in the bazaar without, as we saw in chapter 3, much in the way of accurate information to guide pricing.

Between 1975 and 1977, revenues from direct taxes—primarily income tax—rose substantially in a seemingly anomalous departure from the trend toward the stagnation of direct taxes. The increase, however, did not come because of rising incomes or because of newly powerful extractive institutions: it arose from a campaign by the Rastakhiz Party to squeeze what it could from the bazaar in order to punish merchants for the inflationary crisis (Bashiriyeh 1984, 98–99). Lacking the institutional clout to collect the taxes in an orderly fashion, the government, in an effort organized by Rastakhiz Deputy Secretary General and Commerce Minister Mahdavi, simply used groups of young thugs to seize money from individual merchants

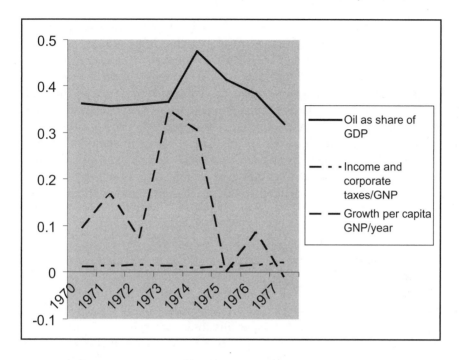

Figure 4.2. Relative changes in Iranian state revenue, 1970–77

Sources: World Bank (2001); Karshenas (1990, 190).

(Afkhami 1985, 84). Revenue collection, in other words, took on a tone not just of politics but of political warfare.

The Rastakhiz Party, standing in for tax collectors, became an instrument of extraction and invasion beginning in August 1975, when hundreds of student party recruits were sent into the bazaars to enforce new price controls and to extract—extort, merchants claimed—the new taxes (Zabih 1979, 30–31; Abrahamian 1982, 442–43). Soon, 10,000 shopkeepers had been fined, over 7,500 had been arrested, and more than 600 shops had been shut down by the Rastakhiz Youth, which group Hoveyda described as "the instruments of Iran's development" (*Kayhan International,* November 26, 1975). Notably, the anti-bazaar campaign was directed not by an existing institution of the state but by a special task force of the Rastakhiz Party (Ashraf 1988, 557). Alleged tax evasion and profiteering by the bazaar were described as late as August 1977 not as a simple problem of economics or policy but as a "problem of the [Rastakhiz] party" (*Ettela'at,* August 23, 1977).

In a strange way, the regime supplanted the underperforming tax bureaucracy with its new official party, hoping that if it could not raise revenues effectively, it could at least shift the blame for inflation to greedy merchants. Thus, the one statistically positive sign in the otherwise negative trends in non-oil revenue collection actually arose from a political decision that had little relation to changing incomes. Moreover, it did much to convince the bazaar as a community to become politically active soon after this episode (Smith 2003a). Meanwhile, the government continued to rely on foreign borrowing to cover the shortfalls from its hastily doubled budget, especially the vast new industrial projects and high-end imports, the former of which were seldom viable and the latter of which were often undeliverable due to lack of infrastructure.

Local Government

The study of provincial and local level government in Iran during the boom has been minimal, and, since the revolution, access to government archives for research is sporadic at best, especially for foreign scholars. Thus, my observations in this section are suggestive rather than conclusive. Nonetheless, based on ethnographic studies of local communities in Iran, it is possible to draw some suggestive conclusions about the focus of the regime's priorities during the 1970s. First, as I mentioned in chapter 2, the apparent decline in the capacity of provincial and local institutions was a predominantly urban trend. Land reform and its accompanying increase in the state's presence in the countryside meant a considerable rise in state authority in rural areas. In this, the Shah's regime may have accomplished as much as the Suharto regime did in rural Indonesia.

What concerns me, and what I suggest ultimately meant the difference in the survival or fall of the regime, is how effectively it could both assert control and provide survival strategies for *urban* citizens. I discuss this in more detail below; for now it is enough to note that in rapidly developing countries such as these, it is likely that urban social groups will be the ones on which the regime's survival depends, notwithstanding Huntington's (1966) imperative to "surround the cities" with conservative peasants. Farhi (1988, 1990) has made the most explicit argument in this vein, adapting Skocpol's (1979) theory of revolution to account for the overwhelmingly urban nature of the antistate coalitions that came to power in Iran and Nicaragua.

In any case, the local institutions charged with administering policy and political life in Iran's cities simply did not keep up with the rate of urban expansion. They failed to do so because the regime gave them little priority, banking that its ability to prevent public politics by potential opposition groups (through SAVAK and the army) would suffice for social control. The Fifth Development Plan—the post-boom revised version—allocated 9.4 billion rials to provincial governments as opposed to 221.2 billion rials for internal security, most of which went to SAVAK. The secret police, in other words, received two and a half times the funding of Iran's entire local system of government.

Most important, this allocation for provincial governments reflected no increase at all over the pre-revision budget, whereas the budgets for the military, SAVAK, and most industrial projects were increased by a factor of anywhere from two to four (Mofid 1987, 106–9). It is clear from these figures that in central decisionmaking, establishing a strong administrative presence at the local level took a back seat to all other priorities.

Several scholars have noted that the first oil boom coincided closely with a marked rise in the autonomy of social groups, particularly the *ulemā*, bazaar, and intellectual communities (Denoeux 1993; Parsa 2000; Smith 2003a). Moreover, they maintain that it was the state's belated attempt in 1976–77 to impose order on Iranian politics that catalyzed the opposition. Thus, for instance, only by essentially launching an invasion of the bazaar in Tehran could new taxes be collected: accomplishing it through normal institutional means was simply not feasible.

The conventional wisdom in the study of the Pahlavi state is that it was somehow both extremely powerful and fatally fragile. Oil revenues enabled the construction of a vast security apparatus and "highly autonomous" decisionmaking (Gasiorowski 1993b) but simultaneously left the regime vulnerable to the opposition. Thus, the revolutionary crisis of 1977–78 is theorized as the result of state breakdown. Yet, Kurzman (1994, 2003), Parsa (1989, 2000), and others have noted that by all objective measures the Iranian state suffered no sudden decline in capacity in the 1977–79 period. The questions remains, then: if the state was so powerful, how did it "collapse" during the crisis of 1977–78?

The answer I propose, one that also reflects this inference about local government and social control more generally, is that the regime may well have retained a high degree of autonomy in decisionmaking and a considerable coercive capacity. However, it never developed the institutional capacity to offer viable survival strategies to a wide array of social groups or the relations with such groups to ensure that they would not turn into the opposition in an economic crisis.

The important distinction here is made by Mann (1987), who distinguishes between despotic power and infrastructural power, respectively the abilities to make policy unconstrained by social pressure and to implement that policy effectively at the local level. Put more bluntly, coercion alone cannot maintain rulers in power. Their survival depends heavily on the ability to monitor the groups that are most likely to turn against them and to provide others with sufficient public goods to gain their support or acquiescence. On the eve of the protests of 1977, the Shah's regime was left with no strong allies in Iranian society, no record of urban social control (as might have been made possible by an effective tax bureaucracy and robust local government), and the extractive and political offenses of the Rastakhiz Party to answer for.

Hard Times in the Lands of Plenty: Two Regimes Face Protests during the Boom

Between 1976 and 1978, Indonesia and Iran both experienced inflationary crises as a result of the rapid influx of revenue during the boom. In part due to the sudden increase in the cost of basic consumer goods and in part because neither of the two regimes was particularly open to popular participation in policymaking, 1977 saw the reemergence of mass politics as a means of expressing discontent with the government. Both the New Order and the Pahlavi regimes had to a large degree staked their legitimacy on development and economic progress. How long they could shrug off demands for more representative politics depended heavily on whether they could provide stable economic growth. Thus, the perception that both were failing to deliver the economic goods played an important role in the timing of these protests.

In both of these countries, the protesters who confronted the regimes were mobilized by urban parties or social movements. It is a regime's ability to monitor dissident groups in the cities and to prevent the growth of demonstrations into broad protest movements that will dictate its chances for survival in a rapidly urbanizing country. One theoretical consequence of rapid urban growth is increasing numbers of recent migrants who have been uprooted from "traditional" social institutions in rural areas. Another is increasing urban unemployment, provided that the number of jobs fails to keep pace with the number of new urban residents. Uprooted and unemployed urban migrants can conceivably provide a base of support for political entrepreneurs. So a significant difference in urban growth figures might explain the variation in outcomes here. However, between 1970 and 1980, urban population growth in both Iran and Indonesia remained fairly consistent, rising at about 5 percent each year. Thus, it is unlikely that rapid urbanization (Huntington 1968) explains the contrast in regime durability.

The urban population remained a considerably higher share of Iran's population than of Indonesia's, of course, ranging from 40 to 50 percent and from 17 to 23 percent, respectively. Indonesia's population was three times that of Iran's, however, and the population of the island of Java alone was nearly twice that of the population of Iran throughout the 1970s. Most important, between 1970 Indonesia's urban population grew from 20 million to nearly 33 million while Iran's grew only from 12 million to 20 million (World Bank 2001). Moreover, if it is simply coercive force that explains the likelihood of regime survival, we would have expected the Shah rather than Suharto to emerge victorious in a confrontation with the opposition. By the early 1970s, even before the Shah embarked on a military spending spree, he had two and a half times the military manpower per 1,000 working age population that Suharto did, at 15.4 to 6.0 (Taylor and Hudson 1972, table 2.4). As a result, by 1971 his army stood at approximately 33 soldiers per 1000 urban residents as opposed to roughly 29 for the Indonesian armed forces. In short, Suharto confronted a consistently larger urban population than the Shah and, subsequently, a potentially higher base of opponents, and he did so with many fewer soldiers per 1,000 citizens, suggesting that raw coercive force alone does not explain why the Shah's opponents were so much more successful than their counterparts in Indonesia.

It is worth describing in at least some detail what I mean by "economic crisis" in these two countries. Table 4.2 provides selected economic indicators for Indonesia and Iran during the 1974–78 period that capture some of the political dynamics of the two economies.[23] The most significant differences across the five-year period are relative dependence on oil exports and economic growth rates. Indonesia's oil export dependence (measured by oil exports as a share of gross domestic product) was roughly half of Iran's during the mid-1970s, and the Indonesian economy continued to expand during the last two years of this period, whereas Iran's economy contracted in both 1977 and 1978. On the surface, there is some reason to believe that the Shah fell simply because the crisis he oversaw was worse than the one Suharto confronted. However, it is important to consider the effects of these crises in the context of each country's demographic and economic background. Economic performance and oil export dependence interact in relation to a government's "rent-paying" capacity. In other words, how many hypothetical petro-dollars do rulers have available to pay out to each citizen? Here the numbers are telling. Taking into account per capita GDP and oil exports as a share of GDP, Suharto's government had on hand during the mid-1970s between US$50 and 55 in oil rents per Indonesian citizen, or about 20 percent of her income. The Shah, on the other hand, had

[23] Thanks to Eva Bellin for suggesting these indicators and for pushing me on the comparison of crises here.

TABLE 4.2.
Selected economic indicators, 1974–78

Country	Indicator	1974	1975	1976	1977	1978
Indonesia	Oil/GDP	20.91	17.98	17.24	16.89	15.72
Iran	Oil/GDP	47.54	41.38	38.37	31.91	24.97
Indonesia	GDP growth (annual %)	8.26	6.18	5.99	8.64	9.21
Iran	GDP growth (annual %)	—	5.45	16.93	−1.10	−11.05
Indonesia	GDP per capita growth (annual %)	5.67	3.71	3.40	6.14	6.82
Iran	GDP per capita growth (annual %)	—	2.18	13.26	−4.20	−13.88
Indonesia	National Gini index*			34.60		38.60
Iran	National Gini index*	42.30**				
Indonesia	Urban Gini index*	—	—	35.00	—	38.00
Iran	Urban Gini index*	49.50***	—	—	—	—
Indonesia	Inflation (annual %)	40.60	19.05	19.86	11.04	8.11
Iran	Inflation (annual %)	14.25	12.88	11.26	27.29	11.72
Indonesia	Avg. Inflation 1974–78:	19.73				
Iran	Avg. Inflation 1974–78:	15.48				

Sources: Data from World Bank Development Indicators 2004 unless otherwise noted. *Deininger and Squire 1996. **Data from 1972, Deininger and Squire 1996. ***Data from 1973, Deininger and Squire 1996.

on average US$690 per citizen, or about 37 percent of an average Iranian's income. These figures reflect the rents available for dealing with potential social dissent and reveal a more complex picture than do raw export dependence scores. The Iranian economy was certainly more dependent on export revenues than Indonesia's, but so too did the Shah have dramatically larger rent resources, even during this economic downturn, which could have been used to mollify social groups. These figures are important in the context of rulers' abilities to use rents to soften the blow of an economic downturn.

Inflation paints a less telling picture. It was higher in Iran in 1977 and 1978 (27 and 12 percent, respectively) but considerably higher in Indonesia in 1974, 1975, and 1976. Yet 40 percent inflation in 1974 failed to catalyze a mass-based opposition movement to Indonesia's New Order. More important, inflation had no statistically significant relationship to either antistate protests or regime failure in the analysis discussed in chapter 1; nor did GDP growth. This suggests not that neither indicator matters, simply that it does not appear to have a systematic effect on the prospects for regimes surviving inflationary or recessionary periods. What matters, ultimately, is the political dynamics that ensue during such periods.

Although comprehensive figures on income distribution are incomplete for both Indonesia and Iran, both national and urban Gini indices for Iran are somewhat higher at 42 and 49 percent, respectively, in 1972 versus 35 percent in Indonesia for 1976 and 39 percent in 1978. The differences are real but not huge, and it seems unlikely that regime outcomes would be explained simply by a 10 or 15 percent increase in Gini coefficients from one country to the next. Again, the importance of inflation as an economic indicator is in its political impact. Protesters in both Indonesia and Iran made use of inflation as a political issue, (rightly) blaming their governments for the effects that windfall revenues had when absorbed too quickly into domestic economies. Simply put, on balance the years 1977–78 were somewhat worse for Iran's than for Indonesia's economy, but not on such a dramatic scale that we can end the story there.

Both of these regimes, which had come to power with the aid of the United States government and maintained close economic and military ties to Washington, were affected by the change of administration in 1977. Incoming president Jimmy Carter had campaigned on a foreign policy platform promoting human rights and had promised to take to task any American client state that did not make improvements in the way its citizens were treated. Suharto and the Shah, along with autocrats around the globe, wondered in January 1977 if the new American leadership meant what it had said during the election campaign. The two leaders were prominently mentioned in human rights campaigns, too, due to the attention paid their abuses, and both governments were singled out in Carter's early human rights speeches.

Many Iran specialists argue that Carter's rhetoric was key in provoking the demonstrations of early 1977, and there is something to this (see for instance Kurzman 2003, 294). What I want to suggest in this section, however, is that given the criticism of both governments and the plausible encouragement to protesters in both countries, it is unlikely that pressure from the United States played the crucial causal role in the ability of either the Shah or Suharto to stay in power through this period. Both regimes drew the attention of Carter's critical speeches, and both tried to deflect the criticism by making limited gestures at liberalization.[24]

In short, a combination of factors manifested themselves domestically in both countries: rising costs, increasingly autocratic policymaking and faltering economic performance, and dissident groups emboldened by offi-

---

[24] It is worth noting that, after initial statements criticizing the human rights records of both governments, the Carter administration backed away from its assertiveness. On January 1, 1978, on a New Year's Day visit to Tehran, President Carter referred to Iran as "an island of stability in a troubled area of the world"; by December 1977 he had accepted Suharto's assurances that political prisoners and East Timor independence guerrillas would be released and treated well, respectively.

cial American human rights rhetoric. In early 1977, student groups took the lead in both Iran and Indonesia, mobilizing street demonstrations that sounded remarkably similar in tone, decrying the dependence on foreign capital, corruption, and undemocratic politics. What differed crucially were (1) the preexisting abilities of the regimes to hold together a coalition and prevent students from building a cross-group, cross-class movement, and (2) the ability to respond flexibly to the demands issuing from protest groups. Both of these factors, I argue below, stem directly from efforts made in the previous two decades to tap into society by building administrative and mobilizing institutions and to maintain contacts with crucial power bases in each society.

Indonesia: Riding Out the Storm into the Second Boom

In late 1977, following several months of tension that emerged from the national elections in May, Indonesia's student movement began to mobilize again. For the most part, student dissent catalyzed around continued inflation, foreign economic dependence, growing economic inequality, official corruption, and the lack of democratic politics. Students at the University of Indonesia (UI) began in particular to voice concern with a series of corruption scandals that emerged after the election. The conviction of the rice procurement director for East Kalimantan on embezzlement charges, an allegation that a Department of Communications official had tried to extort $40 million from GTE for a satellite television contract, and persistent but unproven rumors that the West Java rice crop failure in late 1977 was due to official corruption all overshadowed economic indicators such as rising exports, falling inflation, and a drop in poverty levels.

Over the course of the summer of 1977, student protesters took up several issues in addition to corruption. Suharto's decision to replace a popular governor of the capital district of Jakarta, Ali Sadikin, with his own military secretary, General Tjokropranolo, spurred a "Sadikin for President" campaign on the UI campus. Rising bus fares in Jakarta also provoked student protests and, increasingly, confrontation with government economic policy officials during official student-government meetings. Finally, when the new parliament convened on October 1, the government's outline of its priorities emphasized an intent to build the regime-controlled *Komisi Nasional Pemuda* Indonesia (Indonesian National Youth Committee, or KNPI) and gave no mention at all to other organizations, from KAMI to religious student groups. For many student groups, the statement reflected a plan to monopolize the Indonesian youth movement.

In August 1977, Suharto sent Professor Sumitro, an advisor, to meet with student leaders in Jakarta, Yogyakarta, and Bandung. At UI in Jakarta and Gadjah Mada University in Yogyakarta, students rapidly shifted discussions from economic policy to questioning the military's role in politics. At the Bandung Institute of Technology (ITB), they took over the meeting from the very beginning, issuing a set of impossible conditions for the government and then unilaterally closing down the meeting before discussion could take place (Hariyadhie 1997, 28–33; Bresnan 1993, 197).[25]

Islamic groups, too, registered dissent with New Order policies. The PPP had become for the regime the primary focus of concern, for some of the same reasons that the PKI had frightened Suharto and his fellow officers in the mid-1960s. The PPP's close ties to Nahdlatul Ulama gave it powerful local networks for mobilizing support at election time; it retained popular legitimacy as the party of Islam, and, surprisingly, the regime's strategy of fractionalizing the Islamists in national politics by forcing all Muslim parties to merge into the PPP actually resulted in fusion. Despite the efforts of Soedomo, the head of the Committee to Restore Security and Order (Kopkamtib), and Amir Machmud, the minister of home affairs, to cast Golkar as a good Muslim party, PPP performed well in the 1977 elections and actually won the capital district of Jakarta as well as the province of Aceh.

The same government political outline that had left out independent student organizations also discussed, in several passages, *kepercayaan* (beliefs) and *agama* (religion) as though the former deserved as much official respect as the latter. *Kepercayaan* referred to a system of mysticism that drew from pre-Islamic Javanese, Hindu, and Buddhist traditions; it also registered powerfully with much of the government's leadership, including Suharto, most of whom were raised in central Java, a center of *kepercayaan* practice. For Islamic leaders and their followers, the government's statement smacked of separating the millions of nominal or "statistical Muslims" on Java, called *abangan*, from more devout followers, or *santri* (see Geertz 1960; Liddle 1978b, 181).

As a result of persistent economic complaints and independent grievances by student and Islamic organizations against the regime, numerous protests emerged between October and December 1977. They culminated in a series of parallel protests by student and Islamic organizations on November 10, Heroes' Day in Indonesia, a holiday honoring the soldiers killed in the Battle of Surabaya against British forces in 1945 (Hariyadhie 1997, 45). In the three weeks following the Heroes' Day protests, two of Suharto's advisors gave public speeches in which they criticized the regime's policies

---

[25] The discussion that follows is a brief summary of the events and dynamics of the 1977–78 protests. For more detailed accounts, see Hariyadhie's firsthand recollection of the 1978 student movement (1997) and Bresnan's chronological account of the period (1993, 197–211).

to varying degrees (Liddle 1978b, 184). Suharto, through Army chief of staff Maraden Panggabean, called an emergency staff meeting aimed at cementing and, perhaps more importantly, publicly displaying army unity in the face of substantial public dissent.

On January 6, 1978, the student council at ITB issued a "White Book of the 1978 Students' Struggle" in which it expressed no confidence in Suharto as president and called for an end to corruption, for democratic participation, and for the military's standing above politics on behalf of the Indonesian nation (Hariyadhie 1997, 57; Bresnan 1993, 198).[26] At this juncture, army solidarity was clearer, as troops occupied the ITB campus in Bandung, arrested over 100 students, and closed most of the country's major newspapers for a week. What was less clear was support for Suharto in other areas of the government. The sultan of Yogyakarta, who had been serving as vice president, announced that he would not stand for reelection in the March 1978 vote by the parliament to select a new executive team for the next five years.

When the parliament did convene in March 1978 to elect a president, troops were everywhere in Jakarta, reflecting the regime's real concern. PPP delegates walked out of the Assembly when the government brought to the floor its policy outline with the offending religion/beliefs passages intact. Suharto was ultimately reelected president on March 23, but almost immediately following the election, a group of retired army officers sent a letter to the new army chief of staff, lamenting that the reelection had taken place "in an atmosphere of war" (quoted in Bresnan 1993, 202). Over the next several months, these officers—representing the Forum for Study and Communication, a body made up of former military leaders—sent five more papers to the chief of staff, recommending that the army separate itself from Golkar and, more broadly, from politics. By October, this political vein found its way into official army discussion. The army general staff on October 17 released a paper suggesting that since stability had been achieved, the role of the military in Indonesia's political leadership could begin to shrink (Bresnan 1993, 203).

Over the next year, this question of policy and the prerogatives of the New Order leadership moved from street protest to intra-regime contention. It was noteworthy that despite their recent demands on the regime, the major social organizations whose demonstrations had kicked off this process of political soul-searching largely stayed off the streets. Moreover, there was no "bandwagon" effect. Efforts by the regime to maintain side

---

[26] Note again the use of a three-point demand by student protesters, a symbolic reference to the demands by student organizations in 1965–66 that helped to bring down Sukarno.

payments to civil servants (with regular raises that increased as the second boom took hold) and the urban middle and lower classes (with multiple commodity and fuel subsidies) made it possible to limit the scope of open political dissent. Ultimately, the differences within the army leadership and within the regime itself ceased to take public shape. By 1980, in part due to the largess made possible by the second oil boom and in part because the disagreements among the military leadership were not significant enough to warrant replacing Suharto, the opposition fizzled out.[27]

This period of dissent illustrates how important preexisting patterns of state-society relations were to the long-term viability of the New Order government. Student and Islamic organizations may both have had their complaints about the New Order, but they carried out only one day's worth of collective protests in November 1977. Moreover, neither group succeeded in—nor, apparently, made much effort at—building a coalition across classes or groups. This at the very least would have been necessary to sustain a challenge to the regime, even if the demands were ultimately reformist rather than revolutionary in nature. Throughout the 1970s and even during this period of contention, both the student and Islamic movements had maintained contacts within the upper ranks of the regime. These contacts dated back to the early New Order years and were well established when the regime truly needed them.

In short, what is notable about the protests of the late 1970s in Indonesia is not their magnitude but rather their lack of success. It is tempting, especially given normative concerns about the use of force to deal with dissent, to single out heavy-handed policing of demonstrators as the key explanatory factor in the ability of the regime to ride out this protest episode. As we will see in the case of Iran, however, coercion has much less uniform ability to limit collective action than is often assumed. What mattered crucially for Suharto's ultimate ability to reestablish the regime was the capacity, built over the preceding fifteen years, to know who the "moderates" were in various groups and to separate them from the radicals who were unwilling to reach accommodation. Moreover, the regime's capacity to prevent the emergence of a broad coalition—given the widespread dissatisfaction with New Order politics, the incentive was real—made it possible to avoid facing the volume of opposition that the Shah did in early 1978 and beyond.

[27] Ali Moertopo, a longtime advisor to Suharto, maintained that an attempt by the military to unseat Suharto "would lead to civil war" (*Berita Buana*, July 9, 1980, quoted in Bresnan 1993, 210).

Iran: The End of 2,500 Years of Monarchy

Between 1963 and 1977, the "streets" of Iran were fairly quiet, especially when compared to those in Indonesia. However, opposition to the Pahlavi regime by no means disappeared in the late 1960s and early 1970s. Rather, given the lack of channels for expression, it took on a sporadic and covert character. Since their street protests in the past had accomplished almost nothing, student groups largely restricted their political activities to small group meetings called *dowrehs* (circles), in which individuals would meet regularly to discuss political and social affairs. The more committed militants among the student groups supported or joined small guerrilla movements (see Johnson 1975; Boroujerdi 1996, 40–41).

The Islamist opposition, which had also remained rather quiet during the 1963–77 period, nonetheless managed to retain much of its organizational autonomy despite SAVAK penetration.[28] Only one major protest by the Shi'a community took place in the early 1970s: a demonstration by seminary students in Qom, the center of Shi'a theological training south of Tehran. On June 5, 1975, Qom seminary students staged a gathering to commemorate those injured or killed during the June 1963 protests (Nahzat-e Azadi-ye Iran 1976; Kurzman 2003, 287–89). Despite the prohibition on public use of Khomeini's name, the students began to chant the name of the man best known at the time for leading the 1963 protest. State security forces surrounded the seminary and over the next few days maintained a state of siege until they finally stormed the building on the evening of June 7. Despite the students' calls for support from the residents of the city, frantic (and largely unanswered) phone calls to Qom's religious leaders for help, a hastily organized general strike in Qom on June 7, and the rapid spread of word about the protest around the country, no other social groups joined this demonstration. Nor did Iran's Shi'a leaders issue broader calls to oppose the regime.

There are a number of possible explanations for why this protest event failed to catalyze any kind of broad opposition to the Shah. Kurzman argues that the self-perception of the religious opposition only became revolutionary in late 1977. More specifically, he maintains that it was only after significant mobilization by other groups in Iranian society that Khomeini became convinced that his followers could, and should, begin to try to build

---

[28] In this the Iranian Islamic community was similar to its Indonesian counterpart, even though it was much more hierarchically institutionalized. Shi'a Islam, and in particular the Usuli branch of Shi'ism that is dominant in Iran, has a much more rigid and formal hierarchy than most Sunni sects. The Shi'a "hierocracy" has often been compared to the Catholic Church, in contrast to Sunni Islam, which is less strictly organized and looks rather more like Protestant sects of Christianity.

an anti-regime coalition (2003, 308–10). Another argument for the failure of the June 1975 protest is that Carter's human rights rhetoric opened up a degree of political space in Iran in 1977 that had been absent earlier. Still another possibility is that economic conditions had changed, but evidence for this is notably lacking. I suggest a fourth alternative, albeit one that is not exclusive of the first two theories: by June 1975 the regime had not yet thoroughly antagonized any of the social groups that would take to the streets against it two years later. As a result, the perceived costs of facing repression still seemed higher than the costs of inaction.

The bazaar, for its part, had three more months before the Rastakhiz Party began to attack it in the name of controlling inflation and, in general, merchants were prospering from the first oil boom. Student groups and intellectuals were still generally content to have the regime leave them alone and had not been ordered to endorse the regime actively by joining the party. Although the bazaar and student communities were far from avid supporters of the regime, they might still, in early 1977, have been counted on not to join a broad anti-regime coalition or to be satisfied with limited concessions to their limited demands. This argument is quite consistent with Kurzman's: I simply focus on the incentives for other social groups to mobilize in the two different periods rather than Khomeini's perception of their activities. In any case, it was not until nearly two years after this retrospectively important event that cross-group mobilization began.

Political dissent in Iran grew more vocal in early 1977 as a number of groups that had been specifically targeted by the regime's new Rastakhiz Party voiced their outrage with the new invasiveness of official politics. Importantly, all of these statements and demands were reform-oriented in nature. Only the Ayatollah Khomeini among the opposition demanded the overthrow of the monarchy, but in early 1977 he remained silent, only emerging in November and even then only in response to an emerging coalition of non-*ulemā* groups mobilizing against the regime (Kurzman 2003, 309).[29] Until then, protesting groups never mentioned any thought of bringing down the regime, only of urging reform of certain policies. American political scientist Richard Cottam, who had close ties to Iranian opposition groups in the 1970s, testified before Congress that all of the various groups who became vocal in 1977 "criticized only particular policies rather than the regime itself" before the crisis emerged in 1978 (cited in Kurzman 2003, 308).

---

[29] As was the case with my discussion of Indonesia, I do not by any means give a complete account here of the events of 1977–79 in Iran. There is a number of exhaustive narratives of the revolutionary movement and protest events: see especially, in Persian, Daftar-e Adabiyat-e Enqelab-e Islami (1995) and Aqili (1990, 307–417); in English, Abrahamian (1982, 496–529) and Ashraf and Banuazizi (1985).

Among the newly vocal were Iran's intellectuals. In 1976, after it had become apparent that their human rights defender Jimmy Carter would soon be directing America's policy toward Iran, many long-dormant intellectual associations were revived. These included the Association of Iranian Jurists, the Writers' Association of Iran, and the National Association of University Teachers, all of which began to express their opposition to the Rastakhiz single-party state on such topics as civil and political rights, censorship, and academic freedom (Moghadam 1989, 152; Karimi-Hakkak 1985). These associations had been revived nearly a year before the limited liberalizations of early 1977, suggesting that it was more than the removal of constraints on oppositional mobilization that led to this protest activity. Rather, the timing of this flourish of intellectual resistance suggests that it was the incentives created by the party's attempt to "establish new standards in societal relations and in the people's social and political activities" that spurred it.[30]

When the Shah implemented limited political reforms in early 1977, intellectuals flooded the regime with demands for increased freedom of expression. In March 1977, the regime announced that it would move the national university in Tehran to Isfahan, most likely to distance it from the capital and thus from the center of Iranian politics. In response, students and professors protested, and during the protests the Tehran bazaar remained closed. After the protest, the regime cut faculty salaries; bazaar merchants "quickly established funds to pay faculty salaries in full" (Parsa 1989, 109). In May, a group of lawyers wrote a highly critical letter to the government, the first time since 1963 that the regime had been so publicly and strongly criticized. In June, the Writers' Association of Iran wrote a public letter to Prime Minister and Party Secretary General Hoveyda (Karimi-Hakkak 1985). In July, another group of lawyers wrote a public manifesto criticizing the regime's control of the judiciary (*Ettela'at*, February 7, 1980; Abrahamian 1982, 498), and the bazaar in Tehran formally protested the Rastakhiz Party's price-control campaign (Parsa 1989, 109).

From October 10 to 19, 1977, a Writers' Association poetry meeting gathered some ten thousand participants at the Irano-German Cultural Society (or Goethe Institute) in Tehran (Karimi-Hakkak 1985, 208–11). When it was broken up by the police, students and teachers responded by shutting down nearly all of Tehran's universities for the full ten days. Government judges previously loyal to the regime acquitted all of the demonstrators who were arrested. In support, the bazaars closed throughout the protests. Notably, during these demonstrations, protesters specifically tar-

---

[30] See the "Tasmim ba Mardom Ast" (Decisions are the People's) editorial in *Rastakhiz*, May 10, 1975/ 20 Ardebehesht 1354, p. 4.

geted the local offices of the Rastakhiz Party and not government agencies, suggesting that the party was the center of attention and further illustrating the degree to which the party had polarized the *bazaaris* and intellectuals against the state (Moghadam 1989, 152).

Karimi-Hakkak has argued that the "Ten Nights," as the event became known, "heralds the emergence of popular revolt against the state" (1985, 210). In light of the pattern of protest by *bazaaris* and intellectuals outlined above, though, we might ask whether it also signaled the definitive end of the state-society accommodation that had been steadily collapsing since March 1975. Also, the magnitude of the Ten Nights—as mentioned above, over ten thousand people participated, and thousands more took to the streets to protest its forced stoppage by the state—indicates that by late 1977 a large portion of Iran's bazaar and intellectual communities had turned against the party-state. Throughout 1978, intellectuals made up a substantial portion of the opposition's "foot soldiers." In addition, the bazaars remained closed for several months to communicate, as closures always did, "to other groups in society that some sort of conflict [was] underway" (Parsa 1989, 93).

The Ten Nights demonstrations were arguably the first mass mobilization events of what grew into the revolution. In late 1977, serious attention by the regime might well have accomplished all that was needed to prevent broad mobilization: singling out the moderates and offering limited concessions, as Suharto had done. Had that been accomplished, it is entirely possible that the protests would not have moved beyond what Ashraf and Banuazizi have described as a phase of "nonviolent mobilization" (1985, 4). In fact, their narrative of the escalation of the protests, from this nonviolent phase through cyclical urban riots to mass demonstrations to "disruptive strikes" to an eventual dual sovereignty of regime and opposition leadership, suggests that in the early stages revolutionary movements may be little different from other episodes of contentious politics. As I suggested in chapter 1, what differs crucially in states facing protests such as these are (1) their ability to "reach into" the opposition to assess the scope of demands and respond to them and (2) the capacity to limit mobilization with means other than raw force.

Whereas the New Order regime was able to do just this in the late 1970s, the Shah was not. January 1978 marked the beginning of mass-based mobilization against the regime. Much as the Indonesian opposition had initially been catalyzed to action by an offensive government action, an article published on January 7 in a state-controlled newspaper in Tehran ridiculing Khomeini provoked a riot in Qom on January 9. Even in this incendiary atmosphere, there remained a split among those responding to the article. As Kurzman notes, a group of radical students first went to the city's religious leadership to demand a response. The Ayatollah Ha'eri, for one, was clearly hesitant to react in a radical way: "This sort of thing . . . must be peaceful, not like" the June 1975 protests. On January 8, the protests were apparently limited, and conflict with the police was confined to "verbal sparring" (2003, 290). However, in part because the regime maintained no contacts that it could have utilized to eke out an accommodation with at least some of the students or their leaders, neither Ha'eri nor the general Shi'a leadership in Qom was able to prevent the mass demonstration and rioting of January 9.

According to one eyewitness account, by noon on January 9, enough Qom residents had joined the students for the number of protesters to swell to around ten thousand. Remarkably, the demonstrators remained both nonviolent and silent, marching to the homes of religious leaders and hushing those who began to yell chants at the security forces. When the police ordered them off the streets, however, stones thrown through two nearby windows spurred more rock-throwing, shouting, and physical confrontation with the troops. The troops eventually responded with live fire, and by the end of the day, somewhere between nine (the official version) and a few hundred (the opposition account) had been killed. It was with this incident that the opposition to the Shah made the transition from localized to mass-based mobilization. Forty days later, as per Shi'a custom in commemorating deaths, memorials were held in cities around Iran to honor those killed. This time, it was not merely students; their leaders, *bazaaris*, teachers, and other urban residents also joined the protests. Moreover, the protests spread rapidly to other cities, so that by March 1978 it was common for a protest event in Tehran or Isfahan to be followed within a day or two by major events in ten to twelve other cities, demonstrating not just that mobilizing networks remained robust but also that the vaunted Pahlavi state had much less capacity to penetrate them than had been assumed.

This second, mass-based, phase of anti-regime collective action grew over the next two months and by late summer 1978 workers across many sectors joined the protests by staging strikes. Throughout the spring and summer of 1978, the regime seemed unwilling to face the volume of demands issuing from the protesters. Even at this late date, however, many of them were directed toward reform (for instance, see Parsa 1995, 30–32) rather than toward overthrowing the regime. It was not until late in the fall of 1978 that the regime began to negotiate at all with the opposition and even then only with the clearly marginalized moderates among the opposition. By most accounts, the opportunity to negotiate a transition had vanished by the time Khomeini had emerged as the clear leader of the revolutionary movement in mid-1978. At that point, most major social groups had allied with Khomeini and his supporters either because they genuinely believed in him or because they pragmatically saw him as the best hope for bringing down the Shah. This development made it all but impossible for the regime to salvage any kind of position in a future government that included the opposition (Parsa 1995). The Shah's sole effort at negotiating with moderate opposition leaders consisted of arresting most of them in mid-November 1978 and sounding them out about the prospect of accepting the prime minister's post in a new government that would have preserved the Shah's constitutional monarchy and control of the armed forces (Kurzman 2004, 154).

A common misconception of the revolutionary crisis in Iran is that the Pahlavi state "came apart" in the face of a mass-based movement. The evidence suggests another explanation. While its coercive capacity remained strong, its monitoring, cooptive, and administrative capabilities—its infrastructural power—simply were not developed enough to keep increasing numbers of Iranian citizens from joining the opposition. Kurzman (2004) notes that, by most objective measures, the Shah's state faced no sudden crisis of capacity and that the regime continued to use force in an effort to quell the growing demonstrations. He suggests that what changed was not the capacity of the state but rather the conviction of the opposition that it had sufficient numbers by the late summer of 1978 to bring down the government despite heavy state coercion. Rasler (1996) observes a consistent trend of state repression over the course of 1978 but, contrary to theories that state violence can or could have sustained the Shah's rule, finds that repression was a powerful predictor of expanded antistate protest.

Indeed, Kurzman's respondents pointed repeatedly to incidents of state repression as catalysts mobilizing them from the sidelines into the opposition. It was not, if these respondents represent a sizable portion of those who joined the movement, because the state lacked the will to repress but precisely because it did not (2004, 116–18). Even as the body count continued to increase over the course of 1978 (see Kurzman 2004, 109), ordinary Iranians joined the opposition in ever greater numbers, apparently believing in equally greater numbers that the movement was succeeding. The revolutionary movement began to grow even more rapidly and to incorporate new social groups and new repertoires of contention, during what was arguably the most repressive period of the year—the martial law period that began on September 7, 1978. The first social response to martial law took place the next day and included more than five thousand demonstrators in Jaleh Square in eastern Tehran. The regime's response included helicopter gunships firing on poor slums whose residents had also mobilized and what one journalist at Jaleh Square described as "a firing squad, with troops shooting at a mass of stationary protesters" (*Guardian*, September 17, 1978, cited in Abrahamian 1982, 516). Major strikes in response to this single day took place over the next two weeks in Iran's oil, petro-chemical, banking, mining, heavy industrial sectors, among others, and continued to spread through the end of October.

Not even the establishment of a military government on November 5, 1978, managed to dampen the opposition's growth at all. Indeed, even into December, as it became clear that the Shah would depart—the only re-maining questions being when and to whom he would relinquish power—troops continued to use massive and deadly force to battle protesters. On December 2, 1978, began Muharram, the first month of the new Islamic year. Khomeini and many other opposition leaders had called for strikes, demonstrations, and other forms of protest, and despite political disarray, the state's repressive capacity remained on full display. Hundreds of pro-testers were shot and killed the first night for violating evening curfew. In Qazvin, more than one hundred demonstrators were killed when army tanks simply rolled over the crowds. And in Mashhad, to name just one more among many, approximately two hundred demonstrators were shot as they gathered around the home of a religious opposition leader. As they had failed during the early months of the crisis, episodes of heavy-handed state repression failed in late 1978 to stem the growth of opposition mobi-lization. They did so, the evidence suggests, because protesters and oppo-sitionists gave the regime no credibility when it did try, finally, to negotiate seriously.

In short, it was not because of a crisis of will, as Brzezinski and others have argued (1985, 397), that the Shah failed to regain control in Iran. He and his generals continued to use force to beat back the growing numbers of Iranians who left their homes to join the opposition. What mattered cru-cially is that "Iranians stopped obeying" despite frequent and brutal use of force (Kurzman 2004, 111). The lack of any solid pro-regime coalition com-bined with a weak institutional capacity meant that, as one social group af-ter another defected from the depoliticized status quo, there was little that the regime could do other than to hope that force would suffice. During the first half of 1978, when nearly all protests were reformist in nature and made specific demands that fell well short of regime change, the Shah's gov-ernment could not, did not, reach out to moderates to coopt them. Neither could it manage to prevent cross-class and cross-group collective mobi-lization: years of allowing state capacity to atrophy and overreliance on SAVAK's sanctioned thuggery left the regime with few political resources for managing dissent.

Comparing the use of force in Iran and Indonesia provides a useful lens through which to investigate its role in regime maintenance. Indonesia specialists who assert that violence saved Suharto in 1979 have trouble explaining how it sealed the Shah's fate in the same year. By the same token, scholars of Iran's revolution who argue that state violence undermined the regime confront Suharto's ample use of repression and subsequent survival through the 1978–80 crisis. I have argued here and presented evidence to suggest that it is not coercion that is central to regime survival, although it can have important effects depending on its timing relative to antistate protests (Opp and Roehl 1990; Lichbach 1987; and Karklins and Petersen 1993). Instead, it is the *strategies* that regimes adopt in the years before crises that determine the degree to which rulers can count on limiting the numbers of citizens who decide to challenge the state in the first place. Thus, focusing attention on state-society relations and on institution building during periods of relative calm rather than on the most proximate responses to crisis is a more analytically constructive means of explaining regimes' performance during any given crisis itself.

History and the Limitations of Theory: Iran and Indonesia, 1980–Present

The historical-causal material in this book ends about there, in 1979. Clearly, history continued, and it is worth visiting at least briefly subsequent events in both Indonesia and Iran. The regime that succeeded the Shah's, the Islamic Republic of Iran, survives today, and two of its original architects, Hashemi Rafsanjani and Ali Khamene'i, continue to be key players in the regime. Suharto's New Order collapsed in 1998, however, and has been replaced by a steadily consolidating democracy that despite its problems appears to be stable and growing more so. How good a job does the theory I developed in this book account for the post-1980 years in the two countries? I turn to that question in this section before moving on to a broader consideration of its general scope in the next chapter.

As it happens, I began this study of Iran and Indonesia in early 1998. A few months later, my "most durable" regime ceased to look so unassailable. President Suharto resigned after thirty-two years in power following massive street demonstrations and rioting in Jakarta and other cities and an abrupt withdrawal of support from Golkar and the military. As I began the research, I wondered whether, given the events of the two decades following the endpoint of this study in 1979, the theory would hold much explanatory purchase. The Islamic Republic in Iran shows no signs of falling apart any time soon, and the New Order has now officially been defunct for nearly seven years since the election of Abdurrahman Wahid as president in October 1999.[31] While the global conditions, domestic politics, and economic structure of both countries have changed much since 1980, I believe the answer is that my theory remains useful in understanding the post-1980 trajectories of the Iranian and Indonesian states. But there do exist some important qualifications to its scope.

When Khomeini, his supporters, and a disparate coalition of opposition groups took over the reins of state in early 1979, the uneasy anti-Shah alliance that had propelled them to power quickly came apart. By late 1979, Iran was in a state of civil war, and even after the onset of the Iran-Iraq War in September 1980, it was not until mid-1981 that the Khomeinists had consolidated the Islamic Republican Party (IRP) as the dominant political force in the country. A bomb attack by the Mujahideen-e Khalq Organization (People's Mujahideen, or MKO) early in that year killed fifty of the highest-ranking officials in Khomeini's regime and raised the threat of a continuing civil war, not to mention the possibility that the Khomeini faction in the new government might collapse altogether. Nonetheless, the IRP managed to hold onto power. The new regime began a new autarkic development strategy in the early 1980s but was able to do so only after a protracted and bloody battle with its own opposition. Moreover, the collapse of the Iranian oil industry, followed by an American embargo against Iran in the wake of the hostage crisis, meant that for several years after the regime came to power it had only severely restricted income from oil. In other words, the initial conditions under which the Islamic Republic began to construct an economy based on the revolution's principles corresponded closely to those illustrated in my case study of Indonesia: severe state revenue crisis accompanied by a powerful and well-organized opposition.

Because it was so threatened and because it could not buy the loyalty of potential coalition partners with oil wealth, the Khomeini regime made some major concessions, giving over control of much of the property it had seized to businessmen from the bazaar in the form of directorships of newly established religious foundations.[32] The regime also devoted much energy to building the IRP throughout the early and mid-1980s, and although the party was disbanded in 1987, the mosque- and foundation-based networks that provided the party's power remained in place. By the late 1980s, Kho-

---

[31] Not to mention the numerous "What about Indonesia in 1998?" questions I encountered after I presented parts of the project at numerous conferences, colloquia, and job talks. I thank all participants in these gatherings for spurring an article-length reply (Smith 2003b) simply by asking the question so many times.

[32] These concessions mostly ended what had become a period of serious contention between the bazaar leadership and the new regime. See Smith (2003a) for accounts of several episodes of antistate political mobilization by the bazaar against the Islamic Republic in the first year after the revolution.

meini had succeeded in building a coalition of bazaar and *ulemā*.[33] Finally, not only financial scarcity but also the need to finance a war produced a desperate need for revenues. As a result, "between 1976 and 1985, tax incomes increased by 95 percent whereas oil incomes declined by 42 percent" (Amirahmadi 1990, 166). In short, the experiences of the post-Pahlavi Iranian political economy seem to provide strong support for the argument that the timing of development initiatives relative to the availability of oil revenues and the existence of organized opposition explains the resilience of the Islamic Republic.

Indonesia after the mid-1980s presents some important qualifications to the scope of the argument I have developed in this book. First of all, Suharto, the leader that no observers prior to the Asian economic crisis thought would fall, did just that in May 1998. Despite his fall, however, to my mind the late New Order era lends some support to the general argument I have advanced here: that the political difficulties facing rulers as they embark on important economic policy courses have powerful long-term implications for their survival.[34] First, it is worth noting that it took an economic meltdown far worse than America's Great Depression to bring down Suharto. Neither the oil bust of 1986 nor several subsequent and more minor economic shocks before 1998 managed to do that.

In the 1980s, by most appearances the New Order moved forward as it had in the previous fifteen years. When oil prices took their first, and more minor, plunge in 1982–83, the government moved quickly to restructure the tax system, levying more taxes on the domestic and foreign business communities and also making collection more efficient (Uppal 1986). When the bust came in 1986, the regime was able to cope with that shock, too, and steered itself fairly seamlessly into a reform program that by the late 1980s had generated vastly increased foreign direct investment (FDI) in the Indonesian economy through significant neoliberal restructuring policies. Here, one major change in the state's revenue base occurred.

Where it had had access to vast discretionary revenues during the rich oil boom years, the regime now came to depend much more on FDI revenues and on the sale of debt equity, which in turn were contingent on a stable investment atmosphere, meaning fairly transparent state economic policy. Powerful as it was, however, transparency was not the regime's hall-

---

[33] Interestingly, the reliability of the latter group as a corporate entity was by no means a sure thing, despite their commonality of vocation with Khomeini: eleven of the twelve members of Iran's Shi'a leadership council had in early 1979 rejected his proposal for an Islamic state, maintaining that its principles had no basis in Shi'ism. Thus, bringing the *ulemā* as a whole into the coalition was no sure thing.

[34] This section summarizes an analysis of the last fifteen years of Indonesia's New Order presented in Smith (2003b).

mark in economic policy. Moreover, the competition among developing countries for limited FDI resources meant that the regime's main new revenue base was nowhere near as flexible as oil wealth had been; nor, as a result, were the economic interests of the domestic actors who allied themselves with foreign investors. The political dynamics of this transition to an economic policy based heavily on encouraging foreign investment, one that relied on oil exports for a much smaller portion of the GDP and of state revenues, suggest that it may be not only transitions to late development but also neoliberal reforms that catalyze political trajectories shaped by opposition strength and the ease of acquiring revenues. What happened in Indonesia in the late 1980s was essentially a departure from the "sample" that concerns me in this book: oil export–dependent countries that have embarked on state-dominant late development. A similar process took place in Mexico beginning in the 1980s. Perhaps not coincidentally, the outcomes in Indonesia and Mexico were also similar: transitions from long-lived single-party authoritarian rule within two years of one another.

Two more changes took place that significantly affected the trajectory of the Indonesian political economy and, with it, the regime's prospects. As the "Generation of '45" leaders, who all had fought in the war of independence and had come of age with Suharto, gradually left the government, a new and younger set of leaders entered the highest echelons of political power, which had two effects. First, technically oriented politicians, such as Bacharuddin Jusuf Habibie, constructed a new policy focus for the state: investment in the same kinds of flashy industrial projects, including aeronautics and satellite communications, which had characterized the Shah's boom-era spending spree.[35] These industries were largely prestige-driven and were mostly highly unprofitable. They produced revenue sinkholes that, since they were run by powerful military-business coalitions, were difficult for Suharto to touch during an economic crisis.

Second, the departure of the generals who had built the New Order coalition also meant the end of their ties to the powerful social groups that sustained the "powerhouse state" project of the 1960s and 1970s. By the late 1990s, the regime's social base was much more dependent on economic performance and coercion than it had been twenty years earlier. Moreover, the regime could not count on limited opposition during a crisis, as it could before, because it maintained none of the close contacts with potential opposition leaders that it had in the 1970s and early 1980s. Thus, the late 1980s and 1990s in Indonesia brought a transformation of the structure of

[35] Habibie assumed the presidency in May 1998 following Suharto's resignation, serving until October 1999, when Abdurrahman Wahid was elected president.

the New Order's economic base and of its ties to society, the latter of which mirrored in important ways the Pahlavi regime in the mid-1970s.

Conclusion

A central point in tracing the early phase of protests against both of these regimes has been to argue that during this phase, when demands are nearly all for policy shift rather than regime change, both the Shah and Suharto had the opportunity to salvage their rule, even if it meant jettisoning some policies or making some concessions. To reiterate, there is nothing inevitable about regime breakdown until it has happened. Throughout 1977 and even during the first six months of 1978, it was not at all clear or even likely that the Pahlavi regime would fall. Conversely, in March 1978, it seemed no more assured that Suharto would be able to ride out his political crisis than that the Shah would survive the 1977–78 protests. The accounts I have presented in the last two chapters have been aimed at looking closely at the institutions and state-society relationships that these two regimes built during the 1960s and 1970s to direct their respective development programs.

This chapter has centered on the first oil boom period in Iran and Indonesia. What I have endeavored to illustrate is that, where most accounts attribute causality to the boom itself as the vehicle for creating the institutions and interaction patterns that were cast in such sharp contrast in 1978, it was in fact the trajectories that emerged from initiating late development in the 1960s that enabled Suharto and constrained the Shah.

The boom, shocking as it was to the political economies of Iran, Indonesia, and other exporting states in the developing world, merely magnified prior trajectories: it did not create them. In neither of these cases was the first oil boom centrally responsible for prolonging or undermining their capacities for social control in the late 1970s.

CHAPTER 5

Oil, Opposition, and Late Development

Regime Breakdown and Persistence in Twenty-One Oil-Exporting States

The introduction and the first two chapters of this book demonstrated the existence of, and suggested an answer to, a contradiction between what we thought we knew about the politics of oil wealth and the robust trends that emerged when those "stylized facts" were subjected to empirical scrutiny. Oil wealth generally was held to have a negative influence on regime durability. A central conclusion of this book, however, is that this is only the case in some circumstances. In other cases, the opposite is true, and oil wealth facilitates both state building and robust coalitions. In the third and fourth chapters, I showed how oil's effects on politics in Iran and Indonesia depended strongly on both its timing relative to the onset of late development and the strength of political opposition during the same period. While in Iran the politics of oil looked much as current theories predict, oil had a very different effect in Indonesia, helping both to strengthen the institutions of the New Order state and to bolster the regime's ruling coalition.

In chapter 1, cross-national analysis of the developing world's most oil export–dependent states indicated that regimes in those states tend to enjoy less political strife and longer tenures than rulers in oil-poor countries. In chapter 2, I argued that this phenomenon is largely a function of oil's late arrival to many exporting states. Authoritarian rulers in many late developing states had to build robust coalitions to survive the dual challenges of powerful opposition and rent scarcity. When such rulers gained access to oil revenues later, they incorporated the rents into an already-strong political coalition, and those revenues helped to strengthen both rulers and the institutions they commanded.

In chapters 3 and 4, I tested the depth and sequential logic of the argument's sub-hypotheses and causal mechanisms against the historical experiences of Iran and Indonesia between 1960 and 1980. Those chapters addressed this question: Does the argument explain well the historical dynamics of oil and politics in two states chosen for maximum variation in boom-era crisis management? In Iran, oil preceded late development; oil rents and weak opposition at the onset of late development contributed to the development of weak institutions and weak ties between the regime and society. In Indonesia, political leaders confronted strong opposition and extreme rent scarcity. Because oil revenues arrived late to the New Order regime, they were incorporated into an already-powerful state and regime-building project and actually strengthened both the New Order's hold on power and the capacities of the state. In both countries, markedly divergent state and regime trajectories emerged in the first years of late development.

As I suggested in chapter 2, a structured, focused comparison is the best method of assessing the viability of an explanation meant to overcome the lack of fit between a large body of theorizing on oil's effect on politics and the cross-national results presented in chapter 1. If one is interested not just in explanatory depth but in breadth as well, though, an appropriate next step is to return to a larger sample of cases to gauge how good a job the theory does at accounting for broad trends in regime viability during boom-bust crises across the oil-exporting world. In this chapter I test the theoretical argument using data from Iran, Indonesia, and 19 other oil-exporting states.

Oil, Late Development, and Regime Durability: A First Look at Twenty-One Regimes

Table 5.1 summarizes the crisis and regime histories of the twenty-one developing states most dependent on oil exports between 1974 and 1992. There is an interesting overall trend among exporting states that sheds light on the cross-national findings presented in chapter 1. Oil exporters experienced twenty-one regime crises either during the boom period of 1974–86 (ten) or during the bust of 1986–92 (eleven). Sixteen of them, or more than three quarters of the boom or bust regime crises during this period, ended in regime restabilization, meaning the regime weathered the crisis. Regimes actually collapsed during only four of the twenty crises, belying the received wisdom that "petro-states" are likely to come apart dramatically during such hard times (Karl 1997, 1999).

In sixteen cases, authoritarian regimes regained the upper hand over their opposition and restabilized their rule. Current theories of oil and pol-

TABLE 5.1.
Crisis and regime breakdown in the oil-exporting world

Highly export-dependent states[*]	Boom crisis?	Bust crisis?	No crisis?	Regime breakdown?
Algeria, Angola, Bahrain, Cameroon, Congo (Brazzaville), Ecuador, Egypt, Gabon, Indonesia, Iran, Iraq, Kuwait, Libya, Mexico, Malaysia, Nigeria, Oman, Saudi Arabia, Syria, Tunisia, UAE	Bahrain, Ecuador, Indonesia, Iran, Libya, Nigeria, Oman, Saudi Arabia, Syria	Algeria, Angola, Congo, Ecuador, Egypt, Gabon, Iraq, Malaysia, Nigeria, Saudi Arabia, Tunisia	Kuwait, Mexico, UAE	Congo (1992), Ecuador (1979), Iran (1979), Nigeria (1979)[1], Nigeria (1983)[2]
(21)	(9)	(11)	(3)	(5 in 4 states from 20 crises)

Notes: Brunei and Qatar are excluded from this sample due to extensive missing data. [*] The two democracies in the sample are excluded from the statistical analysis.

itics provide much less satisfying explanations for this much larger set of outcomes since for the most part, the theories predict regime vulnerability during crisis. To revisit one causal link between oil wealth and authoritarian durability, it is the ability to fund, and the willingness to use, repressive apparatuses that sustain authoritarian regimes in oil-rich states (Ross 2001c; Bellin 2004). This line of reasoning would suggest that these fourteen regimes were successful because they cracked down and that the regimes that failed did so because they were unwilling or unable to exercise sufficient coercion to thwart the opposition.

A quick turn back to the case of Iran, however, reveals a massive repressive apparatus and the Pahlavi regime's willingness to use it quite heavy-handedly until very late in the revolutionary crisis.[1] Moreover, there

---

[1] The Jaleh Square incident in Tehran in early September of 1978, for instance, reflects this willingness to use force. Nearly 400 people were killed by Iranian military and police forces during a street demonstration.

is little evidence to support the claim that the United States withdrew its support from the Shah during any crucial phase of the revolutionary crisis, raising questions about these two alternative explanations for regime change and stasis in oil states. In Iran, the evidence suggests, first, that the regime had the will and capacity to exercise coercion until very late in the crisis and, second, that it collapsed despite both its coercive capacities and the continued support of the United States.[2]

In chapter 1, I showed that repression failed to account for the strengthening effect of oil wealth on regimes. This finding makes it unsurprising that the regime failures—in Congo (1991), Ecuador (1978–79), Iran (1979), and Nigeria (1979)—followed significant state repression but also that repression failed to prevent the crises from reaching its tipping point. More generally, scholars have shown that repression often magnifies popular mobilization, even in authoritarian settings.[3] Absent explicit causal linkages between repression and restabilization in particular settings, it remains an open question whether the relationship holds. It is important to look to other explanations for the resilience of authoritarianism in the oil-exporting world.

For example, the New Order regime's response in Indonesia to the protests of 1977–78 illustrates the crucial importance of nonrepressive strategies for long-term regime viability. When student and Islamic organizations took to the streets to protest corruption, nondemocratic policy-making, and the military's role in politics, Suharto immediately sent a close advisor, Professor Sumitro, to meet with student groups. This palliative failed, but the regime also singled out moderate leaders in the student opposition and went to great efforts to coopt them. Subsequently, many became important figures in the ruling Golkar Party. The regime was unable to split the Islamic leadership during this period but it was able to prevent the kind of bandwagoning that produced a mass-based movement in Iran. Significant raises to civil servants and heavy new subsidies on fuel and rice, all made possible by oil revenues, kept the bureaucracy and the emerging middle class on the political sidelines.

By early 1979, popular mobilization had largely ended, and despite some intra-regime tension later that year, the New Order had restabilized its authority. Its ability to coopt and maintain coalition partners, to monitor the opposition, and to prevent the emergence of a broad-based opposition

[2] On the regime's continued use of repression, see Kurzman 1992, esp. chaps. 3 and 7; and Rasler 1996. On U.S. support, see Kurzman 1992, chap. 7; and Rubin 1986. Rubin supplies references to the most authoritative accounts of America's role during the Iranian revolution, which show a clear and consistent pattern of support for the Shah throughout the crisis.

[3] See for instance Opp and Roehl 1990; Lichbach 1987; Francisco 2002; Karklins Petersen 1993.

TABLE 5.2.
Oil, state-led development, and crisis, 1974–1992: A qualitative comparative analysis

	Late development	Strong opposition to late development	Highly oil-dependent at onset of late development	Boom crisis	Bust crisis	Regime change
Algeria	1	1	1	0	1	0
Angola	**0**					
Bahrain	**0**					
Cameroon	1	0	0	0		0
Congo	1	0	1		1	1
Ecuador	1	0	1	1	1	1
Egypt	1	1	0	0	1	0
Gabon	1	0	1	0		0
Indonesia	1	1	0	1	0	0
Iran	1	0	1	1	0	1
Iraq	1	1	1	0	1	0
Kuwait	0					
Libya	0					
Malaysia	1	1	1	0	1	0
Mexico	1	1		0	0	0
Nigeria	1	0	1	1	0	1
Oman	0					
Saudi Arabia	1	0	1	0	0	0
Syria	1	1	0	1	0	0
Tunisia	1	1	0	0	1	0
UAE	**0**					

movement all proved valuable for regime survival. Moreover, all of these capacities were built during the early years of state-led development, when substantial oil revenues were not yet on line, and the regime had to depend on state institutions to extract revenue. Later, when oil revenues did come on line, they were invested back into the same regime and state-building projects that had carried the New Order through the tough first years of its rule. Thus, it is my contention, one well supported by the case of New Order Indonesia, that coalition and state building and not raw coercion are behind the extraordinary durability of many regimes in oil-rich states.[4]

Table 5.2 presents the explanatory variables, regime crises, and outcomes for oil-exporting countries. Authoritarian regimes in fifteen oil-ex-

[4] I use the word *extraordinary* very consciously. Barbara Geddes (1999a, 1999b) discovered that the "triple-threat" regimes in her sample—those that combined elements of personal, military, and single-party rule—lasted for inordinately long periods of time. To my mind, it is no coincidence that three out of the four (Egypt, Indonesia, and Syria—Paraguay is the exception) faced the same strong opposition/low rent access challenges to late development. As I show below, that regime type is itself a product of those initial conditions.

porting countries initiated state-led development: Algeria, Cameroon, Congo (Brazzaville), Ecuador, Egypt, Gabon, Indonesia, Iran, Iraq, Malaysia, Mexico, Nigeria, Saudi Arabia, Syria, and Tunisia. Rulers in eight of these countries—Algeria, Egypt, Indonesia, Iraq, Mexico, Malaysia, Syria, and Tunisia—faced strong and organized social actors that presented a powerful opposition to their plans for late development. All of them experienced a serious crisis during either the booms or the bust, and all eight survived.[5] Further, rulers in all of these countries except Algeria and Iraq had to rely on sources of revenue other than oil exports from the outset of initiating late development. It is noteworthy that Algeria and Iraq have faced perhaps the most long-term civil conflicts within this group, and the effects of initiating late development with ready access to oil rents may explain in part that vulnerability to civil war. Fearon and Laitin (2003), for example, demonstrate that weak states make countries more vulnerable to civil war. The distributional inequities between Sunni Arabs, on the one hand, and Shi'a Arabs and Kurds in Iraq, on the other, and between urban and rural Algerians, respectively, may account for the persistence of domestic conflict despite the two very robust regimes in these two countries.

Of the authoritarian regimes that began state-led development with little or no organized social opposition—Congo, Ecuador, Gabon, Iran, Nigeria, and Saudi Arabia—three fell during the booms (Ecuador, Iran, and Nigeria) and one during the bust (Congo). All of those six regimes also began state-led development in the presence of sizable oil income, obviating the need for domestic extraction and its attendant institutional and coalitional projects. Thus, the weak opposition/plentiful oil rent typology illustrated by Iran in the previous two chapters seems to lead to fragile regimes in other settings as well, and it seems that where the transition to late development is relatively easy, rulers generally opt not to make politically costly decisions about allocating political authority or extracting revenues.

The two regimes that did not fall during the booms or bust, Gabon and Saudi Arabia, have unique characteristics relative to the larger group. Regime stability in Gabon since independence has been guaranteed by its former colonizer, France, and as a result the weak regime has arguably persisted long beyond its expected shelf life. Congolese Labor Party rule, too, relied heavily on French support through 1990; once that support began to erode, the regime's ability to manage dissent went with it. None of the

---

[5] It is important to note that the crisis in Iraq in 1991 occurred not directly because of the bust but in the aftermath of Saddam Hussein's defeat in the 1991 Gulf War against the United States and its allies. One might posit, however, that that defeat arose from a sequence of events related to the bust—rising Iraqi debts and falling oil revenues, subsequent tension with Kuwait, a major source of loans, and the invasion of Kuwait by Iraq.

other regimes in the sample could rely on such reliable external intervention to save them.

Saudi Arabia, engaged in an effort to create a viable industrial sector since the mid-1970s, is only now in the early twenty-first century becoming socially and economically diverse enough to begin to feel the political ramifications of late development. Somewhat unsurprisingly, increasing levels of education and economic diversification in the Saudi kingdom have been accompanied by rising opposition to the royal family, raising the question of how much longer the al-Saud can maintain their rule as it currently exists (Aburish 1995; Fandy 1999; Okruhlik 1999). The socioeconomic environment in which the Saudi regime currently operates is beginning to look more and more like that of early 1970s Iran, and as such a gloomy future may be in store for the royal family if the reforms that so many citizens demand do not become a reality.

In short, a first glance at these twenty-one states appears to support a theory of oil and politics in which, depending on its timing, oil wealth can either bolster authoritarian rulers or undermine them. What that first glance cannot quite do, however, is account for other plausible arguments. It is to this task, and to a broader test of my argument, that I turn in the next section.

Although it would be immensely time-consuming to gather sufficient data to test each of the sub-hypotheses of my argument against all of these 23 states, it is possible to test several of the theory's broader implications (Geddes 2003, 38–40). One is that regimes that face a powerful opposition at the onset of late development should prove more durable than those that do not. Another is that regimes that are oil-poor at the onset of late development should prove more durable than regimes in exporting states in which oil revenues exist to fund late development from the outset. Finally, we should expect that an interaction effect—a combination of low access to oil rents and a powerful opposition—should produce a stronger effect than either factor would alone.

These hypotheses leave a gap between cause and effect, however. Even if they are confirmed, it would still be reasonable to ask *how* and *why* hard times at the onset of late development are associated with more durable regimes. To recall one of the three indicators of state and coalition building from chapter 2, rulers that adopted late development in the face of rent scarcity, a powerful opposition, or both were likely to invest heavily in building official parties even after oil revenues became available to them. Authoritarian institutions, as a result, are themselves an outcome of past political struggles and are properly thought of as intervening variables between initial conditions at the onset of late development and regime durability (boom-bust era crisis management). Thus, another observable and testable implication of the theory is that strong opposition and low rent access at the onset of late development ought to make the emergence of single-party regimes more likely.[6]

Some hypotheses derived from the timing-dependent argument I developed in chapter 2 are as follows:

H₁: Regimes that face strong opposition to their late development programs are less likely to fall during subsequent crises than regimes that do not.

H₂: Regimes that have little or no access to oil rents at the onset of late development are less likely to fall than regimes that can fund late development with already-plentiful oil revenues.

H₃: Rulers who face both rent scarcity and strong opposition at the onset of late development are likely to be the most durable of all.

H₄: Both strong opposition and low oil rent access at the onset of late development make low-cost political planning impossible for authoritarian rulers. As a result, rulers facing these initial conditions are likely to invest in powerful ruling parties, and single-party regimes are more likely to emerge after such conditions.

In the next section, I test these hypotheses using data from twenty-one regimes in the most export-dependent countries in the developing world for the 1974–99 period.[7]

Oil's Changing Political Effects: A Statistical Test of a Historical–Causal Argument

In an effort to test the central arguments of this book—that "when oil" is a more important question than "whether oil," that oil's timing and opposition strength relative to late development are key to later regime viability—I conducted a series of statistical tests using much the same data as in chapter 1. I present the results of these tests below. In this set of analyses, however, I limited the sample to the twenty-one most export-dependent authoritarian states in the developing world (those listed in table 5.1 minus Trinidad and Venezuela, which were democratic for the entirety of the

---

[6] For instance, Geddes's regime types include single-party hybrids with personalist or military components, strict single-party, and "triple-threat," or single-party/military-personalist variants.

[7] All states ruled by authoritarian regimes that relied on oil exports for 10 percent or more of GDP for at least five years between 1974 and 1999 were included in the sample.

time period). In addition to the variables used in the analysis in chapter 1, I incorporated variables for the presence or absence of late development, the strength of political opposition at the onset of late development, and access to oil rents at the onset of late development. I discuss the construction of these variables in detail below and present my coding choices in table 5.5. I also conducted tests to explore the effects of difficult transitions to late development on the emergence of robust authoritarian regime types.

Data, Methods, and Models

I extracted from the data used in chapter 1 cross-section time series data from twenty-one of the twenty-three most oil-export dependent countries in the sample, excluding Trinidad and Tobago and Venezuela. In addition, I truncated the time period to the 1974 to 1999 period, in order to highlight the political effects of the booms and bust of the 1970s and 1980s on regime durability. The result is a dataset comprising 545 country-year observations in all.

Dependent Variables

The outcome of primary interest here is regime durability through the booms and bust of the 1970s and 1980s. As with the analyses in chapter 1, the dependent variable is regime failure as measured by intervening years between regime change in the Polity98 dataset (Jaggers and Marshall 1999). However, I am also interested in explaining, rather than inferring (Waldner forthcoming 2007), why it is that hard times tend to produce durable regimes. I proposed an answer in chapter 2: a transition to late development such as that faced by the New Order regime in Indonesia compels rulers to invest in building powerful ruling parties to "hold" the coalition together. Given the ascending survival rate among Geddes's (1999, 2003) authoritarian regime typology,[8] using this ordinal ranking as a dependent variable essentially predicts increasing regime durability by virtue of the authority structures that make up regimes.[9] This variable is, theoretically speaking, an intervening variable in the causal logic of my argument. It is appropri-

---

[8] Authoritarian regimes of the following types are, in increasing order (and their coding in the Regime Type variable), more likely to survive than preceding ones: (1) Military, (2) Military/Personal, (3) Personal, (4) Single-Party Hybrid (with Military or Personal), (5) Single-Party, and (6) Triple Threat (Single-Party/Military/Personal). Thanks to Barbara Geddes for sharing her regime data with me and to Jason Brownlee for sharing his proportional hazard results and monarchy data.

[9] The dataset includes a final regime type—monarchies, coded "7" in the regime type

ate to test it here as an intermediate outcome rather than simply adding it to a multivariate model.

Independent Variables

For the most part, I have incorporated the same data into this analysis as was used in chapter 1, but there are some important additions. I constructed original variables for late development and opposition strength as well as creating variables for oil rent access at the onset of late development. Late development (Latedev) is a binary variable, coded "1" if a country had engaged in late development and "0" if it did not. I used both quantitative and qualitative assessments to derive this measure, using a benchmark of an increase of at least 25 percent in manufacturing as a share of gross domestic product (GDP) between 1975 and 1990 (World Bank 2001) as well as secondary scholarly analysis of the country in question.[10]

Measuring the strength of the opposition is a more taxing question. Some scholars use proxies such as ethnic fragmentation (Gandhi and Przeworski 2001). The problem with such measures is that without knowing whether such ethnic cleavages are politically active or even salient, it is hard to assess whether they capture much of what is politically important about political opposition. For example, the Kurdish Democratic Party's challenge to the Ba'ath Party in late-1960s Iraq surely qualified as a serious opposition group, but the similarly large Sundanese minority on the island of Java in Indonesia posed no such challenge. Another strategy is to separate moderate from revolutionary, or maximalist, oppositionists and gauge their strength relative to regimes (Brownlee 2002; Snyder 1992). One possible difficulty here is that moderates may become maximalists over time and vice versa. The Shi'a clergy in Iran, for example, did not become truly revolutionary until early 1978, despite several years of repression by the Pahlavi state (Kurzman 2003).

Aiming to measure it in a way that could capture the importance of organization and mobilization, I constructed an index for opposition strength

---

variable, as it is by Brownlee. However, because, unlike the first six types, monarchies are nearly all inherited institutional structures (and were exclusively so during the period covered by the data) rather than regime *choices* constructed in response to political conditions (at least recent conditions), I excluded all country-years for monarchies by qualifying the models in Stata 7.0 with "if RegimeType ~=7." I did so only for the models that use regime type as the dependent variable.

[10] In several of these countries—Mexico, for example—oil revenues became substantial only during this period, and manufacturing appeared to increase less because it was "competing" as a share of GDP with newly discovered oil reserves, an essentially exogenous shock to the economy. In such cases, I took manufacturing as a share of nonoil GDP as the primary measure.

TABLE 5.3.
Late development, opposition, and rent scarcity coding

Country	Late development	LD onset years	Opposition at onset	Oil/GDP at onset	Boom/bust crisis	Regime breakdown
Algeria	1	1965–70	5	0.16	1	0
Angola	0	—	5	0	0	1
Bahrain	0	—	0	0	1	0
Cameroon	1	1977–81	1	0.09	1	0
Congo	1	1973–77	2	0.26	1	1
Ecuador	1	1972–75	1	0.14	1	1
Egypt	1	1956–61	5	0.02	1	0
Gabon	1	1971–76	1	0.30	0	0
Indonesia	1	1966–69	6	0.04	1	0
Iran	1	1961–64	2	0.19	1	1
Iraq	1	1968–71	5	0.30	1	0
Kuwait	0	—	0	0	0	0
Libya	0	—	0	0	1	0
Malaysia	1	1971–75	5	0.03	1	0
Mexico	1	1940–46	4	0.03	0	0
Nigeria	1	1974–77	1	0.23	1	1
Oman	0	—	0	0	0	0
Saudi Arabia	1	1974–78	1	0.69	0	0
Syria	1	1965–71	5	0.015	1	0
Tunisia	1	1962–65	5	0.016	1	0
UAE	0	—	0	0	0	0

(OPPOSITION) at the onset of late development that focuses on (a) its organizational capacity (0–2 points), (b) its capacity to mobilize across numerous classes and groups (0–2 points), and (c) its public challenge to the regime in power (1 point possible each if (a) there existed a maximalist opposition seeking to depose the regime in power and (b) if it staged antistate protests during the onset of late development). The result was a scale ranging from 0 to 6, an ascending ordinal measure of the strength of the opposition at the onset of late development (see table 5.3).

To measure access to oil rents at the onset of late development, I simply used oil exports as a share of GDP. I used the non-oil GDP at the onset of late development as the measure for rent scarcity in these exporting states. The higher the nonoil GDP is as a share of the total, or the smaller oil's share of GDP, the higher rent scarcity is and therefore the less likely regime breakdown should be. I also created a proxy for interaction effects using these variables. First, I multiplied late development by both opposition strength and by non-oil GDP (LateDev × Opposition, LateDev × NonOil-GDP), so that states that did not embark on late development are coded "0." I also multiplied all three variables together to generate an interaction effect (InteractionEffect) to test the impact on regime durability of having faced dual challenges of rent scarcity and strong opposition. I estimate and report the results below both with separate opposition and rent scarcity variables and with the three-way interaction effect.

Control Variables

I have included in all of these models the binary dummy variable for late development. The rationale for including this control is that it could plausibly be late development itself and its subsequent socioeconomic consequences, rather than rent scarcity or opposition at its onset, that are generating any possible regime effects. I include the yearly value of oil export revenues as a share of GDP (OilGDP; see World Bank 2001) to provide another possible constant-cause alternative to my own timing-dependent argument and to capture variation in export dependence among countries in the sample. I also include largely the same controls as those used in the analyses in chapter 1: land area, urban growth, and population. Commonly used controls such as per capita GDP, GDP growth in the previous year, and ethnic fragmentation were included in the regime type models but were all insignificant in preliminary analyses and were excluded from the final regime failure models. I included regional fixed-effects dummy variables for the Middle East, sub-Saharan Africa, Latin America, and Asia in early models as well; none of them were significant, so all were excluded from the final regime failure models. They were retained, however, in the models for which regime type is the dependent variable. Finally, since no regime among the Gulf monarchies (all members of the Gulf Cooperation Council) has ever collapsed, I include a dummy variable for GCC membership to control for this extremely long-lived group of dynastic regimes.[11]

I employed probit regression in estimating the regime failure models, where regime failure takes a value of "1" in any failure year and "0" otherwise; positive coefficients, in these models, indicate that a variable increases the likelihood of regime failure as its value rises and vice versa if its coefficient is negative. In estimating the models in which regime type is the outcome, I employ ordered logistic regression. In these models, a positive coefficient indicates a variable's effect of "moving" a regime up the ordinal durability ranking.

---

[11] I estimated the same models with the GCC states excluded, and the coefficients for each of the independent variables—the opposition, nonoil GDP, and interaction effect variables—grew larger with the data from those six countries left out.

TABLE 5.4.
Oil, opposition, late development, and regime breakdown, 1974–1999

Independent variable	Model 1	Model 2
Late development	−.155	−.591
	(.495)	(.456)
Opposition at onset	**−.213***	—
of late development	**(.106)**	
Rent scarcity at onset	**−.773**	—
of late development	**(.563)**	
Opposition-rent scarcity	—	**−.304*****
interaction effect		**(.082)**
Oil/GDP	−1.585	−1.58
	(.966)	(.113)
Land area	.0000006**	.0000006**
	(.0000002)	(.0000002)
Urban growth	−.160	−.158
	(.090)	(.089)
GCC	−1.081*	−1.017*
	(.487)	(.484)
Population	.000000004	.000000005*
	(.000000003)	(.000000003)
Constant	.130	.034
	(.647)	(.626)
N=	394	394
Log likelihood	74.993	−75.70
Pseudo R^2	.217	.210

Notes: Analysis is by Probit regression. Entries are unstandardized coefficients; standard errors are in parentheses. *, **, and *** indicated significance at <.05, <.01, and <.001, respectively.

Results

The first column in table 5.4 presents the results from the first set of models, which estimate the effects of opposition strength and oil rent scarcity on later regime durability. They confirm broadly the effects of a "hard" transition to late development such as the one I outlined in tracing the trajectory followed in early New Order Indonesia. Opposition strength has a strong and significant positive effect on the likelihood of regime survival. Indeed, the predicted likelihood of *failure* is .034 with all explanatory variables set at their means (opposition set at its mean of 2.33). When opposition at the onset of late development rises to 5 (as Egypt is coded), the likelihood of regime failure drops to just over a quarter of the mean likelihood, at .009. Rent scarcity also exerts a positive effect on regime durability, although its effect fails to reach significance, at .05. Nonetheless, when nonoil GDP rises from its mean of .559 to .980 (Egypt's nonoil GDP at the onset of late development), the likelihood of failure drops again by nearly half, to .005. These effects remain robust when controlling for land area, urban growth, population size, yearly oil export dependence, and GCC membership, as well as under more stringent statistical tests for time- and panel-specific effects. Having faced a strong and well-organized opposition at the onset of late development dramatically improved the prospects for these regimes in dealing with the crises of the boom and bust years, even though late development itself had a weak negative impact on regime survival.

The second column presents the results of the same model, but with an interaction effect to capture the cumulative long-term impact of facing both a powerful opposition and rent scarcity. The combined challenge to the regimes adopting late development represented in the group is an even stronger positive predictor of regime durability (negative predictor of failure) than either opposition or rent scarcity alone, providing powerful support for the proposition that it is not just one or the other but both challenges together that tends to produce such durable authoritarian regimes such as those in Egypt, Indonesia, Malaysia, Syria, and Tunisia. In sum, analysis of the twenty-one most export-dependent authoritarian regimes in the developing world suggests that the political and economic circumstances facing rulers as they initiated late development strongly affected the decisions they made about coalition and state building. Where rulers faced rent scarcity and a tough challenge from the opposition, they tended to build political organizations—ruling parties—that improved their chances of surviving the tumultuous boom and bust years. I turn next to the impact of the late development juncture on regime formation.

Table 5.5 presents the results for ordered logistic analysis of the determinants of authoritarian regime type. To reiterate, types 4, 5, and 6 are variants on single-party regimes in increasing order of expected durability, and both rent scarcity and opposition strength are predicted to result in more durable (higher-ranked) regimes. The first column of table 5.5 includes the separate measures for opposition strength and rent scarcity at the onset of late development. Both exert strong and robust upward pressure on regime type, supporting the hypothesis that the construction of powerful ruling parties is an important causal link tying these challenging transitions to late development to later regime viability. Interestingly, these variables run in the opposite direction of both the late development dummy and yearly oil export dependency. That is, late development by itself is associated with more fragile regime types; so, too, is a high degree of oil export dependence. These two controls are robust predictors of more fragile regime types, suggesting that it is neither the mere adoption of late development nor the mere presence of oil wealth that generates powerful variants of single-party rule but rather late development initiated under very difficult conditions.

TABLE 5.5.
Rent scarcity, opposition, and regime type

Independent variable	Model 1	Model 2
Late development	−30.509***	−10.638***
	(4.250)	(1.899)
Oil/GDP	−10.368***	−11.521***
	(2.207)	(1.940)
Opposition at onset	**5.363***	—
of late development	**(.967)**	
Rent scarcity at onset	**24.457***	—
of late development	**(2.912)**	
Opposition-rent scarcity	—	**5.381***
interaction effect		**(.620)**
Middle East	−1.323	7.937***
	(1.689)	(1.766)
Sub-Saharan Africa	18.720***	17.754***
	(3.373)	(2.304)
Latin America	3.353	10.262***
	(2.272)	(1.898)
Ethnic diversity	−1.594	11.166***
	(2.902)	(2.733)
GDP per capita$_{ln}$	−2.974***	.046
	(.547)	(.246)
Urban growth	−.301	−.377
	(.243)	(.201)
N=	270	270
Log likelihood	−141.472	−182.733
Pseudo R^2	.631	.523

Notes: Analysis is by ordered logistic regression. Entries are unstandardized coefficients; standard errors are in parentheses. *, **, and *** indicate significance at <.05, <.01, and <.001, respectively.

Back again to Some Cases: A Brief Look at Congo and Egypt

Beyond Indonesia and Iran, these effects manifested themselves in trajectories of institutional and political change. In Tunisia, for instance, the onset of late development under Habib Bourgiba in the early 1960s faced active opposition from organized labor and from student organizations. In addition, Tunisia had in the early 1960s almost no oil industry at all; exports provided only 1.6 percent of the gross domestic product (World Bank 2001). The Neo-Destour regime in Tunisia, in other words, faced circumstances of strong opposition and high rent scarcity. Its response to these challenges, and to the task of embarking on late development, looked much like the New Order's response in Indonesia: heavy investment in re-organizing the Neo-Destour Party to extend the central leadership's authority into local settings combined with equally heavy investment in local governmental institutions.

The result was a stronger state *and* a stronger ruling party. When Tunisia's oil reserves began to produce significant revenue for the state in the late 1970s, the regime invested those revenues too back into the state and its coalition. As a result, it was possible to defuse a 1987 crisis that could well have brought down the regime by removing Bourgiba from power and replacing him from within the party. State and regime trajectories such as this one emerged in Egypt, Iraq, and Malaysia as well, going far to protect the regimes in these countries from numerous crises.[12]

By contrast, Ecuador's military government under Guillermo Rodriguez Lara began full-scale late development in 1972 after marginalized the opposition and becoming highly dependent on oil export revenues to fund the state. Where other military regimes—Nasser's in Egypt, Suharto's in Indonesia, to take two examples—built auxiliary organizations such as ruling parties to cement their grip on power in response to fiscal and political challenges, Lara's government had the same luxury of options available to the Shah and subsequently invested little in institution or coalition building. Only four years later, opposition from Ecuador's business community and from conservative army officers brought down Lara's regime and began a process of democratic transition that culminated in a return to civilian rule in 1979. In the remainder of this section, I explore briefly the trajectories that Congo and Egypt followed after the onset of late development.

Congo, 1968–92

The origins of Congolese Labor Party (Parti congolais du Travail, PCT) rule under Marien Ngouabi and of late development in the Republic of Congo in the early 1970s reflect conditions of substantial rent access and weak opposition also found in Iran and Ecuador. The Congolese government that preceded the PCT—the National Revolutionary Movement (MNR) under Alphonse Massemba-Débat—accomplished what the PCT would subsequently not need to: purging the country's strongest organized opposition and effectively clearing the political playing field of the most dangerous challengers. After the 1963 revolution, Massemba-Débat's regime attacked pro-Catholic unions and social organizations and consolidated existing labor unions into a single state-run one, the Congolese Trade Union Confederation (Confédération Syndicale Congolaise, CSC; see Radu and Somerville 1989, 165–67; Thompson and Adloff 1984, 11–12). Despite his

---

[12] Again, the regime in Iraq is now defunct, but it survived twelve years of crippling sanctions and two major wars, only falling after a full-scale invasion by the United States and Britain in the spring of 2003.

efforts, these groups and, much more important, disaffected elements in the military combined to overthrow Massemba-Débat in 1968 and to replace him with Marien Ngouabi.

It took Ngouabi the first three years of his rule to consolidate power over the civil servants (who went on strike in 1969), rioting students (1971), and the People's Militia (which he defeated in 1972). As a result, "the weakening of the radical left . . . seemed to indicate that by the end of 1972 the military had won the struggle for power" (Radu and Somerville 1989, 173). In comparative perspective, the hard times of early PCT rule provide additional confirmation of what the Shah's purges in 1950s Iran suggested: that rulers working to consolidate their rule who are not simultaneously trying to jump-start late development do not seem to carry forward the lessons of those early years. If they are not trying to restructure the economic bases of their societies but simply want to stamp out opposition forces, these early domestic battles do not appear to have long-term strengthening effects for the rulers themselves. As a result, the PCT faced weak and disorganized opposition to state-led late development when it first responded to the first oil boom in 1974 (Clark 1997, 66). Labor unions and radical student groups were considerably weakened as a result of the MNR's purges and could not mount a concerted challenge.

The Congolese government already relied heavily on oil exports for more than a quarter of GDP (World Bank 2001). As a result, Ngoaubi could nationalize, create, and endow industrial enterprises without any need to raise the money domestically. Like the Shah and like Lara in Ecuador, Ngouabi went on a developmental spending binge that was completely unconstrained by any domestic revenues sources or tax base. Because he did so in the absence of a sustained opposition to his policies, Ngouabi could also opt not to devote much attention to building his formally Soviet-styled PCT into the organizational weapon that the original had become. Instead, he could pursue ideology, rhetoric, and state-run development projects on the cheap and neglect the tougher tasks of constructing a mass movement party to reflect a broad and deep social coalition to undergird his rule.

As a result, the PCT's ruling coalition remained quite narrow, centered on the M'bochis from northern Congo (Ngouabi's own ethnic group and home region) and on the political class created with rent-bought bureaucratic expansion from 3,300 civil servants in 1960 to 73,000 by 1986 (Radu and Somerville 1989, 159). Organizationally, the party failed to become much of a mass-mobilizing or coalition-maintaining political force: "The PCT had its political role and influence strictly limited by the army" (174). In the same way that Iran Novin and then the Rastakhiz remained organizationally weak because the Shah felt no sense of desperation to build a party apparatus around his rule and also feared that a party could acquire an independent support base and challenge him, Ngouabi never dedicated himself to building the party he had created into a proper regime maintenance vehicle. As a result, the PCT was "never able to really control student, youth or labor unions, though they are nominally its ancillary organs. It remained a lethargic instrument" (Young 1982, 37).

State building and the quest for domestic revenue sources took no higher priority in Ngouabi's regime. Even given the regime's social and military support from the M'bochi, the PCT invested very little in expanding the state's administrative power into the northern parts of Congo or even in building roads into the region.[13] Despite the regime's officially Marxist/ planned economy ideology and state-directed line on development, relatively little priority went to building a state that could accomplish such lofty goals.

In part because of the lag between Socialist rhetoric and reality and in part because of the economic distortion caused by the regime's mismanagement of the first oil windfalls of the 1973–74 boom, the late 1970s brought political crisis, just as they had in Iran, Indonesia, and elsewhere. Ngouabi's regime had little in the way of resources with which to confront the opposition that had mobilized against it except violence, and that proved insufficient. On March 18, 1977, Ngouabi was assassinated and replaced by an interregnal regime led by Joachim Yhombi-Opango, which lasted until February 1979, when the PCT's Central Committee voted overwhelmingly against his presidency and elected another M'bochi army officer and party elite, Denis Sassou-Nguesso, to replace him.

If Ngouabi, Yhombi-Opango, and Sassou-Nguesso had not all come from the army and from the PCT—both organizations were heavily cleaved by both ethnic and ideological tensions—the substantive turn taken after this succession would probably have hit the political science radar screen as a regime change. Because it remained formally an intra-PCT succession, however, it did not. In any case, Sassou-Nguesso came to power just as the second oil boom of 1979 made it possible for him to consolidate his own power with a massive new round of rent payoffs to the civil service and the urban poor via newly expanded bureaucratic employment and subsidies, respectively. During his first five years in power, oil's share of Congo's gross domestic product never dropped below 40 percent and rose as high as 57 percent (World Bank 2001). Moreover, the discovery of new oil deposits in Congo, which French and Italian corporations quickly brought into

[13] Thanks to John Clark for his discussions on this topic. See also Decalo (1990, 42–44).

production, augmented the patronage-encouraging increase in oil prices spurred by the revolutionary crisis in Iran and further magnified Sassou-Nguesso's access to rents.

Because his accession to power took place as a result of intraparty intrigues and military splits and because there continued to exist no opposition organization capable of threatening his military support base, Sassou-Nguesso took few steps to reinvigorate the cohesion of the PCT. He pursued the same sort of institutional decimation that Ngouabi had, purging both the army and the party of "actual, former, and perceived opponents" and ensuring that his own power remained "centralized and personalized" (Radu and Somerville 1989, 183). As the Shah's inability to cope with spreading opposition and eventual downfall suggests, this optimal strategy in the short term tends to leave rulers with few long-term means of ensuring their survival through crises other than coercion and rent patronage.

The country's small population enabled the regime to buy acquiescence during the boom years by spreading windfall rents broadly in Congolese society. French military protection also helped to prolong Sassou-Nguesso's rule, but a severe economic crisis that began with the oil bust in 1986 brought down the PCT in 1991–92.[14] When oil prices collapsed in 1986, Sassou-Nguesso turned to the austerity measures the IMF had been demanding, including attempts to rein in civil service salaries, to scale back inefficient Socialist-inspired state-owned enterprises, and to cut subsidies to the urban poor (Clark 1997, 67; Radu and Somerville 1989, 184–85). By 1989 opposition mobilization had compelled the regime to liberalize parliamentary politics, a step that was followed in 1990 by the emergence of a cross-ideological alliance against Sassou-Nguesso's government. Finally, the CSC organized a strike in August 1990 that proved to be the critical opposition mass needed to force the regime to negotiate. The CSC extracted government permission to hold an independent Congress, during which it declared its autonomy from the government. Shortly after that setback, an unscheduled meeting of the PCT's Central Committee agreed to legalize the formation of other political parties, setting the stage for multiparty elections in 1992 and the end of the regime's uncontested hold on power.[15]

---

[14] This section draws largely on Clark (1997b, 67–70).

[15] Since 1992, the transition to democracy has derailed, and Congo's political history since then has been punctuated by several civil conflicts. See Clark (2002) and Englebert and Ron (2004).

Egypt, 1952–Present

The Free Officers overthrew Egypt's monarchy on July 23, 1952, amidst violent antistate protests, parliamentary disintegration, and demands that the king end what the officers referred to as his loyalty to western investors. These conditions—a weak head of state, broad-based opposition mobilization in the streets, an ineffective parliament—presented the Free Officers with a political landscape much like the one that Suharto and his allies in the Indonesian Armed Forces confronted in late 1965. Moreover, economic disarray presented a similarly strong set of incentives to retool the economy. Very soon after taking power, the regime began to implement its vision of Arab Socialist planned development under the direction of the Permanent Council for the Development of National Production to direct the country's long-term industrial transformation (Waterbury 1983, 61).[16]

As in Indonesia in 1966–67, Muhammad Naguib's regime faced powerful organized opposition from both sides of the political spectrum. The Egyptian Communist Party (ECP) demanded wholesale social engineering and truly revolutionary political change. The Muslim Brotherhood, on the other side of the political spectrum, opposed Socialist planned development and pressured the Free Officers not to follow such an economic path (Hinnebusch 1985, 12–15). Naguib himself, finally, faced stiff opposition from Gamal Abdel Nasser, who led his supporters to build a political organization, the Liberation Rally, specifically to challenge Naguib (Fahmy 2002, 56–57). Nasser's strategy during this period, reflecting conditions of strong opposition, rested in significant part on building an alliance through the LR with the Cairo Transport Workers Union, whose support and mobilization against Naguib's government was crucial to the LR's success in seizing power (Waterbury 1983, 312).

In 1954 Nasser succeeded in forcing Naguib from power. His LR regime then had to confront four major social groups: the ECP, the Muslim Brotherhood, the remnants of Naguib's supporters in the government and wider political arena, and large rural landowners who bristled at the new regime's economic rhetoric and who held sizable capital. The LR under Nasser felt the greatest threat from Naguib supporters and from the Muslim Brotherhood; arrest figures for the 1954–56 period show over 1,400 of the former in the first three months of 1954 alone and 3,000 members or supporters of the latter between October 1954 and July 1956 (Waterbury 1983, 341). Between 1952 and 1956, in short, as a crucial step toward the goal of rapid

---

[16] This similarity is all the more striking given the markedly different ideological orientations of the two regimes: center-right and western-oriented in Indonesia and avowedly left and anti-West in Egypt.

state-driven economic development, Nasser's government had little choice but to pursue costly strategies of survival very similar to those undertaken in Indonesia a decade and a half later.

In a departure from the strong opposition/rent scarcity onset of late development illustrated by New Order Indonesia, however, the LR's fiscal situation was not as dire as it might have been even though oil production would not kick in until the 1970s. As Waterbury notes, Egypt "emerged from the Second World War with £425 million in sterling reserves and thus foreign exchange was no particular problem" (1983, 61). Consequently, the regime faced a mixed set of political and economic incentives. It could not avoid dealing with the opposition, but it could to some degree avoid the politically costly option of extracting revenues from domestic elites. Egypt's major capital holders were large landowners, and the regime's 1952 land reform took them on squarely, breaking their rural political power, redistributing land to peasants, and pressuring them to invest their capital in industry rather than in agriculture (Waterbury 1983, 61–62). However, the LR government did not extend itself to make taxes a substantial source of revenues, although in 1955 a new law did begin to provide new tax funding for local infrastructure projects (Waterbury 1983, 66; Fahmy 2002, 184).

Tax extraction did not accelerate in Egypt as it later did in Indonesia. As a result, tax evasion remained widespread, and this central mechanism of state formation did not have the same strengthening effect that it might otherwise have had. Taking a look back at the cross-national results analyzing the effects that opposition strength and rent access had at the onset of late development, the case of Egypt helps to corroborate the causal story. The results in table 5.3 suggest that opposition strength has a relatively stronger effect on later regime durability than does rent access and, further, that rulers who face both challenges—fiscal scarcity and powerful opposition—tend to fare better. They suggest that a regime like Nasser's LR in Egypt, facing the conditions that it did, would likely invest heavily in social control and coalition building—via the geographical expansion of infrastructural power into the countryside and the construction of a powerful ruling party—rather than emphasizing revenue extraction.

What did take place in the arena of state formation was a fairly rapid extension of central government authority into local settings. Notably, this extension of the state's infrastructural power was predominantly politically motivated: "*Out of political necessity,* the Junta had from the outset expressed a special interest in the countryside, triggered first by their desire to destroy the power of the large landowners who represented a political threat to their rule, and second by the need to gain support among the rural masses to legitimize the new regime" (Fahmy 2002, 184, emphasis added). Whereas there had existed a fairly strong and capable bureaucracy at the national level, under Nasser the state quickly moved into local settings and established itself politically as the only game in town (Harik 1972, 291–96).

Created in 1953 as a vehicle through which Nasser could build the support needed to challenge Naguib, the LR was the first of three political organizations[17] that the regime used to mobilize support, to hold together a ruling coalition, and to control access to government-granted perks such as civil service employment. The LR served to consolidate the regime by bringing organized labor into the coalition (Waterbury 1983, 312); in 1956 Nasser jettisoned the LR and created a new group called the National Union. As Waterbury notes, the NU was formed after the regime's major opposition had been purged; nonetheless, the legacy of past struggles provided a strong motivation to maintain and to expand the party's institutions: "Once firmly established in power after 1956, Nasser sought to move beyond preemption to the *structuring of political life in support of the regime*" (1983, 313, emphasis added).

Following the failure of the Arab Socialist Union between Egypt and Syria in 1961, Nasser replaced the National Union with the Arab Socialist Union. The ASU was in principle a voluntary membership organization, but in practice membership was necessary to stand for election to all levels of government and even to participate in certain professions. It also took a much more explicitly populist tone and implemented a stronger social outreach program than had the NU, assertively reaching out to the "working forces," meaning peasants, industrial workers, intellectuals, soldiers, and "native capitalists" (Fahmy 2002, 58). The party also required that half the seats on all committees—including the National Assembly—be composed of workers and peasants. In addition, the party increased its capacity in social control over the NU's by extending basic units beyond space—cities and the countryside—into work, establishing units as well "in factories, offices, schools, universities, banks and even in government ministries and agencies" (Fahmy 2002, 58).

Investment in the ruling party continued into the 1970s, even as the party's name and even social support base changed with the changing political needs of the leadership and with the succession of Anwar Sadat to replace Nasser after his death in 1970. At first, however, Sadat turned to the National Assembly as his major base of organizational support while fighting a battle of regime consolidation against ASU leader Ali Sabri. Sabri

---

[17] Like Suharto had done with Golkar in Indonesia, Nasser refused to classify the LR or either of its two immediate successors, the National Union and the Arab Socialist Union, as "political parties," preferring instead to call them "organizations." This was in large part due to the past vilification of political parties in both countries as the causes of their economic and political instability.

had gone far to build the ASU into a genuine organizational weapon capable of exerting serious social and political influence in Egyptian society and, more ominously for Sadat, opposing Sadat openly. By outflanking Sabri's ASU and relying on the Assembly for support, Sadat could also curry favor with rural landowners, who were overrepresented in the Assembly due to districting and many of whom were not happy with Sabri's efforts during the late Nasser years to expropriate their lands (Fahmy 2002, 61). By the spring of 1971, Sadat had managed to consolidate his own power; on May 2 he removed Sabri from the ASU leadership and from the vice presidency, beginning a purge of the ASU ranks to replace them with men loyal to Sadat.

Until 1974, Sadat left the ASU in a state of relative neglect, focusing on economic policy reform and the creation of a new political coalition around Egypt's commercial classes. However, Sadat's decision to introduce limited political liberalization with the opening of the economy in the early 1970s brought a willingness to experiment with multiparty politics, meaning that the regime would again face electoral competition, however limited by the legacy of Nasser's emasculation of opposition parties. The regime organized contestation across the political spectrum, creating blocs within the ASU representing left, center (the government's coalition, termed the Egypt Party), and right. Center candidates running on the government ticket won 280 of 344 seats in the Assembly, giving Sadat a sense of vindication.[18] In the aftermath of the elections, Sadat allowed the formation of additional political parties, renaming his regime's group the National Democratic Party (NDP), which has ruled since 1978.

State and party building between 1950 and 1980 would prove crucial to the regime's survival. Nasser and his successors faced several major crises beginning with Egypt's crushing defeat in the 1967 Arab-Israeli War. Nasser's death in 1970, the food riots of 1977, the turmoil surrounding the 1979 peace treaty with Israel, and Anwar Sadat's assassination all threatened the regime, as did later challenges to NDP dominance (Brownlee 2007). Like the New Order in Indonesia, successive rulers in Egypt found themselves confronting periodic challenges to their hold on power—economic crises, economic policy shifts, external shocks, contributed to moments of potential political danger. As in Indonesia, what mattered in Egypt was the

---

[18] There appears to have been minimal cheating on the election days (October 2 and the runoff election on November 4 for candidates who had not won an outright majority previously); see *The Economist*, November 6, 1976, p. 86. The real interference took place before the elections, when Sadat's coalition, known as the "Egypt Party," commanded near-total control over the media and could exert influence on the civil service and bureaucracy through veiled references to employment security, and afterwards, when parliament loyalists dutifully voted to expel opposition members who criticized Sadat (see Waterbury 1982, 373–75).

ability of elites to hold together their coalitions by continuing to offer credible commitments via status in the ruling party. Contrary to earlier, modernization theory–driven accounts of ruling parties as channels for participation (for example, see Huntington 1968, 1970; Binder 1966), evidence from these countries and others suggests that the real political value of ruling parties is as institutional guarantees of "in-group" status for workers, religious organizations, business elites, and other social groups that make up the support base of various authoritarian regimes.

Conclusion

This book began with three puzzles: Why did the Shah of Iran fail to maintain power through the political crisis of 1977–79 while President Suharto of Indonesia, facing a similar challenge, rode out the crisis and stayed in power for twenty more years? Why does oil wealth coexist with weak states in some developing countries and strong ones in others? And why have social scientists not found a way to explain the multiple effects that resource wealth can have on domestic politics? In chapter 2, I suggested an answer to the third of these questions by way of answers to the first two. The structured comparison of Iran's and Indonesia's political economies in chapters 3 and 4 allowed me significant purchase on the first question. Cross-national analysis of Iran, Indonesia, and nineteen other highly export-dependent countries between 1974 and 1999 suggested a powerful general role for the transition to late development as a critical juncture in shaping state and regime trajectories in the boom and bust years, suggesting an answer to the second question. In this chapter, I summarize the findings of the book and outline its implications and contributions for the study of the politics of resource wealth and state building in the developing world. I also make the case for linking origins-focused arguments like the one driving this book to the newly invigorated study of authoritarian persistence. Finally, I outline the contribution that this study makes to recent theorizing on temporal sequences as causes of social outcomes and as an illustration of the value of a mode of inquiry I refer to as integrated comparative analysis.

It is often said that a theory's "punch" rests on its ability to force the rethinking of commonly held conclusions. In Iranian studies, scholars have reached a loose consensus that oil wealth had something to do with both the increasingly weak ties between Iranian society and the Pahlavi state and with the weakness of the state itself. And, in Indonesian studies, some scholars have looked to oil rents as a major factor in the ability of the New Order regime to hold together its coalition. However, there has been little or no attention paid to a phenomenon present in Indonesia, one that has crucial implications: to wit, that under certain conditions, oil wealth can *facilitate* institutional development. This is perhaps the most substantively important implication of the book. It is this surprising finding, rather than simply repression or rent distribution, I argue, that accounts for the extraordinary tenacity of many regimes in oil-rich states through some very hard times, and it takes us far beyond the presumption that these regimes have lasted as long as they have solely or even primarily because of patronage or raw force.

To state the argument again in its briefest form, the effect of oil wealth on politics and institutions is not a question of *whether* oil but *when*. Like a host of other important macro-structural variables whose effects have been theorized and traced by other scholars in the comparative historical tradition (Gerschenkron 1962; Moore 1966; Rueschemeyer, Stephens, and Stephens 1992; for general outlines of these principles, see Ragin 1987; Hall 2003), the world oil market and its domestic manifestations exert influences that depend heavily on the timing of and circumstances surrounding their entry into national political economies. Where state leaders embarked on late development with ready rent access, and where they confronted only weak opposition, they could pursue low-cost early strategies of consolidating their own "developmental states." As I have shown, these enviable early years came back to haunt them in the form of weak ties to society and few resources with which to manage dissent.

In a variation on the "no pain, no gain" adage, rulers such as Suharto in Indonesia who set late development in motion in the face of rent scarcity and stiff opposition made difficult choices early on that paid off later. Even when initial coalition partners left the coalition and joined the opposition, as the Indonesian student movement did in the 1970s, the early ties that rulers had built to these groups allowed for a dialogue to continue even during protest periods. Moreover, because the regime had reached out to the opposition in the past, it had credibility when it did so again. As a result, identifying moderates and placating or coopting them was a viable strategy and went far to defuse crises that could have developed into regime-threatening upheavals such as those that brought down the governments of Congo, Ecuador, Iran, and Nigeria.

This finding—that late-arriving oil can bolster a carefully built coalition in an authoritarian regime—has gloomy implications for those interested in democracy promotion and consolidation. In essence, it predicts long life spans for some of the most visible dictatorships in the developing world—in Iraq, Syria, and elsewhere. In Iraq, to take a particularly visible case, the most surprising (to military and civilian planners in the U.S. government) and disturbing aspect of postwar nation-building has been the persistence of the Ba'ath Party's organizational coherence long after there ceased to be a regime. That is, to use Migdal's (1988) language, the party has proven to be a major rival rule-maker and provider of survival strategies to the Coalition Provisional Authority and now to successive Iraqi Unity governments and the major obstacle to pacifying Iraq, despite prewar depictions of the regime as a personal or neopatrimonial one revolving around Saddam Hussein. In Indonesia too, the fall of Suharto has overshadowed the persistence of both Golkar and the Indonesian Armed Forces as major organizational players in national politics. In short, we can reasonably expect transitions from such regimes, if and when they occur, to lead to the persistence of old regime structures than in other post-authoritarian settings.[1]

Oil and Politics in Iran, Indonesia, and Beyond

I posited in chapter 2 that access to revenues from the sale of oil—rent access—would have different effects depending on its timing relative to the onset of late development. In addition to oil wealth, I suggested that, at that juncture, the presence or absence of an organized opposition is critical to understanding the decisions that rulers made about building coalitions and state institutions. Iran and Indonesia began late development beginning within a few years of one another in the 1960s. Anti-Communist authoritarian regimes in each country initiated this development push, and the 1973–74 oil boom flooded both economies and state coffers with windfall revenues.

Iran and Indonesia shared a history of ethnoregional separatism, failed constitutional democracy, a left-nationalist coalition whose rule produced institutional decay and economic stagnation, the ascent of U.S.-supported autocratic regimes, and the 1973–74 oil boom. As a result, we could be reasonably sure that these factors did not account for the difference in outcomes. That Suharto's regime faced more frequent protests during the 1970s and yet managed to survive rules out the theory that he simply survived by being less unpopular than the Shah. And the Shah's frequent use

---

[1] Indeed, in the April 5, 2004, parliamentary elections in Indonesia, Golkar won over 21 percent of the votes, making it the biggest party bloc in the incoming parliament. Yusuf Kalla, a longtime high-level figure in Golkar, also was elected to the vice presidency in September 2004 and was later elected to lead the party.

of coercion during the growing crisis of 1978 suggests that it is not repression that explains why his regime fell and Suharto's did not. Constructing a most-similar research design that paired Iran and Indonesia through roughly the same period made it possible to address multiple rival hypotheses and to ensure that they did not covary with the outcome: regime durability. But there were important differences, both in the circumstances surrounding the onset of late development and in the subsequent institutional trajectories into which those windfalls were incorporated.

The theory I proposed also contains what many of these other possible arguments do not: a specific set of mechanisms tying initial conditions to early coalition and institution building and to subsequent trajectories. The cases of Iran and Indonesia assess the explanatory accuracy of the theory by confirming sequential propositions across several institutional and organizational settings. They illustrate the argument in detail by tracing the institutions and patterns of state-society relations present during the first boom back to their origins in the onset of late development. Where many other accounts place the causal weight on ad hoc decisions made by the Shah and Suharto, aspects of their personalities, or the boom itself, I show that it was in the 1960s and early 1970s that these regimes developed the tools with which to handle later societal opposition, for better or for worse. That the Shah was forced to flee Iran into exile in January 1979 and Suharto enjoyed nearly another two decades in office result directly from the early years of late development. Much more than on-the-spot decisions in the late 1970s, preexisting institutions and relations with social groups determined whether leaders had the flexibility and resources to deal with rising social dissent.

After analyzing in chapters 3 and 4 the processes through which oil shaped regimes and state institutions in Iran and Indonesia, I pursued in chapter 5 a cross-national test of two key implications of the argument. First, analysis of data from twenty-one exporters in the years since the 1973–74 oil boom provides powerful general support for a timing-sensitive theory of oil and late development. Regimes that began late development under conditions of rent scarcity and stiff opposition tended to fare significantly better in later years, when the oil shocks created economic disturbances that manifested themselves politically. Second, it appears that these regimes fared better precisely because they built powerful political organizations—ruling parties—that could hold together coalitions by providing a stable and predictable set of expectations about how rulers would respond to and protect the interests of coalition partners. In short, the conscious decisions by rulers to invest in building strong parties, and the robust party-regimes that result, are key causal links between early hard times and subsequent regime resilience.

Just as Gerschenkron (1962) found that industrialization had profoundly different implications in the eighteenth century than in the twentieth, the emergence of the world oil market as a key factor in domestic political economies has had widely different effects in exporting states depending on the circumstances and timing of entry. It has done so because, depending on its timing, oil wealth has acted through a different set of mechanisms, setting in motion varying trajectories. As a result, the ultimately fragile regimes in Iran and Congo and robust ones in Syria and Tunisia are all representative outcomes of oil wealth. This finding resolves the either-or debate over the political impact of oil wealth by illustrating how oil's effects are so heavily dependent on the timing of its arrival.

Timing, Rationality, and the Importance of Institutional Origins

Most scholarly work in political science on the politics of oil wealth to date has been heavily influenced by dependency theory. That is, the global oil market, driven by the demands of consuming states in the advanced industrial world, creates a set of political constraints common to all exporting countries. While this is undoubtedly true in some respects—for instance, price volatility is to some degree a reality that all exporters have to confront—I have endeavored to show in this book that the world oil market displays different effects depending on the circumstances and timing of its entry into domestic contexts. Far from being a static, purely structural variable with which rulers in exporting countries have to contend, the world oil market and its domestic manifestation in export revenues exert widely varying effects.

This point is empirically important because a theory that can account for this can explain much more compellingly the various kinds and strengths of political regimes in the oil-exporting world. In a broader sense, it is equally important because it demonstrates clearly the importance of research methods and theoretical frameworks that are sensitive to timing. In this study, I have followed a comparative-historical analytic framework in which critical junctures in time are central to explaining subsequent political pathways and outcomes. More specifically, *when* those critical junctures happen—whether we are talking about the onset of late development or the emergence of a country as one highly dependent on oil exports—is often a more significant question than *whether* they happen.

Only by paying close attention to issues of timing and sequence is it possible to understand how major events or processes can have varied impacts on politics. I have argued that the initial conditions surrounding late development powerfully shaped the dynamics of subsequent institutional and social change, in some settings sharply limiting the range of options available to rulers and in others expanding them. In other words, I have tried to theorize and to illustrate what Pierson and Skocpol (2000), Katznelson (1997), and Waldner (2002), among others, have called for: close attention to institutional origins. Katznelson, in particular, has openly lamented what Waldner refers to as the "loss of ambition" suffered by comparative historical analysts: The loss of ambition, he writes, "is the consequence of shifting attention from extraordinary moments of regime creation and transformation to the routinized contours of normal politics in different democratic capitalist regimes. But this relocation runs the risk of detaching the two kinds of enterprises and of recusing historical-institutional work from its more assertive ambitions" (85).

The theory I developed in chapter 2 and assessed in subsequent chapters explicitly links these two enterprises. It reflects a return to a focus on those "extraordinary moments" during which the roots of later politics are born, providing a theory as to how routine politics are likely to take shape as a result. A large body of work in this vein has made more than clear the immense fruitfulness and benefit of studying such moments of economic transformation. Gerschenkron's (1962) study of late industrialization in Europe, Moore's (1966) analysis of agricultural commercialization, and Migdal's (1988) focus on postcolonial rural economic incorporation into global markets, among many others, all point to a need for close historical attention to the politics of critical economic junctures. More importantly, they reflect a common analytical framework. From the conditions that surround those initial economic transitions, it is possible to hypothesize institutional outcomes, whether in terms of state economic intervention, regime type, or state capability.

Here, I have theorized likely institutional and coalitional outcomes based on initial conditions at the time of initiating late development. In doing so within a comparative-historical approach to studying the impact of timing, I make a clear choice to throw in my lot with these macro-oriented scholars. The argument maintains that early decisions, once reflected in institutional and coalitional choices, shape both the number and kind of later options. However, it is crucial to provide a mechanism or mechanisms through which initial macro-conditions lead to institutional and coalitional outcomes.

To my mind, synthesizing insights from both microeconomic (that is, rational choice) theory and the logic of historical causality suffers from no inherent contradiction; on the contrary, the two approaches provide much more explanatory bite than either can alone. In theorizing how initial conditions lead to institutions and coalitions, I drew from rational choice theory to argue that, assuming rulers would (a) rather stay in power than not and (b) prefer to consolidate their development programs at the lowest possible cost, the availability of oil wealth and a lack of organized opposition to their programs would constitute the first choice of option. When this option is unavailable, rulers must choose from a less attractive set of options. The strategies chosen by rulers and the subsequent coalitions and institutional results that emerge are the mechanisms through which initial conditions produce long-term outcomes (for a more general statement, see Waldner 2002).

When oil revenues are plentiful, rulers are most likely to choose the option of substituting oil wealth for state and regime building. When I hypothesized that leaders who had no other viable options—in other words, who faced a forced move because they had no such oil revenues—would make real concessions and invest in institution-building strategies despite the political costs, I based the logic of such choices on immediate constraints. That is to say, I made no assumptions that leaders facing tough circumstances were somehow capable of thinking with longer time horizons than those who had access to oil wealth and who faced no organized opposition.[2] Rather, I hypothesized that short-term calculations aimed at consolidating late development would produce longer-term outcomes affecting not only development but also regime viability.

A primary goal of mine in this book has been to show that oil and oil wealth do not carry around one set of incentives and constraints that hang over actors in all times and all places. Rather, the incentives provided by oil rents present options to rulers that appear to vary according to timing. To put the theoretical argument another way, oil rents that coincide with the onset of late development in Iran and elsewhere became a crucial part of the political landscape that defined how rulers thought about the politics of economic transformation. Rent access allowed them to make direct payoffs to potential supporters and to avoid difficult decisions about how to extract revenues from domestic elites. When oil rents were scarce or absent during the transition in Indonesia and other states, though, rent scarcity was a challenging and central component of the political equation facing rulers. Supporters demanded something for their support and, without easy access to rents that could provide an early source of patronage, a seat at the policy table or real power in national politics was all that new rulers could offer. Moreover, revenues had to come from somewhere, and the cost of forging bargains with domestic elites seemed less than the costs of not doing so in such cases.

To tie these issues back into the larger discussion of comparative his-

[2] Thanks to Steve Hanson and David Waldner for their lengthy discussions on the issues covered in this section.

torical analysis, I argued that decisions made at the onset of late development actually shaped the institutional settings and state-society relations to which rulers had access in later periods. Once established, both institutions and patterns of state-society relations were much more difficult to reverse than in earlier periods. Thus, the wider array of options available to the Shah—who could have chosen not to pursue the oil-based route and build a strong party that could guarantee him a powerful coalition or could have chosen to emphasize local political institutions and extraction—provided powerful incentives to take a low-cost approach to embarking on development. Later, paradoxically, the relatively low degree to which his choices were initially determined gave him fewer options for dealing with an emerging opposition in the late 1970s.

Suharto, conversely, faced much more highly constrained options; initial conditions made his choices highly determined but led to choices that, over time, produced a much wider array of options for dealing with crises. Thus, during the crises that both regimes faced between 1977 and 1979, the difference was not that Suharto reacted rationally or optimally and that the Shah did not. Rather, I argued and showed in chapter 5 that what mattered crucially was the resources in hand—institutions, coalitions, and ties to social groups—that enabled effective responses. The most strategically savvy leader, in other words, would have probably failed, given resources as limited as the Shah's.

In other words, the choices that Suharto and the Shah made in the 1960s explain not the ultimate outcomes (regime survival or failure) but rather the institutional trajectories that emerged from the onset of late development. It is the trajectories themselves that explain the outcomes, for there is little reason to believe that either of the two leaders acted more or less rationally than the other unless we impute rationality from the benefits or costs of downstream outcomes. In the late 1970s, both rulers tried to manage emerging crises with a combination of carrots and sticks, and both rulers had imperfect knowledge about the scope of opposition. Suharto, however, had much more access to the opposition as a result of the ties his regime had built to social groups that, in the late 1960s and early 1970s, were still, whether explicitly or tacitly, part of the ruling coalition. Absent those ties, his regime would probably have been no more capable of managing dissent than the Shah's was.

Beyond Iran and Indonesia, the political fallout of late development remains intact with few exceptions. With some notable exceptions, few highly export-dependent states have gone very far toward reforming their economies. Oil production—and with it oil revenues—dropped off in these two states earlier than in others; unsurprisingly, they are among the only oil exporters to democratize (with Ecuador, Trinidad and Tobago, and

Venezuela). Many, including Egypt, Syria, and Tunisia, have taken the minimum steps that their rulers think will satisfy international lenders. Only when both oil prices and production drop off substantially does it seem that either economic or political reform is very likely in the world's major exporting states, and this group of holdout governments has been able to ride the legacies of late development and of late-arriving oil into the twenty-first century.

Beyond Oil and Late Development: Regime Change and the Persistence of Authoritarianism

A recent and growing research agenda (see, for instance, Brownlee 2004; Geddes 1999; Levitsky and Way 2002; Waldner 2004) has focused on the political regimes that have bucked the Third Wave and remained resolutely nondemocratic since the mid-1970s. This is a research program with many questions left to be answered, to be sure, but the central concern is how these regimes resisted pressures that led to democratic transitions in dozens of other countries. Moreover, with the exception of Waldner's, these studies tend to focus on proximate factors that explain regime durability—for instance, "single-party regimes last longer than others" or "strong parties help to maintain competitive authoritarianism." These are valuable contributions, but they leave open an important question: Where do strong parties, or single-party regimes, come from? Why do strong parties emerge in some places but not others? Why, for instance, did the Shah's Rastakhiz Party in Iran or Marcos's New Society Movement in the Philippines fail to develop into the same kind of regime-cohering organizations as Suharto's Golkar in Indonesia or Asad's Ba'ath party in Syria?

I have endeavored to show in this book that political organizations, no less than state institutions, take shape according to the circumstances surrounding their creation. In the same way in which parties that had control of the state's patronage resources took on a different character than those in the opposition in the United States (Shefter 1994), ruling parties in authoritarian states vary in their ability to hold together coalitions. Thus, it is a promising avenue of inquiry to investigate the origins of durable authoritarian regime types (for instance, see Smith 2003b, 2005), and this book suggests two important initial conditions that influence the long-term viability of authoritarian regimes: constraints on patronage rents and opposition strength.

The pattern of transition to late development illustrated by evidence from New Order Indonesia also sheds light on an important question in Middle East studies: Why has authoritarianism been so much more stubborn in that region than in Africa, Asia, and Latin America in an "era of de-mocratization"? Rather than ascribing the "robustness" of Middle East au-thoritarianism to religion, culture, repression, or superpower meddling, the analysis in this book suggests that it is the contingent configuration of late development, fiscal scarcity that is mitigated only later by oil rents, and the presence of powerfully organized opposition movements such as Com-munist parties, the Muslim Brotherhood, or Kurdish separatist parties that accounts for some of the most tenacious dictatorships in the region. Many countries in the Middle East share a trend toward political mobilization by Islamists, Communists, or ethnic minorities into strongly organized par-ties or movements that coincided with the onset of late development in the 1960s and 1970s. Where those phenomena did coincide, the result was of-ten the establishment of powerful authoritarian regimes that, like Syria and Tunisia, joined the family of oil-rich states later. The emergence of oil ex-ports as a major part of the economies of these states meant that already powerful regimes became even more so as rulers could both expand pa-tronage networks and invest in further strengthening their party appara-tuses and the institutions of state. Boom- or bust-era crises that likely would have brought down weaker regimes failed to do so in Algeria, Egypt, Iraq, Syria, and Tunisia, and the evidence presented here suggests that it is in significant part because of these governments' challenging transitions to late development.

Synthesizing Inference and Explanation: Integrated Comparative Analysis

Throughout this study, I have endeavored to illustrate important points and sequences that combine macro- and micro-approaches and that employ a wide range of methodological tools. In constructing the case studies, I used comparative macrosociology and cross-national statistics mixed with ground-level data, such as memoirs and seminar minutes documenting in-teractions between Indonesian army officers and student leaders in late 1965, interviews with tax officials in provincial Iran paired with time-series direct tax data, and the like. I also used the historical logic of the argument and its illustration in a structured comparison to provide an explanatory framework in order to make sense of two sets of cross-national statistical tests. My goal has been to show that central concerns in comparative social inquiry are often best accomplished by combining multiple methods. Chap-ters 3 and 4 of this book, for example, are integrated with chapters 1 and 5 rather than simply being "nested" within them. So, too, are Iran and In-donesia better thought of as integrated with the large-N analyses of 105 other countries in chapter 1 and nineteen others in chapter 5.

This is by no means a novel statement of methodological predilection. From nested induction and nested analysis to statements of "shared standards" and whole books devoted to multiple method research,[3] scholars in comparative politics have been debating how to construct fruitful relationships between aggregate data analysis and comparative-historical, case study, or fieldwork-based research for some time. I wish to suggest here simply that by using both, it is possible to derive broad inferences as well as to provide deep explanations of major social phenomena. Not any less importantly, it makes what looked like a polarized debate in the late 1990s between "area studies" and "social science" appear more clearly as an unnecessary tradeoff obscuring a fruitful middle ground.

Comparative historical analysis provides causal leverage over questions for which statistical inquiry can provide only inferential conclusions (Rueschemeyer, Stephens, and Stephens 1992; Waldner 2004). Numerous case studies of oil-rich countries over the last twenty years or so generated a host of theoretical conclusions about oil's effect on politics; my aggregate tests of these conclusions turned up some misfits between theory and the empirical record. While large-N analysis of cross-national data in chapter 1 provided a starting point for rethinking the politics of oil wealth, gauging the explanatory depth of the theoretical argument was only possible by engaging in the comparative analysis of cases. It is also the case that tracing how oil's impact varied according to its timing could not be accomplished solely by large-N analysis. Lacking a coherent temporal account of how that impact might be different, there would be little to guide timing-sensitive statistical analysis.

However, the confirmation of a theory's causal logic provided by structured, focused comparison can be a stepping stone to incorporating qualitatively derived and tested variables back into statistical datasets for analysis involving large numbers of country-years.[4] Once I established the internal validity of the theory against the cases of Iran and Indonesia, I could be more confident of the external validity of the variables in question—and consequently of the theory itself. The analysis in chapter 5 bolstered the theory's analytical breadth by confirming the robust and significant relationship between difficult transitions to late development and later regime viability. The interpretation of those results, though, would have made little sense without the historical causal logic demonstrated in the previous two chapters. I could have claimed that the results were com-

---

[3] See Lieberman (2005) and Coppedge (2001), Brady and Collier (2004) and King, Keohane, and Verba (1994), and Creswell and Clark (2007), respectively.

[4] Note, however, that there is no inherent reason that one must employ the two modes in this order or employ them to these ends. As Lieberman notes, nested analysis may move from small-N to large-N and back again to small-N, depending on the project, or may utilize only two steps or modes (2005).

patible with my hypotheses, but without (1) a coherent causal theory tying initial conditions to outcomes and (2) a structured comparison validating that causal account, it would necessarily have remained an interesting correlation compatible with an interesting story. Integrating large- and small-N analysis within a single research design provides a means for cross-methodological dialogue. To give but one possible example of an integrated approach based on the structure of this study, large-N analysis provided a basis for case selection and the elimination of rival arguments. Structured comparative analysis assessed the causal depth and sequential logic of the theoretical argument and provided conceptual clarification for incorporating new independent variables into a dataset.

Structured comparison, however, also rests on the adequacy of causal stories. In this case and undoubtedly in many others, compelling causal stories must begin with extended field research, the product of which is often referred to as "area studies."[5] There are several reasons for this. First, it is often the case that reliance on secondary literatures on given countries leaves the scholar dependent on the choice of topics—in scientific language, the measurement of variables—that previous researchers found attractive or interesting. Almost by default, this reliance can funnel research along well-trodden paths, but a fresh look made possible by new research can unearth important new findings. Moreover, the kind of familiarity that in-depth exposure to a fairly small number of national settings enables scholars to assess rival arguments as they go, taking culture, historical specificity, and other local factors into account early in the theory-building process. The ability to control for, or at least to address and set aside, such rival explanations, is much easier when one can rely on a degree of "local knowledge" to assess their relative weight.

At a time when the "fragmentation of comparative politics" (Huber 2002) is often cast as a black-and-white debate between area studies and social science, I side with others in consciously avoiding the dichotomy. That is, provided that we share a common commitment to explaining outcomes that interest many comparativists,[6] there is no good reason to throw out any tools or to limit the toolkit to a single one: "Give a small boy a ham-

---

[5] Indeed, my colleagues in Asian studies at the University of Florida, for lack of a better "area" with which to categorize me, have settled on "Southwest-Southeast Asianist."

[6] It is important to acknowledge the following dynamic: one group of scholars in comparative politics is interested in understanding rather than explaining, and a second group (there may be some overlap) is interested in specific cases or outcomes rather than in general theorizing. In my view, the latter group has gotten an inexplicably bad rap in comparative politics. Their single-case analyses are no less valuable than excellent works in international relations that focus on the outbreak of World War I, the resolution of the Cuban missile crisis, or a host of other equally important single-case studies. There are clear analogies in the natural sciences as well—no one would argue that a theoretically informed study of the extinction of the dinosaurs is lacking in import or merit because it seeks to explain only that one temporally proximate set of species extinctions.

mer, and he finds that everything he encounters needs pounding" (Kaplan 1998). To the contrary, there are many reasons to pursue multiple methods beyond a simple, laudable commitment to ecumenism. Integrating comparative analysis combines inference and explanation in ways that can help provide compelling answers to big questions while at the same time addressing those questions across multiple methodological and empirical arenas.

Appendix

TABLE A.1.
Summary of variables

Variable	Obs	Mean	Std. Dev.	Min	Max
oilgdp	2159	.0759178	.1626896	0	1.219637
civilwar	3998	.3764382	.8664168	0	3
democracy	3666	−2.36743	6.844403	−10	10
tprotest	3392	1.147111	3.317007	0	49
elf85	4240	.5297925	.2633405	.003	.984
urbangro	4240	4.676197	2.700443	−44.15816	23.41692
gdpgrow	3507	4.058124	6.714938	−50.6	81.88776
boomeffect	2248	.170217	.7927611	0	10.8226
busteffect	2248	.1304891	.6521709	0	8.291536
pastfail	3887	2.284024	2.939099	0	26
trend	4173	20	11.25598	1	39
regimefall	3887	.1155132	.3196815	0	1
logpoptotal	4280	15.51183	1.722056	10.71442	20.94928
logarea	4141	12.15344	1.989721	6.063785	16.04847
democracy^2	3666	52.43781	27.70497	0	100
logpopdensity	4141	3.357724	1.523284	−.4648309	8.776274

Table A.2.
Country list for the dataset

1. Afghanistan	35. Ethiopia	72. Nepal
2. Algeria	36. Gabon	73. Nicaragua
3. Angola	37. Gambia	74. Niger
4. Argentina	38. Ghana	75. Nigeria
5. The Bahamas	39. Guatemala	76. Oman
6. Bahrain	40. Guinea	77. Pakistan
7. Bangladesh	41. Guinea-Bissau	78. Panama
8. Barbados	42. Guyana	79. Papua New Guinea
9. Belize	43. Haiti	80. Paraguay
10. Benin	44. Honduras	81. Peru
11. Bhutan	45. India	82. Philippines
12. Bolivia	46. Indonesia	83. Qatar
13. Botswana	47. Iran	84. Rwanda
14. Brazil	48. Iraq	85. Saudi Arabia
15. Brunei	49. Israel	86. Senegal
16. Burundi	50. Jamaica	87. Sierra Leone
17. Cambodia	51. Jordan	88. Singapore
18. Cameroon	52. Kenya	89. Somalia
19. Central African	53. South Korea	90. South Africa
Republic	54. Kuwait	91. Sri Lanka
20. Chad	55. Laos	92. Sudan
21. Chile	56. Lebanon	93. Swaziland
22. China (PRC)	57. Lesotho	94. Syria
23. Colombia	58. Liberia	95. Tanzania
24. Congo, Democratic	59. Libya	96. Thailand
Republic (Kinshasa)	60. Madagascar	97. Togo
25. Congo, Republic	61. Malawi	98. Trinidad and Tobago
(Brazzaville)	62. Malaysia	99. Tunisia
26. Costa Rica	63. Mali	100. Turkey
27. Cote d'Ivoire	64. Mauritania	101. Uganda
28. Cuba	65. Mauritius	102. United Arab Emirates
29. Djibouti	66. Mexico	103. Uruguay
30. Dominican Republic	67. Mongolia	104. Venezuela
31. Ecuador	68. Morocco	105. Yemen Arab Republic
32. Egypt	69. Mozambique	106. Zambia
33. El Salvador	70. Myanmar	107. Zimbabwe
34. Equatorial Guinea	71. Namibia	

Bibliography

Abar, Akhmad Zaini. 1995. *1966–1974: Kisah Pers Indonesia* [1966–1974: A story of the Indonesian press]. Yogyakarta, Indonesia: LKiS.

Abrahamian, Ervand. 1980. Structural Causes of the Iranian Revolution. *MERIP Reports* 87 (May): 21–27.

———. 1981. The Strengths and Weaknesses of the Labor Movement in Iran, 1941–1953. In *Continuity and Change in Modern Iran*, ed. Michael Bonine and Nikki Keddie. Albany: State University Press of New York.

———. 1982. *Iran between Two Revolutions*. Princeton: Princeton University Press.

———. 1989. *The Iranian Mojahedin*. New Haven: Yale University Press.

Aburish, Säid K. 1995. *The Rise, Corruption, and Coming Fall of the House of Saud*. New York: St. Martin's Press.

———. 2000. *Saddam Hussein: The Politics of Revenge*. New York: Bloomsbury.

Achen, Christopher. 2000. Why Lagged Dependent Variables Can Suppress the Explanatory Power of Other Independent Variables. Paper presented at the Annual Meeting of the Political Methodology Section of the American Political Science Association, UCLA, Los Angeles, California, July 20–22, 2000.

Afkhami, Gholam. 1985. *The Iranian Revolution: Thanatos on a National Scale*. Washington, DC: Middle East Institute.

———, ed. 2001. *Siyasat va Siyasatgozari-ye Eqtesadi dar Iran 1350–1360* [Ideology, politics, and process in Iran's economic development, 1960–1970]. Bethesda, MD: Foundation for Iranian Studies.

Ahmad Khan, Sarah. 1994. *Nigeria: The Political Economy of Oil*. Oxford: Oxford University Press.

Aïssaoui, Ali. 2001. *Algeria: The Political Economy of Oil and Gas*. Oxford: Oxford University Press, Oxford Institute for Energy Studies.

Akhavi, Shahrough. 1986. State Formation and Consolidation in Twentieth-century Iran: The Reza Shah Period and the Islamic Republic. In *The State, Reli-*

gion, and Ethnic Politics: Afghanistan, and Pakistan, ed. Ali Banuazizi and Myron Weiner. Syracuse: Syracuse University Press.

——. 1992. Shi'ism, Corporatism, and Rentierism in the Iranian Revolution. In *Comparing Muslim Societies: Knowledge and the State in a World Civilization,* ed. Juan R. I. Cole, 261–93. Ann Arbor: University of Michigan Press.

Alam, Asadollah. 1991. *The Shah and I: The Confidential Diary of Iran's Royal Court, 1969–1977.* London: I. B. Tauris.

Alatas, Farid, Syed. 1997. *Democracy and Authoritarianism in Indonesia and Malaysia: The Rise of the Post-Colonial State.* New York: St. Martin's Press.

Alesina, Alberto, and Robert Perotti. 1996. Income Distribution, Political Instability, and Investment. *European Economic Review* 40: 1203–28.

Alexander, Yonah, and Allan Nanes, eds. 1980. *The United States and Iran: A Documentary History.* Frederick, MD: University Publications of America.

Alimard, Amin, and Cyrus Elahi. 1976. Modernization and Changing Leadership in Iran. In *Iran: Past, Present and Future,* ed. Jane W. Jacqz. New York: Aspen Institute for Humanistic Studies.

Allen, Chris, Michael Radu, Keith Somerville, and Joan Baxter. 1989. *Benin, the Congo, Burkina Faso: Economics, Politics, and Society.* London: Pinter.

Al-Khuri, Fu'ad Isaq. 1980. *Tribe and State in Bahrain: The Transformation of Social and Political Authority in an Arab State.* Chicago: University of Chicago Press.

Alvarez, Mike, José Antonio Cheibub, Fernando Limongi, and Adam Przeworski. 1996. Classifying Political Regimes. *Studies in Comparative International Development* 31, no. 2: 3–36.

——. 1999. *ACLP Political and Economic Database.* Available at www.ssc .upenn.edu/~cheibub/data/, accessed May 24, 2001.

Amal, Ichlasul. 1992. *Regional and Central Government in Indonesian Politics.* Yogyakarta, Indonesia: Gadjah Mada University Press.

Amin, Adimir. 1976. The Role of Oil in Indonesia's Economic Development. *Prisma* 3: 106–13.

Amirahmadi, Hooshang. 1988. Middle-Class Revolutions in the Third World. In *Post-Revolutionary Iran,* ed. Hooshang Amirahmadi and Manoucher Parvin. Boulder, CO: Westview Press.

——. 1990. *Revolution and Economic Transition: The Iranian Experience.* Albany: State University of New York Press.

Aminzade, Ronald. 1992. Historical Sociology and Time. *Sociological Methods and Research* 20, no. 4: 456–80.

Amjad, Mohammed. 1989. *Iran: From Royal Dictatorship to Theocracy.* New York: Greenwood Press.

Amphas-Mampoua. 2000. *Political Transformations of the Congo.* Durham, NC: Pentland Press.

Amuzegar, Jahangir. 1999. *Managing the Oil Wealth: OPEC's Windfalls and Pitfalls.* London: I. B. Tauris.

Amuzegar, Jahangir, and M. Ali Fekrat. 1971. *Iran: Economic Development under Dualistic Conditions.* Chicago: University of Chicago Press.

Anderson, Benedict. 1971. *A Preliminary Analysis of the October 1, 1965, Coup in Indonesia.* Ithaca: Cornell University Modern Indonesia Project.

——. 1983. Old State, New Society: Indonesia's New Order in Comparative Historical Perspective. *Journal of Asian Studies* 42, no. 3 (May): 477–96.

——. 2000. Petrus Dadi Ratu. *New Left Review* 3 (May–June): 7–15.

Anderson, Leslie. 2005. Graduate Education in a Pluralist Context: The Metaphor of a Toolbox. In *Perestroika: The Raucous Rebellion in Political Science,* ed. Kirsten Renwick Monroe, 421–33. New Haven: Yale University Press.

Anderson, Lisa. 1986. *The State and Social Transformation in Tunisia and Libya, 1830–1980.* Princeton: Princeton University Press.

Anonymous. 1983. Current Political Attitudes in an Iranian Village. *Iranian Studies* 16, nos. 1–2: 3–29.

——. 1984. Political Attitudes in an Iranian Village: A Follow-Up. *Iranian Studies* 17, no. 4: 453–65.

Antlöv, Hans. 1995. *Exemplary Centre, Administrative Periphery: Rural Leadership and the New Order in Java* Richmond, U.K.: Curzon Press.

Anwar, Yozar. 1979. *Angkatan 66: Sebuah Catatan Harian Mahasiswa* [Generation of '66: Memoirs of a student daily]. Jakarta, Indonesia: Pustaka Sinar Harapan.

Aqili, Baqir. 1990/1369. *Ruzshomar-i Tarikh-i Iran* [Daily chronology of Iranian history]. Tehran: Nashr–e Goftar.

Arbetman, Marina, and Jacek Kugler. 1997. *Political Capacity and Economic Behavior.* Boulder, CO: Westview Press.

Arjomand, Said Amir. 1986. *Turban for the Crown.* New York: Oxford University Press.

Arthur, W. Brian. 1994. *Increasing Returns and Path Dependence in the Economy.* Ann Arbor: University of Michigan Press.

Ascher, William. 1999. *Why Governments Waste Natural Resources: Policy Failures in Developing Countries.* Baltimore, MD: Johns Hopkins University Press.

Asher, Mukul G., and Anne Booth. 1992. Fiscal Policy. In *The Oil Boom and After,* ed. Anne Booth, 39–76. Singapore: Oxford University Press.

Ashraf, Ahmad. 1988. Bazaar-Mosque Alliance: The Social Basis of Revolts and Revolutions. *Politics, Culture, and Society* 1: 538–67.

——. 1996. From the White Revolution to the Islamic Revolution. In *Iran after the Revolution: Crisis of an Islamic State,* ed. Saeed Rahnema and Sohrab Behdad. New York: I. B. Tauris.

Ashraf, Ahmad, and Ali Banuazizi. 1985. The State, Classes and Modes of Mobilization in the Iranian Revolution. *State, Culture and Society* 1, no. 3: 3–40.

Ashraf, Ahmad, and Cyrus Elahi. 1976. Social Mobilization and Participation in Iran. In *Iran: Past, Present, and Future,* ed. Jane W. Jacqz. New York: Aspen Institute for Humanistic Studies.

Atiqpur, Muhammad. 1979/1358. *Naqshi-i Bazar va Bazari'ha dar Inqilab-i Iran* [The role of the bazaar and bazaaris in the Iranian Revolution]. N.p.

Auty, Richard. 1990. *Resource-Based Industrialization: Sowing the Oil in Eight Developing Countries.* Oxford, U.K.: Clarendon Press.

——. 1994. Industrial Policy Reform in Six Large Newly Industrializing Countries: The Resource Curse Thesis. *World Development* 22, no. 1: 11–26.

Azca, M. Najib. 1998. *Hegemoni Tentara* [Military hegemony]. Yogyakarta, Indonesia: LKiS.

Bachtiar, Harsja W. 1968. Indonesia. In *Students and Politics in Developing Nations*, ed. Donald K. Emmerson. New York: Praeger.

Bahasoan, Awad. 1982. Golongan Karya: The Search for a New Political Format. *Prisma* 25: 55–82.

Baker, Richard W., M. Hadi Soesastro, J. Kristiadi, and Douglas E. Ramage, eds. 2000. *Indonesia: The Challenge of Change.* Jakarta: Center for Strategic and International Studies and East-West Center.

Bakhash, Shaul. 1984. *The Reign of the Ayatollahs: Iran and the Islamic Revolution.* New York: Basic Books.

Bakhtiar, Ali. 1974. The Royal Bazaar of Isfahan. *Iranian Studies* 7, nos. 1–2: 320–47.

Banani, Amin. 1961. *The Modernization of Iran, 1921–1941.* Stanford, CA: Stanford University Press.

Bank Indonesia. 1978. *Statistik Ekonomi-Kuangan Indonesia* [Indonesian economic-fiscal statistics]. October.

Banks, Arthur S. 1996. *Cross-National Time Series Data Archive.* Binghamton: Center for Social Analysis, State University of New York at Binghamton.

Baraheni, Reza. 1977. *The Crowned Cannibals: Writings on Repression in Iran.* New York: Vintage.

Baram, Amatzia. 1991. *Culture, History, and Ideology in the Formation of Ba'thist Iraq, 1968–89.* New York: St. Martin's.

Barkey, Henri J. 1989. State Autonomy and the Crisis of Import Substitution. *Comparative Political Studies* 22, no. 2 (October): 291–314.

Bashiriyeh, Hossein. 1984. *The State and Revolution in Iran, 1962–1982.* New York: St. Martin's.

Bates, Robert. 1981. *Markets and States in Tropical Africa.* Berkeley: University of California Press.

——, ed. 1988. *Toward a Political Economy of Development: A Rational Choice Perspective.* Berkeley: University of California Press.

——. 1990. Macropolitical Economy in the Field of Development. In *Perspectives on Positive Political Economy,* ed. James E. Alt and Kenneth A. Shepsle. New York: Cambridge University Press: 31–54.

——. 1997. *Open-Economy Politics: The Political Economy of the World Coffee Trade.* Princeton: Princeton University Press.

——. 2001. *Prosperity and Violence: The Political Economy of Development.* New York: W. W. Norton.

Bates, Robert, Avner Greif, Margaret Levi, Jean-Laurent Rosenthal, and Barry Weingast. 1998. *Analytic Narratives.* Princeton: Princeton University Press.

Bawazier, Fuad. 1988. Central-Local Fiscal Relations in Indonesia. Ph.D. dissertation, University of Maryland.

Beattie, Kirk J. 1994. *Egypt during the Nasser years: Ideology, Politics, and Civil Society.* Boulder, CO: Westview.

Beblawi, Hazem, and Giacomo Luciani. 1987. *The Rentier State.* London: Croom Helm.

Beck, Lois. 1990. Tribes and the State in Nineteenth- and Twentieth-Century Iran. In *Tribes and State Formation in the Middle East,* ed. Philip S. Khoury and Joseph Kostiner, 185–225. Berkeley: University of California Press.

———. 1991. *Nomad: A Year in the Life of a Qashqa'i Tribesman in Iran.* Berkeley: University of California Press.

Beck, Nathaniel, and Jonathan N. Katz. 1995. What to Do (and Not to Do) with Time-Series Cross-Section Data. *American Political Science Review* 89, no. 3 (September): 634–47.

Beck, Nathaniel, Jonathan N. Katz, and Richard Tucker. 1998. Taking Time Seriously: Time-Series Cross Section Analysis with a Binary Dependent Variable. *American Journal of Political Science* 42, no. 4 (October): 1260–88.

Behnam, M. Reza. 1986. *Cultural Foundations of Iranian Politics.* Salt Lake City: University of Utah Press.

Bellin, Eva. 1994. The Politics of Profit in Tunisia: Utility of the Rentier Paradigm? *World Development* 22, no. 3: 427–36.

———. 2002. *Stalled Democracy: Capital, Labor, and the Paradox of State-Sponsored Development.* Ithaca: Cornell University Press.

———. 2004. The Robustness of Authoritarianism in the Middle East: Exceptionalism in Comparative Perspective. *Comparative Politics* 36, no. 2: 139–57.

Benjamin, Nancy C., Shantayanan Devarajan, and Robert Weiner. 1989. The "Dutch Disease" in a Developing Country: Oil Reserves in Cameroon. *Journal of Development Studies* 30: 71–92.

Bennett, Andrew. 1997. Lost in the Translation: Big (N) Misinterpretations of Case Study Research. Paper presented at the 38th annual meeting of the International Studies Association. Toronto, Canada, March 18–22.

Bennett, Andrew, and Alexander L. George. 1997. Process Tracing in Case Study Research. Paper presented at the MacArthur Foundation Workshop on Case Study Methods, Belfer Center for Science and International Affairs. Harvard University, Cambridge, Massachusetts, October 17–19.

Bernard, Mitchell. 1996. States, Social Forces, and Regions in Historical Time: Toward a Critical Political Economy of Eastern Asia. *Third World Quarterly* 17, no. 4: 649–65.

Bertocchi, Graziella, and Michael Spagat. 2001. The Politics of Co-optation. *Journal of Comparative Economics* 29: 591–607.

Bharier, Julian. 1971. *Economic Development in Iran 1900–1970.* London: Oxford University Press.

Bienen, Henry. 1983. *Oil Revenues and Policy Choice in Nigeria.* Washington, DC: World Bank.

———. 1985. *Political Conflict and Economic Change in Nigeria.* Totowa, NJ: Frank Cass.

Bill, James A. 1963. The Social and Economic Foundations of Power in Contemporary Iran. *Middle East Journal* 17, no. 4 (Autumn): 400–413.

———. 1968. *The Iranian Intelligentsia: Class and Change.* Ph.D. dissertation, Princeton University.

———. 1969. The Politics of Student Alienation: The Case of Iran. *Iranian Studies* 2: 8–26.

———. 1970. Modernization and Reform from Above: The Case of Iran. *Journal of Politics* 32, no. 1 (February): 19–40.

———. 1972. Class Analysis and the Dialectics of Modernization in the Middle East. *International Journal of Middle East Studies* 3: 417–34.

——. 1988. *The Eagle and the Lion: The Tragedy of American-Iranian Relations*. New Haven: Yale University Press.

Binder, Leonard. 1966. Political Recruitment and Participation in Egypt. In *Political Parties and Political Development*, ed. Joseph LaPalombara and Myron Weiner, 217–40. Princeton: Princeton University Press.

Biro Statistik Daerah Istimewa Yogyakarta. 1970. *Statistik Pemda DIY 1969* [Statistics for the regional government of the special district of Yogyakarta].

Biro Pusat Statistik Indonesia. 1963. *Statistical Yearbook* of Indonesia. Jakarta: BPS.

——. 1964. *Statistical Yearbook of Indonesia*. Jakarta: BPS.

——. 1965. *Statistical Yearbook of Indonesia*. Jakarta: BPS.

——. 1966. *Statistical Yearbook of Indonesia*. Jakarta: BPS.

——. 1967. *Statistical Yearbook of Indonesia*. Jakarta: BPS.

——. 1968. *Statistical Yearbook of Indonesia*. Jakarta: BPS.

Boileau, Julian M. 1983. *GOLKAR: Functional Group Politics in Indonesia*. Jakarta, Indonesia: Center for Strategic and International Studies.

Bonine, Michael. 1981. Shops and Shopkeepers: Dynamics of an Iranian Provincial Bazaar. In *Continuity and Change in Modern Iran*, ed. Michael Bonine and Nikki Keddie. Albany: State University Press of New York.

Booth, Anne. 1986. In *Central Government and Local Development in Indonesia*, ed. Colin MacAndrews. East Asian Social Science Monographs. Singapore: Oxford University Press.

Boroujerdi, Mehrzad. 1996. *Iranian Intellectuals and the West: The Tormented Triumph of Nativism*. Syracuse: Syracuse University Press.

Boswell, Terry, ed. 1989. *Revolution in the World-System*. New York: Greenwood.

Boudreau, Vincent. 1998. *Styles of Repression and Mobilization in Southeast Asia*. Manuscript, City College of New York.

Box-Steffensmeier, Janet, and Bradford Jones. 1997. Time Is of the Essence: Event History Models in Political Science. *American Journal of Political Science* 41, no. 4 (October): 1414–61.

Brady, Henry, and David Collier. 2004. *Rethinking Social Inquiry*. Lanham, MD: Rowman and Littlefield.

Bratton, Michael. 1994. Civil Society and Political Transitions in Africa. In *Civil Society and the State in Africa*, ed. John W. Harbeson, Donald Rothchild, and Naomi Chazan. Boulder, CO: Lynne Rienner.

——, and Nicolas van de Walle. 1994. Neopatrimonial Regimes and Political Transitions in Africa. *World Politics* 46: 453–89.

Bresnan, John. 1993. *Managing Indonesia: The Modern Political Economy*. New York: Columbia University Press.

Brogan, Christopher. 1984. *The Retreat from Oil Nationalism in Ecuador, 1976–1983*. London: University of London, Institute of Latin American Studies.

Brown, David W. 2001. Why Governments Fail to Capture Economic Rent: The Unofficial Appropriation of Rain Forest Rent in Insular Southeast Asia between 1970 and 1999. Ph.D. dissertation, University of Washington.

Brownlee, Jason. 2002. . . . . And Yet They Persist: Explaining Survival and Transition in Neopatrimonial Regimes. *Studies in Comparative International Development* 37, no. 3 (Fall): 35–63.

Brownlee, Jason. 2007. *Authoritarianism in an Age of Democratization.* New York: Cambridge University Press.

Brzezinski, Zbigniew. 1985. *Power and Principle: Memoirs of the National Security Adviser 1977–1981.* New York: Farrar, Straus and Giroux.

Buchori, Mochtar. 1996. *Culture and Politics in Indonesia: Personal Reflections.* Jakarta: Center for Strategic and International Studies.

Bueno de Mesquita, Bruce, and Randolph M. Siverson. 1995. War and the Survival of Political Leaders: A Comparative Study of Regime Types and Political Accountability. *American Political Science Review* 89, no. 4 (December): 841–55.

Bunce, Valerie. 1985. The Empire Strikes Back: The Evolution of the Eastern Bloc from a Soviet Asset to a Soviet Liability. *International Organization* 39, no. 1 (Winter): 1–46.

——. 1999. *Subversive Institutions: The Design and the Destruction of Socialism and the State.* New York: Cambridge University Press.

Cage, N. 1978. Iran: The Making of a Revolution. *New York Times,* December 17.

Cahyono, Heru. 1992. *Peranan Ulama Dalam GOLKAR 1971–1980: Dari Pemilu Sampai Malari* [The role of the Islamic scholars in GOLKAR, 1971–1980: From the general election to the January 15 disaster]. Jakarta: Pustaka Sinar Harapan.

Campbell, Donald T. 1975. "Degrees of Freedom" and the Case Study. *Comparative Political Studies* 3, no. 2 (July): 178–93.

Carey, Jane Perry Clark, and Andrew Galbraith Carey. 1960. Oil and Economic Development in Iran. *Political Science Quarterly* 75, no. 1 (March): 66–86.

Carlson, Sevinc. 1977. *Indonesia's Oil.* Boulder, CO: Westview.

Center for Information Analysis, Indonesia. 1999. *Gerakan 30 September: Antara Fakta dan Rekayasa* [The September 30 movement: Between fact and construction]. Yogyakarta, Indonesia: Penerbit Media Pressindo.

Chatelus, Michel. 1987. Rentier or Producer Economies in the Middle East? In *The Economic Development of Jordan,* ed. B. Khader and A. Badran, 204–20. London: Croom Helm.

Chaudhry, Kiren Aziz. 1992. Economic Liberalization in Oil-Exporting States: Iraq and Saudi Arabia. In *Privatization and Liberalization in the Middle East,* ed. Ilya Harik and Denis J. Sullivan. Bloomington: Indiana University Press.

——. 1993. The Myths of the Market and the Common History of Late Developers. *Politics and Society* 21, no. 3: 245–74.

——. 1994. Economic Liberalization and the Lineages of the Rentier State. *Comparative Politics* 26 (October): 1–25.

——. 1997. *The Price of Wealth: Economies and Institutions in the Middle East.* Ithaca: Cornell University Press.

Chehabi, Houchang. 1990. *Iranian Politics and Religious Modernism: The Liberation Movement of Iran under the Shah and Khomeini.* Ithaca: Cornell University Press.

Chiabi, Emmanuel. 1997. *The Making of Modern Cameroon.* Lanham, MD: University Press of America.

Cilliers, Jakkie, and Christian Dietrich, eds. 2000. *Angola's War Economy: The Role of Oil and Diamonds.* Pretoria, South Africa: Institute for Security Studies.

Clark, John F. 1997. Petro-Politics in the Republic of Congo. *Journal of Democracy* 8, no. 3: 62–76.

Clark, John F., and David Gardinier, eds. 1997. *Political Reform in Francophone Africa.* Boulder, CO: Westview Press.

Clarke, Angela. 1990. *Bahrain: Oil and Development, 1929–1989.* Boulder, CO: International Research Center for Energy and Economic Development.

Cockcroft, James D. 1980. On the Ideological and Class Character of Iran's Anti-Imperialist Revolution. In *Iran: Precapitalism, Capitalism, and Revolution,* ed. Georg Stauth. Saarbrücken, Germany: Breitenbach.

Cohen, Youssef, Brian R. Brown, and A. F. K. Organski. 1981. The Paradoxical Nature of State Making: The Violent Creation of Order. *American Political Science Review* 75, no. 4 (December): 901–10.

Collier, David. 1998. Comparative Method in the 1990s. *APSA-CP* (Winter 1998): 1–5.

Collier, David, and James E. Mahon. 1993. Conceptual "Stretching" Revisited: Adapting Categories in Comparative Analysis. American Political Science Review 87, no. 4 (December): 845–55.

Collier, David, and James Mahoney. 1996. Insights and Pitfalls: Selection Bias in Qualitative Research. *World Politics* 49 (October): 56–91.

Collier, Paul, and Anke Hoeffler. 1998. On Economic Causes of Civil War. *Oxford Economic Papers* 50: 563–73.

Collier, Ruth Berins, and David Collier. 1991. *Shaping the Political Arena: Critical Junctures, the Labor Movement and Regime Dynamics in Latin America.* Princeton: Princeton University Press.

Conybeare, John A. C. 1982. The Rent-Seeking State and Revenue Diversification. *World Politics* 35, no. 1 (October): 25–42.

Cooley, Alexander. 2000. Booms and Busts: Theorizing Institutional Formation and Change in Oil States. *Review of International Political Economy* 7, no. 4: 163–80.

Coppedge, Michael. 1999. Thickening Thin Concepts and Theories: Combining Large N and Small in Comparative Politics. *Comparative Politics* 31, no. 4: 465–76.

——. 2005. Explaining Democratic Deterioration in Venezuela through Nested Inference. In *Advances and Setbacks in the Third Wave of Democratization in Latin America,* ed. Frances Hagopian and Scott Mainwaring. New York: Cambridge University Press.

Corden, W. Max, and J. Peter Neary. 1982. Booming Sector and De-Industrialisation. *Economic Journal* 92, no. 368 (December): 825–48.

Coronil, Fernando. 1997. *The Magical State: Nature, Money, and Modernity in Venezuela.* Chicago: University of Chicago Press.

Cottam, Richard. 1968. Political Party Development in Iran. *Iranian Studies* 1: 82–95.

——. 1988. *Iran and the United States: A Cold War Case Study.* Pittsburgh: University of Pittsburgh Press.

Creswell, John, and Vicki Plano Clark. 2007. *Designing and Conducting Mixed Methods Research.* Thousand Oaks, CA: Sage.

Cribb, Robert, ed. 1990. *The Indonesian Killings, 1965–1966: Studies from Java and Bali.* Clayton, Australia: Monash University Centre for Southeast Asian Studies.

Cribb, Robert, and Colin Brown. 1995. *Modern Indonesia: A History since 1945.* New York: Longman.

Crone, Donald K. 1988. State, Social Elites, and Government Capacity in Southeast Asia. *World Politics* 40, no. 2 (January): 252–68.

Cronin, Stephanie. 1997. *The Army and the Creation of the Pahlavi State in Iran, 1910–1926.* London: I. B. Tauris.

Crouch, Harold. 1978. *The Army and Politics in Indonesia.* Ithaca: Cornell University Press.

Crystal, Jill. 1989. Coalitions in Oil Monarchies: Kuwait and Qatar. *Comparative Politics* 21, no. 4 (July), 427–44.

——. 1990. *Oil and Politics in the Gulf.* New York: Cambridge University Press.

Cueva, Agustín. 1982. *The Process of Political Domination in Ecuador.* New Brunswick, NJ: Transaction Books.

Daftar-e Adabiyat-e Enqelab-e Islami. 1995/1374. *Ruz Shomar-e Enqelab-e Islami* [Daily chronology of the Islamic revolution]. Tehran: Office of Literature on the Islamic Revolution.

Dapice, David O. 1980. An Overview of the Indonesian Economy. In *The Indonesian Economy,* ed. Gustav F. Papanek. New York: Praeger.

Davey, Kenneth. 1989. Central-Local Financial Relations. In *Financing Local Government in Indonesia,* ed. Nick Devas. Athens: Ohio University Monographs in International Studies.

David, Paul. 1985. CLIO and the Economics of QWERTY. *American Economic Review* 75, no. 2: 332–37.

David, Steven R. 1997. Internal War: Causes and Cures. *World Politics* 49, no. 4: 552–76.

Davidheiser, Evelyn. 1992. Strong States, Weak States: The Role of the State in Revolution. *Comparative Politics* 24: 463–75.

Davis, Graham A. 1995. Learning to Love the Dutch Disease: Evidence from the Mineral Economies. *World Development* 23, no. 10: 1765–79.

Decalo, Samuel. 1998. *The Stable Minority: Civilian Rule in Africa, 1960–1990.* Gainesville, FL: FAP Books.

Decalo, Samuel, Virginia Thompson, and Richard Adloff. 1996. *Historical Dictionary of Congo.* Lanham, MD: Scarecrow Press.

Dekmejian, R. Hrair. 1971. *Egypt under Nasir: A Study in Political Dynamics.* Albany: State University of New York Press.

Delacroix, Jacques. 1980. The Distributive State in the World System. *Studies in Comparative International Development* 15: 3–20.

Denoeux, Guilain. 1993. *Urban Unrest in the Middle East: A Comparative Study of Informal Networks in Egypt, Iran, and Lebanon.* Albany: State University of New York Press.

Devas, Nick. 1989. Local Revenue Sources: Charging for Services and Profits from Local Government Enterprises. In *Financing Local Government in Indonesia,* ed. Nick Devas. Athens: Ohio University Monographs in International Studies.

Dewan Pimpinan Pusat Golongan Karya. 1978. *Laporan Pertanggungjawaban*

Dewan Pimpinan Pusat Golongan Karya Periode 1973–1978 Kepada Mus-yawarah Nasional II Golongan Karya [Accountability report of the Golkar Central Leadership Council for the 1973–1978 period to the Second National Golkar Conference]. Jakarta, Indonesia.

Dey, Oey Hong, ed. 1974. *Indonesia after the 1971 Elections.* London: Oxford University Press.

Deyo, Frederick C., ed. 1987. *The Political Economy of the New Asian Industrialism.* Ithaca: Cornell University Press.

Dillman, Bradford L. 2000. *State and Private Sector in Algeria: The Politics of Rent-Seeking and Failed Development.* Boulder, CO: Westview.

Dix, Robert H. 1983. The Varieties of Revolution. *Comparative Politics* 15: 281–94.

Djamaluddin, Dasman. 1998. *Jenderal TNI Anumerta Basoeki Rachmat dan SUPERSEMAR* [TNI General Anumerta Basoeki Rachmat and the executive order of March 11]. Jakarta: PT Gramedia Widiasarana Indonesia.

Djohan, Djohermansyah. 1990. *Problematik Pemerintahan dan Politik Lokal: Sebuah Kasus Dari Daerah Sumatera Barat* [Problematics of local government and politics: A case from West Sumatra]. Jakarta: Bumi Aksara.

Donges, Juergen B., Bernd Steccher, and Frank Wolter. 1980. Industrialization in Indonesia. In *The Indonesian Economy*, ed. Gustav F. Papanek. New York: Praeger.

Dunn, John. 1985. Understanding Revolutions. In *Rethinking Modern Political Theory*, ed. John Dunn, 68–86. Cambridge: Cambridge University Press.

Dydo, Todiruan. 1989. *Pergolakan Politik Tentara Sebelum dan Sesudah G 30 S/PKI* [Upheaval of military politics before and after the September 30 movement of the Indonesian Communist Party]. Jakarta: Golden Terayon Press.

Easterly, William, and Ross Levine. 1997. Africa's Growth Tragedy: Policies and Ethnic Divisions. *Quarterly Journal of Economics* 112, no. 4 (November): 1203–50.

Eckstein, Harry. 1975. Case Study and Theory in Political Science. In *Handbook of Political Science*, ed. Fred Greenstein and Nelson Polsby. Reading, MA: Addison-Wesley.

Economist. 1977. The Dutch Disease. November 26: 82–83.

Elm, Mostafa. 1992. *Oil, Power, and Principle: Iran's Oil Nationalization and its Aftermath.* Syracuse: Syracuse University Press.

Elster, Jon. 1989. *Nuts and Bolts for the Social Sciences.* New York: Cambridge University Press.

Emmerson, Donald. 1976. *Indonesia's Elite: Political Culture and Cultural Politics.* Ithaca: Cornell University Press.

Ertman, Thomas. 1997. *Birth of the Leviathan.* New York: Cambridge University Press.

Evans, Peter. 1979. *Dependent Development.* Princeton: Princeton University Press.

——. 1989. Predatory, Developmental, and Other Apparatuses: A Comparative Political Economy Perspective on the Third World State. *Sociological Forum* 4, no. 4 (December): 561–87.

——. 1995. *Embedded Autonomy: States and Industrial Transformation.* Princeton: Princeton University Press.

——. 1997. The Eclipse of the State? Reflections on Stateness in an Era of Globalization. *World Politics* 50, no. 1: 62–87.

Evans, Peter B., Dietrich Rueschemeyer, and Theda Skocpol, eds. 1985. *Bringing the State Back In.* New York: Cambridge University Press.

Fahmy, Ninette S. 2002. *The Politics of Egypt: State-Society Relationship.* New York: Routledge Curzon.

Fandy, Mamoun. 1999. *Saudi Arabia and the Politics of Dissent.* New York: St. Martin's Press.

Farazmand, Ali. 1989. *The State, Bureaucracy, and Revolution in Modern Iran: Agrarian Reforms and Regime Politics.* New York: Praeger.

Farhi, Farideh. 1988. State Disintegration and Urban-Based Revolutionary Crisis: A Comparative Analysis of Iran and Nicaragua. *Comparative Political Studies* 21: 231–56.

——. 1990. *States and Urban-Based Revolutions.* Chicago: University of Illinois Press.

Farmanfarmaian, Manucher, and Roxane Farmanfarmaian. 1997. *Blood and Oil: Inside the Shah's Iran.* New York: Modern Library.

Farman Farmaian, Sattareh. 1992. *Daughter of Persia: A Woman's Journey from her Father's Harem Through the Islamic Revolution.* New York: Crown.

Farmayan, Hafez F. 1971. Politics during the Sixties: A Historical Analysis. In *Iran Faces the Seventies,* ed. Ehsan Yar-Shater. New York: Praeger.

Farouk-Sluglett, Marion, and Peter Sluglett. 2001. *Iraq since 1958: From Revolution to Dictatorship.* London: I. B. Tauris.

Fatemi, Khosrow. 1982. Leadership by Distrust: The Shah's *Modus Operandi.* *Middle East Journal* 36, no. 1: 48–61.

Fearon, James D., and David D. Laitin. 2003. Ethnicity, Insurgency, and Civil War. *American Political Science Review* 97, no. 1: 75–90.

Feith, Herbert. 1962. *The Decline of Constitutional Democracy in Indonesia.* Ithaca: Cornell University Press.

——. 1963a. Indonesia's Political Symbols and their Wielders. *World Politics* 16, no. 1 (October): 79–97.

——. 1963b. The Dynamics of Guided Democracy. In *Indonesia,* ed. Ruth T. McVey. New Haven: Yale University Press.

——. 1964. President Soekarno, the Army, and the Communists: The Triangle Changes Shape. *Asian Survey* 4, no. 8 (August): 969–80.

——. 1982. Repressive-Developmentalist Regimes in Asia. *Alternatives* 7, no. 4 (Spring), 491–506.

Firoozi, Ferydoon. 1974a. The Iranian Budgets: 1964–1970. *International Journal of Middle East Studies* 5, no. 3 (June): 328–43.

——. 1974b. Tehran: A Demographic and Economic Analysis. *Middle Eastern Studies* 10, no. 1: 60–76.

——. 1978. Income Distribution and Taxation Laws of Iran. *International Journal of Middle East Studies* 9, no. 1 (January): 73–87.

Fischer, Michael. 1977. Persian Society: Transformation and Strain. In *Twentieth-Century Iran,* ed. Hossein Amirsadeghi. London: Heinemann.

Fishman, Robert M. 1990. Rethinking State and Regime: Southern Europe's Transition to Democracy. *World Politics* 42, no. 3 (April): 422–40.

Foran, John. 1992. A Theory of Third World Social Revolutions: Iran, Nicaragua, and El Salvador Compared. *Critical Sociology* 19: 3–27.

——. 1993. Theories of Revolution Revisited: Toward a Fourth Generation? *Sociological Theory* 11: 1–20.

——, ed. 1994. *A Century of Revolution: Social Movements in Iran.* Minneapolis: University of Minnesota Press.

——, ed. 1997. *Theorizing Revolutions.* New York: Routledge.

Forje, John W. 1981. *The One and Indivisible Cameroon: Political Integration and Socio-Economic Development in a Fragmented Society.* Lund, Sweden: University of Lund.

Forrest, Tom. 1995. *Politics and Economic Development in Nigeria.* Boulder, CO: Westview.

Francisco, Ronald. 2002. After the Massacre: Mobilization in the Wake of Harsh Repression. Presented at the annual meeting of the American Political Science Association, Boston, MA: September.

Frank, Lawrence P. 1984. Two Responses to the Oil Boom: Iranian and Nigerian Politics after 1973. *Comparative Politics* 16: 295–314.

Fremerey, Michael. 1976. *Students and Politics in Indonesia: An Analysis of Political Attitudes Among the Young Indonesian Intelligentsia.* Frankfurt: Deutsche Institut für Internationale Pädagogische Forschung.

Friedman, Thomas. 2005. The Geo-Green Alternative. *New York Times.* January 30.

Gaffar, Afan. 1992. *Javanese Voters: A Case Study of Election under a Hegemonic Party System.* Yogyakarta, Indonesia: Gadjah Mada University Press.

Gandhi, Jennifer, and Adam Przeworski. 2001. Dictatorial Institutions and the Survival of Dictators. Paper presented at the annual meeting of the American Political Science Association. San Francisco, CA, August.

Gasiorowski, Mark J. 1987. The 1953 Coup D'etat in Iran. *International Journal of Middle East Studies* 19: 261–86.

——. 1991. *U.S. Foreign Policy and the Shah: Building a Client State in Iran.* Ithaca: Cornell University Press.

——. 1993a. The Qarani Affair and Iranian Politics. *International Journal of Middle East Studies* 25, no. 4: 625–44.

——. 1993b. Policymaking in a Highly Autonomous State: Iran Under the Shah, 1963–1978. *Iranian Journal of International Affairs* 5, no. 2: 440–82.

——. 1995. Economic Crisis and Political Regime Change: An Event History Analysis. *American Political Science Review* 89, no. 4 (December): 882–97.

Gause, F. Gregory. 1994. *Oil Monarchies: Domestic and Security Challenges in the Arab Gulf States.* New York: Council on Foreign Relations Press.

Gauze, René. 1973. *The Politics of Congo-Brazzaville.* Stanford, CA: Hoover Institution Press.

Geddes, Barbara. 1991. How the Cases You Choose Affect the Answers You Get: Selection Bias in Comparative Politics. *Political Analysis* 2: 131–50.

——. 1994. *Politician's Dilemma: Building State Capacity in Latin America.* Berkeley: University of California Press.

——. 1999. Authoritarian Breakdown: Empirical Test of a Game Theoretic Argument. Paper presented at the annual meeting of the American Political Science Association. Atlanta, GA, September.

——. 2003. *Paradigms and Sand Castles: Theory Building and Research Design in Comparative Politics.* Ann Arbor: University of Michigan Press.

Geertz, Clifford. 1960. *The Religion of Java.* Chicago: University of Chicago Press.

Gelb, Alan. 1986a. From Boom to Bust: Oil Exporting Countries over the Cycle 1970–84. *IDS Bulletin* 17, no. 4: 22–29.

——. 1986b. Adjustment to Windfall Gains: A Comparative Analysis of Oil-Exporting Countries. In *Natural Resources and the Macroeconomy,* ed. J. Peter Neary and Sweder van Wijnbergen. Cambridge, MA: MIT Press.

——. 1988. *Oil Windfalls: Blessing or Curse?* New York: Oxford University Press for the World Bank.

George, Alexander L. 1979. Case Studies and Theory Development: The Method of Structured, Focused Comparison. In *Diplomacy: New Approaches in History, Theory, and Policy,* ed. Paul G. Lauren. New York: Free Press.

George, Alexander L., and Timothy J. McKeown. 1985. Case Studies and Theories of Organizational Decision Making. *Advances in Information Processing in Organizations* 2: 21–58.

Gereffi, Gary. 1989. Rethinking Development Theory: Insights from East Asia and Latin America. *Sociological Forum* 4, no. 4 (December): 505–33.

Gerschenkron, Alexander. 1962. Economic Backwardness in Historical Perspective. In *Economic Backwardness in Historical Perspective: A Collection of Essays,* ed. Alexander Gerschenkron. Cambridge, MA: Belknap Press of Harvard University.

Ghandchi-Tehrani, Davoud. 1982. Bazaaris and Clergy: Socio-Economic Origins of Radicalism and Revolution in Iran. Ph.D. dissertation, City University of New York.

Gheissari, Ali. 1998. *Iranian Intellectuals in the 20th Century.* Austin: University of Texas Press.

Gie, The Liang. 1995. *Pertumbuhan Pemerintah Daerah di Negara Republik Indonesia* [The development of regional government in Indonesia]. 2nd edition. Yogyakarta, Indonesia: Liberty.

Gilbar, Gad. 1977. The Big Merchants (tujjar) and the Persian Constitutional Revolution of 1906. *Asian and African Studies* 11, no. 3: 275–303.

Gitisetan, Dariush. 1985. *Iran: Politics and Government Under the Pahlavis, An Annotated Bibliography.* London: Scarecrow.

Glassburner, Bruce. 1976. In the Wake of General Ibnu: Crisis in the Indonesian Oil Industry. *Asian Survey* 16, no. 12 (December): 1099–1112.

——. 1978a. Political Economy and the Soeharto Regime. *Bulletin of Indonesian Economic Studies* 14, no. 3: 24–51.

——. 1978b. Indonesia's New Economic Policy and its Sociopolitical Implications. In *Political Power and Communications in Indonesia,* ed. Karl Jackson and Lucian Pye. Berkeley: University of California Press: 137–70.

Gleditsch, Nils Petter, Peter Wallensteen, Mikael Eriksson, Margareta Sollenberg, and Havard Strand. 2002. Armed Conflict 1946–2001: A New Dataset. *Journal of Peace Research* 39, no. 5: 615–37.

Goldstone, Jack A. 1980. Theories of Revolution: The Third Generation. *World Politics* 32: 425–53.

——, ed. 1986a. *Revolutions: Theoretical, Comparative, and Historical Studies.* New York: Harcourt Brace Jovanovich.

——. 1986b. Superpowers and Revolutions. In *Superpowers and Revolutions*, ed. J. R. Adelman. New York: Praeger.

——. 1991a. Ideology, Cultural Frameworks, and the Process of Revolution. *Theory and Society* 20: 405–53.

——. 1991b. *Revolution and Rebellion in the Early Modern World*. Berkeley: University of California Press.

Gomez, Edmund Terence, and Kwame Sundaram Jomo. 1999. *Malaysia's Political Economy: Politics, Patronage and Profits*. New York: Cambridge University Press.

Goode, James. 1991. Reforming Iran during the Kennedy Years. *Diplomatic History* 15, no. 1: 13–29.

Gordon, Joel. 1992. *Nasser's Blessed Movement: Egypt's Free Officers and the July Revolution*. New York: Oxford University Press.

Gourevitch, Peter. 1986. *Politics in Hard Times: Comparative Responses to International Economic Crises*. Ithaca: Cornell University Press.

Government of Indonesia. 1974. *Pidato Kenegaraan Presiden RI Jendral Soeharto* [State speeches of Indonesian President General Soeharto].

Graham, Robert. 1979. *Iran: The Illusion of Power*. New York: St. Martin's.

Green, Jerrold. 1980. Pseudoparticipation and Countermobilization: Roots of the Iranian Revolution. *Iranian Studies* 13, nos. 1–4: 31–53.

——. 1982. *Revolution in Iran: The Politics of Countermobilization*. New York: Praeger.

Gros, Jean-Germain, ed. 2003. *Cameroon: Politics and Society in Critical Perspective*. Lanham, MD: University Press of America.

Gudarzi, Manuchehr, Khodadad Farmanfarmaian, and Abdol-Majid Majidi. 1999. *Barnameh Rizi Amrani va Tasmimgiri-ye Siyasi* [Ideology, process, and politics in Iran's development planning]. Bethesda, MD: Foundation for Iranian Studies.

Gullick, J. M. 1981. *Malaysia: Economic Expansion and National Unity*. Boulder, CO: Westview.

Gurr, Ted Robert. 1980. *Handbook of Political Conflict*. New York: Free Press.

——. 1994. Peoples against States: Ethnopolitical Conflict and the Changing World System. *International Studies Quarterly* 38, no. 3 (September), 347–477.

Haber, Stephen, and Armando Razo. 1998. Political Instability and Economic Performance: Evidence from Revolutionary Mexico. *World Politics* 51, no. 1: 99–143.

Haggard, Stephen. 1986. The Newly Industrializing Countries in the International System. *World Politics* 38, no. 2: 343–70.

——. 1990. *Pathways from the Periphery: The Politics of Growth in the Newly Industrializing Countries*. Ithaca: Cornell University Press.

Haggard, Stephan, and Robert Kaufman, eds. 1992. *The Politics of Economic Adjustment*. Princeton: Princeton University Press.

——. 1995. *The Political Economy of Democratic Transitions*. Princeton: Princeton University Press.

Hagopian, Frances. 1994. Traditional Politics against State Transformation in Brazil. In *State Power and Social Forces*, ed. Joel Migdal, Atul Kohli, and Vivienne Shue. New York: Cambridge University Press.

Hall, Peter. 2003. Aligning Ontology and Methodology in Comparative Research.

In *Comparative Historical Analysis in the Social Sciences*, ed. James Mahoney and Dietrich Rueschemeyer, 373–404. New York: Cambridge University Press.

Hall, Peter, and Rosemary Taylor. 1996. Political Science and the Three New Institutionalisms. *Political Studies* 44, no. 5: 936–57.

Halliday, Fred. 1979. *Iran: Dictatorship and Development.* London: Penguin.

Halm, Heinz. 1997. *Shi'a Islam From Religion to Revolution.* Princeton: Markus Weiner.

Hansen, Gary E. 1971. Rural Administration and Agricultural Development in Indonesia. *Pacific Affairs* 44, no. 3: 390–400.

——. 1972. Indonesia's Green Revolution: The Abandonment of a Non-Market Strategy Toward Change. *Asian Survey* 12, no. 11 (November): 932–46.

——. 1975. Indonesia 1974: A Momentous Year. *Asian Survey* 15, no. 2 (February): 148–56.

——. 1976. Indonesia 1975: National Resilience and Continuity of the New Order Struggle. *Asian Survey* 16, no. 2 (February): 146–58.

——. 1978. Bureaucratic Linkages and Policy-Making in Indonesia: BIMAS Revisited. In *Political Power and Communications in Indonesia*, ed. Karl Jackson and Lucian Pye. Berkeley: University of California Press.

Harik, Iliya. 1972. Mobilization Policy and Political Change in Rural Egypt. In *Rural Politics and Social Change in the Middle East*, ed. Richard Antoun and Iliya Harik, 287–314. Bloomington: Indiana University Press.

Hariyadhie. 1997. *Perspektif Gerakan Mahasiswa 1978 Dalam Percaturan Politik Nasional* [Perspectives on the student movement of 1978 in the chess game of national politics]. Jakarta: PT Golden Terayon Press.

Harris, Lillian Craig. 1986. *Libya: Qadhafi's Revolution and the Modern State.* Boulder, CO: Westview.

Haskel, Barbara G. 1980. Access to Society: A Neglected Dimension of Power. *International Organizations* 34: 89–120.

Haydu, Jeffrey. 1998. Making Use of the Past: Time Periods as Cases to Compare and as Sequences of Problem Solving. *American Journal of Sociology* 104, no. 2 (September), 339–71.

Hedström, Peter, and Richard Swedberg, eds. 1998. *Social Mechanisms: An Analytical Approach to Social Theory.* New York: Cambridge University Press.

Hegre, Havard, Tanja Ellingsen, Scott Gates, and Nils Peter Gleditsch. 2001. Toward a Democratic Civil Peace? Democracy, Political Change, and and Civil War, 1816–1992. *American Political Science Review* 95, no. 1: 33–48.

Heller, Mark, and Nadav Safran. 1985. *The New Middle Class and Regime Stability in Saudi Arabia.* Cambridge, MA: Center for Middle Eastern Studies, Harvard University.

Herb, Michael. 1999. *All in the Family: Absolutism, Revolution, and Democracy in the Middle Eastern Monarchies.* Albany: State University of New York Press.

——. 2005. No Representation Without Taxation? Rents, Development, and Democracy. *Comparative Politics* 37, no. 3 (April): 297–316.

Herbst, Jeffrey. 2000. *States and Power in Africa: Comparative Lessons in Authority and Control.* Princeton: Princeton University Press.

Heston, Alan, and Robert Summers. 1998. Penn World Tables. Mark 5.6. Available at datacentre2.chass.utoronto.ca/pwt56/, accessed March 22, 2002.

Heyat, Z. 1983. *Iran: A Comprehensive Study of Socio-Economic Conditions.* n.p.: Eastern Publishing Society.

Hill, Hal, ed. 1989. *Unity and Diversity: Regional Economic Development in Indonesia since 1970.* Singapore: Oxford University Press.

——. ed. 1994. *Indonesia's New Order: The Dynamics of Socio-Economic Transformation.* Honolulu: University of Hawaii Press.

——. 2000. *The Indonesian Economy.* New York: Cambridge University Press.

Hindley, Donald. 1967. Political Power and the October 1965 Coup in Indonesia. *Journal of Asian Studies* 26, no. 2 (February): 237–49.

——. 1971. Indonesia 1970: The Workings of Pantjasila Democracy. *Asian Survey* 11, no. 2 (February): 111–20.

——. 1972. Indonesia 1971: Pantjasila Democracy and the Second Parliamentary Elections. *Asian Survey* 12, no. 1 (January): 56–68.

Hinnebusch, Raymond. 1985. *Egyptian Politics under Sadat: The Post-Populist Development of an Authoritarian-Modernizing State.* Cambridge: Cambridge University Press.

——. 1990. *Authoritarian Power and State Formation in Ba'thist Syria: Army, Party, and Peasant.* Boulder, CO: Westview.

——. 2001. *Syria: Revolution from Above.* New York: Routledge.

Hodges, Tony. 2001. *Angola: From Afro-Stalinism to Petro-Diamond Capitalism.* Bloomington: Indiana University Press.

——. 2004. *Angola: Anatomy of an Oil State.* 2nd ed. Bloomington: Indiana University Press.

Hooglund, Eric. 1982. *Land and Revolution in Iran, 1960–1980.* Austin: University of Texas Press.

Horowitz, Donald. 1985. *Ethnic Groups in Conflict.* Berkeley: University of California Press.

Hout, Wil. 1996. Development Strategies and Economic Performance in Third World Countries, 1965–92. *Third World Quarterly* 17, no. 4: 603–24.

Hoveyda, Fereydun. 1980. *The Fall of the Shah.* London: Weidenfeld and Nicolson.

Huber, Evelyne. 2002. The Fragmentation of Comparative Politics. *APSA-CP* 13, no. 1 (Winter): 1–2, 24–25.

Humphreys, Macartan. 2005. Natural Resources, Conflict, and Conflict Resolution: Uncovering the Mechanisms. *Journal of Conflict Resolution* 49, no. 4: 508–37.

Huntington, Samuel P. 1966. The Political Modernization of Traditional Monarchies. *Daedalus* (Summer): 763–88.

——. 1968. *Political Order in Changing Societies.* New Haven: Yale University Press.

——. 1991. *The Third Wave: Democratization in the Late Twentieth Century.* Norman: University of Oklahoma Press.

Huntington, Samuel P., and Clement H. Moore, eds. 1970. *Authoritarian Politics in Modern Society: The Dynamics of Established One-Party Systems.* New York: Basic Books.

Hurtado, Osvaldo. 1985. *Political Power in Ecuador.* Trans. Nick Mills. Boulder, CO: Westview.

Hyden, Goran. 1980. *Beyond Ujamaa in Tanzania: Underdevelopment and an Uncaptured Peasantry.* Berkeley: University of California Press.

International Monetary Fund. 1994. *International Financial Statistics.* CD-Rom, Washington, DC: IMF.

Isaacs, Anita. 1993. *Military Rule and Transition in Ecuador, 1972–92.* Pittsburgh: University of Pittsburgh Press.

Ismael, Jacqueline S. 1993. *Kuwait: Dependency and Class in a Rentier State.* Gainesville, FL: University Press of Florida.

Issawi, Charles. 1971. *The Economic History of Iran.* Chicago: University of Chicago Press.

Jackman, Robert. 1993. *Power Without Force: The Political Capacity of Nation-States.* Ann Arbor: University of Michigan Press.

Jacqz, Jane W., ed. 1976. *Iran: Past, Present and Future.* New York: Aspen Institute for Humanistic Studies.

Jazayeri, Ahmad. 1986. Prices and Output in Two Oil-Based Economies: The Dutch Disease in Iran and Nigeria. *IDS Bulletin* 17, no. 4: 14–21.

Jones Luong, Pauline, and Erika Weinthal. 2001. Prelude to the Resource Curse: Explaining Oil and Gas Development Strategies in the Soviet Successor States and Beyond. *Comparative Political Studies* 34, no. 4 (May): 367–99.

Johnson, Mark. 1977. Oil I: Recent Developments. *Bulletin of Indonesian Economic Studies* 13, no. 3: 34–47.

Kadhim, Mihssen. 1983. *The Political Economy of Revolutionary Iran.* Cairo: Cairo Papers in Social Science.

Kano, Hiromasa. 1978. City Development and Occupational Change in Iran: A Case Study of Hamadan. *Developing Economies* 16, no. 3: 298–328.

Kang, David C. 2002. *Crony Capitalism: Corruption and Development in South Korea and the Philippines.* New York: Cambridge University Press.

Kaplan, Abraham. 1998. *The Conduct of Inquiry.* Reprint edition. New Brunswick: Transaction.

Karimi-Hakkak, Ahmad. 1985. Protest and Perish: A History of the Writers' Association of Iran. *Iranian Studies* 18.

Karklins, Rasma, and Roger Petersen. 1993. "Decision Calculus of Protesters and Regimes: Eastern Europe 1989." *The Journal of Politics* 55, no. 3 (August): 588–614.

Karl, Terry. 1997. *The Paradox of Plenty: Oil Booms and Petro-States.* Berkeley: University of California Press.

——. 1999. Reflections on the Paradox of Plenty. *Journal of International Affairs* 53, no. 1 (Fall): 31–48.

Karshenas, Massoud. 1990. *Oil, State, and Industrialization in Iran.* New York: Cambridge University Press.

Kartanegara, M. Fahrud. 1994. *Catatan Seorang Aktivis Kampus* [The notes of a campus activist]. Jakarta: PT Golden Terayon Press.

Kartodirdjo, Sartono. 1977. Peasant Mobilization and Political Development in Indonesia. *Indonesian Quarterly* 5, no. 2 (April): 94–115.

——. 1996. *Komunikasi dan Kaderisasi Dalam Pembangunan Desa: Intisar Laporan-laporan Penelitian P3PK (LSPK) UGM 1974–1981* [Communication and "cadreization" in rural development: research reports of the Center for Rural and Village Development Research, 1974–81]. Yogyakarta, Indonesia: Aditya Media.

Katopo, Aristides, ed. 2000. *Menyingkap Kabut Halim 1965* [Lifting the Halim fog of 1965]. Jakarta: Pustaka Sinar Harapan.

Katouzian, M. A. 1974. Land Reform in Iran: A Case Study in the Political Economy of Social Engineering. *Journal of Peasant Studies* 1, no. 2: 220–39.

——. 1981. *The Political Economy of Modern Iran: Despotism and Pseudo-Modernism, 1926–1979.* London: Macmillan Press.

Katzenstein, Peter. 1985. *Small States in World Markets: Industrial Policy in Europe.* Ithaca: Cornell University Press.

Katznelson, Ira. 1997. Structure and Configuration in Comparative Politics. In *Comparative Politics: Rationality, Culture, and Structure,* ed. Mark Lichbach and Alan Zuckerman. New York: Cambridge University Press.

Kazemi, Farhad. 1980a. Urban Migrants and the Revolution. *Iranian Studies* 13, nos. 1–4: 257–77.

——. 1980b. *Poverty and Revolution in Iran: The Migrant Poor, Urban Marginality and Politics.* New York: New York University Press.

——. 1996. Civil Society and Iranian Politics. In *Civil Society in the Middle East,* ed. Augustus Richard Norton, vol. 2. Leiden, the Netherlands: E. J. Brill.

Kazemi, Farhad, and Ervand Abrahamian. 1978. The Nonrevolutionary Peasantry of Modern Iran. *Iranian Studies* 11: 259–303.

Keddie, Nikki. 1981. *Roots of Revolution: An Interpretive History of Modern Iran.* New Haven: Yale University Press.

Kelly, Roy. 1989. Property Taxation. In *Financing Local Government in Indonesia,* ed. Nick Devas. Athens: Ohio University Monographs in International Studies.

Keshavarzian, Arang. 1996. From Holy Alliance to Enemy of Islam. MA thesis, University of Washington.

Khadduri, Majid. 1978. *Socialist Iraq: A Study in Iraqi Politics since 1968.* Washington, DC: Middle East Institute.

Khalifa, Ali Mohammed. 1979. *The United Arab Emirates: Unity in Fragmentation.* Boulder, CO: Westview.

Al-Khalil, Samir. 1989. *Republic of Fear: The Politics of Modern Iraq.* Berkeley: University of California Press.

Kheirabadi, Masoud. 1991. *Iranian Cities: Formation and Development.* Austin: University of Texas Press.

King, Gary, Robert Keohane, and Sidney Verba. 1994. *Designing Social Inquiry.* Princeton: Princeton University Press.

Knight, Jack. 1992. *Institutions and Social Conflict.* New York: Cambridge University Press.

Kohli, Atul. 1987. The Political Economy of Development Strategies: Comparative Perspectives on the Role of the State. *Comparative Politics* 19, no. 2: 233–46.

——. 1994. Centralization and Powerlessness: India's Democracy in a Comparative Perspective. In *State Power and Social Forces,* ed. Joel Migdal, Atul Kohli, and Vivienne Shue. New York: Cambridge University Press.

Korps Pegawai Republik Indonesia, Daerah Istimewa Yogyakarta [Korpri-DIY]. 1981. *Hari Ulang Tahun Korpri & Rapat Kerja Daerah Korpri Se Daerah Is-*

timewa Yogyakarta [Korpri's birthday and the regional working meeting of the special district of Yogyakarta]. Yogyakarta, Indonesia.

van der Kroef, Justus M. 1971. *Indonesia after Sukarno.* Vancouver, Canada: University of British Columbia Press.

Kunio, Yoshihara. 1988. *The Rise of Ersatz Capitalism in South-East Asia.* Singapore: Oxford University Press.

Kurzman, Charles. 1992. *Structure and Agency in the Iranian Revolution of 1979.* Ph.D. dissertation, University of California at Berkeley.

——. 1994. A Dynamic View of Resources: Evidence from the Iranian Revolution. *Research in Social Movements, Conflicts and Change* 17: 53–84.

——. 1996. Structural Opportunity and Perceived Opportunity in Social-Movement Theory: The Iranian Revolution of 1979. *American Sociological Review* 61: 153–70.

——. 2003. The Qum Protests and the Coming of the Iranian Revolution, 1975 and 1978. *Social Science History* 27, no. 3 (Fall): 287–325.

——. 2004. *The Unthinkable Revolution in Iran.* Cambridge: Harvard University Press.

Lamborn, Alan C. 1983. Power and the Politics of Extraction. *International Studies Quarterly* 27.

Latham, Michael E. 2000. *Modernization As Ideology: American Social Science and "Nation Building" in the Kennedy Era.* Chapel Hill: University of North Carolina Press.

Lenczowski, George. 1960. *Oil and State in the Middle East.* Ithaca: Cornell University Press.

Lenczowski, George, ed. 1978. *Iran Under the Pahlavis.* Stanford, CA: Hoover Institution Press.

Lev, Daniel S. 1966. Indonesia 1965: The Year of the Coup. *Asian Survey* 6 (February): 103–10.

——. 1972. *Islamic Courts in Indonesia.* Berkeley: University of California Press.

——. 1985. Colonial Law and the Genesis of the Indonesian State. *Indonesia* 40 (October): 57–74.

Levy, James. 1981. *The Challenge to Democratic Reformism in Ecuador.* Albuquerque: University of New Mexico Press.

Levi, Margaret. 1988. *Of Rule and Revenue.* Berkeley: University of California Press.

——. 1997. A Model, A Method, and a Map: Rational Choice in Comparative and Historical Analysis. In *Comparative Politics,* ed. Mark Lichbach and Alan Zuckerman. New York: Cambridge University Press.

Levitsky, Steven, and Lucan Way. 2002. The Rise of Competitive Authoritarianism. *Journal of Democracy* 13, no. 2 (April): 51–65.

Levy, Daniel, and Gabriel Székely. 1987. *Mexico: Paradoxes of Stability and Change.* Boulder, CO: Westview.

Lewis-Beck, Michael. 1986. Interrupted Time Series. In *New Tools for Social Scientists,* ed. William Berry and Michael Lewis-Beck. Beverly Hills, CA: Sage.

Lichbach, Mark Irving. 1987. Deterrence or Escalation? The Puzzle of Aggregate Studies of Repression and Dissent. *Journal of Conflict Resolution* 31, no. 2 (June): 266–97.

Liddle, R. William. 1973. Evolution from Above: National Leadership and Local

Development in Indonesia. *Journal of Asian Studies* 32, no. 2 (February): 287–309.

——. 1977. Indonesia 1976: Challenges to Suharto's Authority. *Asian Survey* 17, no. 2 (February): 95–106.

——. 1978a. Participation and the Political Parties. In *Political Power and Communications in Indonesia,* ed. Karl Jackson and Lucian Pye, 171–95. Berkeley: University of California Press.

——. 1978b. Indonesia 1977: The New Order's Second Parliamentary Election. *Asian Survey* 18, no. 2 (February): 175–85.

——. 1996. *Leadership and Culture in Indonesian Politics.* Sydney: Allen and Unwin.

Lieberman, Evan S. 2001. Causal Inference in Historical Institutional Research: A Specification of Periodization Strategies. *Comparative Political Studies* 34, no. 9 (November): 1011–35.

——. 2003. *Race and Regionalism in the Politics of Taxation in Brazil and South Africa.* New York: Cambridge University Press.

——. 2005. Nested Analysis as a Mixed-Method Strategy for Comparative Research. *American Political Science Review* 99, no. 3 (August): 435–52.

Lijphart, Arend. 1971. Comparative Politics and the Comparative Method. *American Political Science Review* 65, no. 3 (September): 682–93.

Linz, Juan J. 2000. *Totalitarian and Authoritarian Regimes.* Boulder, CO: Lynne Rienner.

Logsdon, Martha Gay. 1974. Neighborhood Organization in Jakarta. *Indonesia* 18 (October): 53–70.

Looney, Robert E. 1982. *Economic Origins of the Iranian Revolution.* New York: Pergamon.

Lowi, Miriam. 2004. Oil Rents and Political Breakdown in Patrimonial States: Algeria in Comparative Perspective. *Journal of North African Studies* 9, no. 3 (Autumn): 83–102.

Luciani, Giacomo. 1987 Allocation vs. Production States: A Theoretical Framework. In *The Rentier State,* ed. Hazem Beblawi and Giacomo Luciani. London: Croom Helm.

——. 1994. The Oil Rent, The Fiscal Crisis of the State and Democratization. In *Democracy without Democrats? The Renewal of Politics in the Muslim World,* ed. Ghassan Salame. London: I. B. Tauris: 130–52.

MacAndrews, Colin, ed. 1986a. *Central Government and Local Development in Indonesia.* Singapore: Oxford University Press.

——. 1986b. Central Government and Local Government in Indonesia: An Overview. In *Central Government and Local Development in Indonesia,* ed. Colin MacAndrews. Singapore: Oxford University Press.

——. 1986c. The Structure of Government in Indonesia. In *Central Government and Local Development in Indonesia,* ed. Colin MacAndrews. Singapore: Oxford University Press.

MacDougal, John A. 1978. Patterns of Military Control in the Indonesian Higher Central Bureaucracy. *Indonesia* 33: 89–121.

MacIntyre, Andrew. 1991. *Business and Politics in Indonesia.* Sydney: Allen and Unwin.

——. 1994. Power, Prosperity, and Patrimonialism: Business and Government in

Indonesia. In *Business and Government in Industrialising Asia*, ed. Andrew MacIntyre. Ithaca: Cornell University Press.

——. 1999. Political Institutions and the Economic Crisis in Thailand and Indonesia. In *The Politics of the Asian Economic Crisis*, ed. T. J. Pempel. Ithaca: Cornell University Press.

——. 2000. Funny Money: Fiscal Policy, Rent-Seeking, and Economic Performance in Indonesia. In *Rents, Rent-Seeking, and Economic Development: Theory and Evidence in Asia*, ed. Mushtaq Khan and Jomo K. S. New York: Cambridge University Press.

——. 2001. Investment, Property Rights, and Corruption in Indonesia. In *Corruption: The Boom and Bust of East Asia*, ed. J. E. Campos. Manila: Ateneo University Press.

Mackie, Jamie. 1974. *Konfrontasi: The Indonesia-Malaysia Dispute, 1963–1966.* Kuala Lumpur: Oxford University Press.

Mackie, Jamie, and Andrew MacIntyre. 1994. Politics of New Order Indonesia. In Indonesia's *New Order: The Dynamics of Socio-Economic Transformation*, ed. Hal Hill. St. Leonards, Australia: Allen and Unwin.

Mahdavy, Hossein. 1970. The Patterns and Problems of Economic Development in Rentier States: The Case of Iran. In *Studies in the Economic History of the Middle East*, ed. M. A. Cook. London: Oxford University Press.

Mahoney, James. 2000a. Path Dependence in Historical Sociology. *Theory and Society* 29: 507–48.

——. 2000b. Rational Choice Theory and the Comparative Method: An Emerging Synthesis? *Studies in Comparative International Development* 35, no. 2 (Summer): 83–94.

——. 2001. *The Legacies of Liberalism: Path Dependence and Political Regimes in Central America.* Baltimore: Johns Hopkins University Press.

Majd, Mohammed Gholi. 2000a. Small Landowners and Land Distribution in Iran, 1962–71. *International Journal of Middle East Studies* 32, no. 1 (February): 123–53.

——. 2000b. *Resistance to the Shah: Landowners and Ulama in Iran.* Gainesville: University Press of Florida.

Makka, A. Makmur, and Dhurorudin Mashad. 1997. *ICMI: Dinamika Politik Islam di Indonesia* [ICMI: Dynamics of Islamic politics in Indonesia]. Jakarta: PT Pustaka CIDESINDO.

Mahasin, Aswab. 1983. On the Outskirts of the Periphery: Popular Movements in the New Order. *Prisma* 47: 25–33.

Malley, Michael. 1999. Resource Distribution, State Coherence, and Political Centralization in Indonesia, 1950–1997. Ph.D. dissertation, University of Wisconsin at Madison.

Mann, Michael. 1987. The Autonomous Power of the State: Its Origins, Mechanisms and Results. In *States in History*, ed. John Hall. New York: Basil Blackwell.

Manzano, Osmel, and Roberto Rigobon. 2001. *Resource Curse or Debt Overhang?* Manuscript.

de Marenches, Count. 1988. *The Evil Empire: The Third World War Now.* London: Sidgwick and Jackson.

Marshall, Monty G., and Keith Jaggers. 2000. *Polity IV Project: Political Regime*

Characteristics and Transitions 1800–1999. Available at www.bsos.umd.edu/
cidcm/polity, accessed September 26, 2002.

Martha, Ahmaddani G., Christianto Wibisono, and Yozar Anwar. 1984. *Pemuda
Indonesia: Dalam Dimensi Sejarah Perjuangan Bangsa* [Indonesian youth: In
the history of struggle for the nation]. Jakarta: Yayasan Sumpah Pemuda.

Martz, John D. 1987. *Politics and Petroleum in Ecuador.* New Brunswick, NJ:
Transaction.

Mas'oed, Mochtar. 1983. The Indonesian Economy and Political Structure during the Early New Order, 1966–1971. Ph.D. dissertation, Ohio State University.

——. 1984. The State Reorganisation of Society under the New Order. *Prisma* 47:
3–24.

McDaniel, Tim. 1991. *Autocracy, Modernization, and Revolution in Russia and
Iran.* Princeton: Princeton University Press.

McKeown, Timothy J. 1999. Case Studies and the Statistical Worldview: Review
of King, Keohane, and Verba's *Designing Social Inquiry: Scientific Inference in
Qualitative Research. International Organization* 53, no. 1: 161–90.

Middlebrook, Kevin J. 1995. *The Paradox of Revolution: Labor, the State, and
Authoritarianism in Mexico.* Baltimore: Johns Hopkins University Press.

Migdal, Joel S. 1988. *Strong Societies and Weak States: State-Society Relations
and State Capabilities in the Third World.* Princeton: Princeton University
Press.

——. 1997. Studying the State. In *Comparative Politics: Rationality, Culture,
and Structure,* ed. Marc Lichbach and Alan Zuckerman, 208–35. New York:
Cambridge University Press.

——. 2001a. *Through the Lens of Israel: Explorations in State and Society.* New
York: SUNY Series in Israel Studies.

——. 2001b. *State in Society: How States and Societies Transform and Constitute One Another.* New York: Cambridge University Press.

Migdal, Joel S., Atul Kohli, and Vivienne Shue, eds. 1994. *State Power and Social
Forces.* New York: Cambridge University Press.

Milani, Abbas. 2000. *The Persian Sphinx: Amir Abbas Hoveyda and the Riddle
of the Iranian Revolution.* Washington, DC: Mage.

Milani, Mohsen M. 1988. *The Making of Iran's Islamic Revolution: From Monarchy to Islamic Republic.* Boulder, CO: Westview.

Mill, John Stuart. 1860. *A System of Logic, Ratiocinative and Inductive: Being a
Connected View of the Principles of Evidence and the Methods of Scientific
Investigation.* New York: Harper and Brothers.

Miller, William Green. 1969a. Political Organization in Iran: From Dowreh to Political Party I. *Middle East Journal* 23, no. 2: 159–67.

——. 1969b. Political Organization in Iran: From Dowreh to Political Party II.
Middle East Journal 23, no. 3: 343–50.

Milne, Robert Stephen, and Diane K. Mauzy. 1999. *Malaysian Politics under Mahathir.* London and New York: Routledge.

Mitchell, Timothy. 1991. The Limits of the State: Beyond Statist Approaches and
Their Critics. *American Political Science Review* 85, no. 1 (March): 77–96.

Moaddel, Mansoor. 1986. The Shi'i Ulama and the State in Iran. *Theory and Society* 15: 519–56.

———. 1993. *Class, Politics, and Ideology in the Iranian Revolution.* New York: Columbia University Press.

Moertopo, Ali. 1981. *Strategi Pembangunan Nasional* [Strategy for national development]. Jakarta: Center for Strategic and International Studies.

Mofid, Kamran. 1987. *Development Planning in Iran: From Monarchy to Islamic Republic.* Cambridgeshire, U.K.: Middle East and North African Studies Press.

Moghadam, Valentine M. 1989. Populist Revolution and the Islamic State in Iran. In *Revolution in the World-System,* ed. Terry Boswell. New York: Greenwood.

Moghissi, Haideh. 1994. *Populism and Feminism in Iran: Women's Struggle in a Male-Defined Revolutionary Movement.* New York: St. Martin's.

Mohammadi-Nejad, Hassan. 1976. The Iranian Parliamentary Elections of 1975. *The Indian Political Science Review* 10: 201–15.

Moore, Barrington. 1966. *Social Origins of Dictatorship and Democracy: Lord and Peasant in the Making of the Modern World.* Boston: Beacon.

Morfit, Michael. 1986. Strengthening the Capacities of Local Government: Policies and Constraints. In *Central Government and Local Development in Indonesia,* ed. Colin MacAndrews. Singapore: Oxford University Press.

Mottahedeh, Roy. 1985. *Mantle of the Prophet.* New York: Pantheon.

Movahid, Mohammed Ali. 1970/1349. *Naft-e Ma va Masayel-e Huquqi-ye An* [Our oil and its legal issues]. Tehran: National Publishers.

Mozaffari, Mehdi. 1991. Why the Bazar Rebels. *Journal of Peace Research* 28, no. 4: 377–91.

Mubyarto and Sartono Kartodirdjo. 1988. *Pembangunan Pedesaan di Indonesia* [Rural development in Indonesia]. Yogyakarta, Indonesia: Liberty.

Mufti, Malik. 1996. *Sovereign Creations: Pan-Arabism and Political Order in Syria and Iraq.* Ithaca: Cornell University Press.

Nabavi, J. 1978. The Rastakhiz Party: A Year after Its Creation. *The Indian Political Science Review* 12: 8–24.

Nahzat-e Azadi-ye Iran, Khariz az Kishvar. 1976/1354. *Gozaresh-e Kamel-e Tazahorat-e 15–17 Khordad '54* [Complete report on the demonstrations of June 5–7, 1975]. Document 20:42. Reprinted in *Iranian Opposition to the Shah,* ed. Wolfgang Behn. Zug, Switzerland: Inter Documentation Company, 1984.

Najmabadi, Afsaneh. 1987a. Depoliticisation of a Rentier State: The Case of Pahlavi Iran. In *The Rentier State,* ed. Hazem Beblawi and Giacomo Luciani. London: Croom Helm.

———. 1987b. *Land Reform and Social Change in Iran.* Salt Lake City: University of Utah Press.

———. 1993. States, Politics, and the Radical Contingency of Revolutions: Reflections on Iran's Islamic Revolution. *Research in Political Sociology* 6: 197–215.

Najmabadi, Farokh. 1976. Strategies of Industrial Development in Iran. In *Iran: Past, Present, and Future,* ed. Jane W. Jacqz. New York: Aspen Institute for Humanistic Studies.

Nakhleh, Emile A. 1976. *Bahrain: Political Development in a Modernizing Society.* Lexington, MA: Lexington.

Naraghi, Ehsan. 1994. *From Palace to Prison.* Chicago: Ivan R. Dee.

Nasr, Vali. 2000. Politics within the Late-Pahlavi State: The Ministry of Economy and Industrial Policy, 1963–69. *International Journal of Middle East Studies* 32, no. 1 (February): 97–122.

Nategh, Homa. 1994/1373. *Bazarganan* [Merchants]. Tehran, Iran: Intisharat-i Tus.

National Security Archives. 2002a. *Sukarno's Confrontation with the United States: December 1964–September 1965.* Electronic Briefing Book no. 52: Indonesia Document Collection. Available at www.gwu.edu/~nsarchiv/NSAEBB/NSAEBB52/, accessed May 19, 2002.

——. 2002b. *The Secret CIA History of the Iran Coup.* Electronic Briefing Book no. 28: Iran Document Collection. Available at www.gwu.edu/~nsarchiv/NSAEBB/NSAEBB28/index.html, accessed May 23, 2002.

Ngoh, Victor Julius. 1987. Cameroon, 1884–1985: A Hundred Years of History. Yaounde, Cameroon: Navi-Group Publications.

Nitisastro, Widjojo, ed. 1965. *Masalah-masalah Ekonomi dan Faktor-faktor IPOLSOS* [Economic problems and international, political, and social factors]. Jakarta: LEKNAS/LIPI.

Nordlinger, Eric A. 1987. Taking the State Seriously. In *Understanding Political Development,* ed. Samuel P. Huntington and Myron Weiner. Boston: Little, Brown.

North, Douglass C. 1981. *Structure and Change in Economic History.* New York: W. W. Norton.

——. 1990. *Institutions, Institutional Change, and Economic Performance.* New York: Cambridge University Press.

Okruhlik, Gwenn. 1999. Rentier Wealth, Unruly Law, and the Rise of Opposition: The Political Economy of Oil States. *Comparative Politics* 31, no. 3 (April), 295–315.

Olson, Mancur. 1965. *The Logic of Collective Action: Public Goods and the Theory of Groups.* Cambridge, MA: Harvard University Press.

——. 1986. A Theory of the Incentives Facing Political Organizations: Neo-Corporatism and the Hegemonic State. *International Political Science Review* 7, no. 2 (April): 165–89.

——. 1993. Dictatorship, Democracy, and Development. *American Political Science Review* 87, no. 3 (September): 567–76.

Opp, Karl-Dieter, and Wolfgang Roehl. 1990. Repression, Micromobilization, and Political Protest. *Social Forces* 69, no. 2 (December): 521–47.

Ottaway, David, and Marina Ottaway. 1970. *Algeria: The Politics of a Socialist Revolution.* Berkeley, University of California Press.

Ottaway, Marina. 2003. *Democracy Challenged: The Rise of Semi-Authoritarianism.* Washington, DC: Carnegie Endowment for International Peace.

Overland, Jody, Kenneth L. Simons, and Michael Spagat. 2000. *Political Instability and Growth in Dictatorships.* Manuscript, University of London.

Padmo, Soegijanto. 2000. *Land Reform dan Gerakan Protes Petani Klaten 1959–1965* [Land reform and the Klaten farmers' protest movement of 1950–1965]. Yogyakarta, Indonesia: Media Pressindo.

Pahlavi, Mohammed Reza. 1967. *The White Revolution.* Tehran: Kayhan Press.

——. 1977. *Bi-su-yi tamaddun-i buzurg* [Toward the great civilization]. Tehran: Kitabkhanah-i Pahlavi.

——. 1980a. *The Shah's Story.* London: Michael Joseph.

——. 1980b. *Answer to History.* New York: Stein and Day.

Palangi, A. n.d. *Shahr va Shahrdari-ye Qazvin* [The city and municipality of Qazvin]. Tehran.

Palmer, Ingrid. 1978. *The Indonesian Economy since 1965: A Case Study of Political Economy.* London: Frank Cass.

Panter-Brick, Keith. 1978. *Soldiers and Oil: The Political Transformation of Nigeria.* Totowa, NJ: Cass.

Parsa, Misagh. 1988. Theories of Collective Action and the Iranian Revolution. *Sociological Forum* 3, no. 1: 44–71.

——. 1989. *Social Origins of the Iranian Revolution.* New Brunswick: Rutgers University Press.

——. 1994. Mosque of Last Resort: State Reform and Social Conflict in the Early 1960s. In *A Century of Revolution: Social Movements in Iran,* ed. John Foran, 135–59. Minneapolis: University of Minnesota Press.

——. 1995. Conversion or Coalition: Ideology in the Iranian and Nicaraguan Revolutions. *Political Power and Social Forces* 9, 23–60.

——. 2000. *States, Ideologies, and Social Revolutions.* New York: Cambridge University Press.

Parsa, Misagh, and Azar Tabari. 1983. Land, Politics and Capital Accumulation. *MERIP Reports* 113 (March–April): 26–30.

Pesaran, M. H. 1998. Economic Trends and Macroeconomic Policies in Post-Revolutionary Iran. Unpublished paper, Cambridge University.

Peters, B. Guy. 1998. *Comparative Politics: Theory and Methods.* New York: New York University Press.

Pierson, Paul. 1994. *Dismantling the Welfare State? Reagan, Thatcher, and the Politics of Retrenchment.* New York: Cambridge University Press.

——. 2000a. Not Just What But When: Timing and Sequence in Political Processes. *Studies in American Political Development* 14.

——. 2000b. Increasing Returns, Path Dependence, and the Study of Politics. *American Political Science Review* 94, no. 2 (June): 251–67.

——. 2003. Big, Slow-Moving, and . . . Invisible: Macro-Social Processes in the Study of Comparative Politics. In *Comparative Historical Analysis in the Social Sciences,* ed. James Mahoney and Dietrich Rueschemeyer, 177–98. New York: Cambridge University Press.

Pierson, Paul, and Theda Skocpol. 2002. Historical Institutionalism in Contemporary Political Science. In *Political Science: The State of the Discipline,* ed. Ira Katznelson and Helen Milner. New York: Norton. 693–721.

Poggi, Gianfranco. 1978. *The Development of the Modern State: A Sociological Introduction.* Stanford: Stanford University Press.

Prasetyantoko, A. 1999. *Kaum Profesional Menentang Rezim Otoriter* [Professionals confront an authoritarian regime]. Jakarta: PT Gramedia Widiasarana Indonesia.

Przeworski, Adam, and Henry Teune. 1970. *The Logic of Comparative Social Inquiry.* Malabar, FL: Krieger.

Pusat Data Propinsi DIY [Data Center for the Special District of Yogyakarta]. 1980. *Propinsi DIY Dalam Angka* [The special district of Yogyakarta in figures].

Pusat Informasi Nasional Departemen Penerangan [Information Center, National Department of Information]. 1997. *Susunan Kabinet Republik Indone-*

sia, 1945–1998 [Composition of cabinets of the Republic of Indonesia, 1945–1998]. Jakarta: Departemen Penerangan.

Quandt, William B. 1969. *Revolution and Political Leadership: Algeria, 1954–1968.* Cambridge, MA: MIT Press.

Radu Michael S., and Keith Somerville. 1989. The People's Republic of The Congo. In *Benin, The Congo, Burkina Faso,* ed. Chris Allen, Joan Baxter, Michael S. Radu, and Keith Somerville, 145–236. London: Pinter Publishers.

Ragin, Charles C. 1989. *The Comparative Method.* Berkeley: University of California Press.

——. 1997. Turning the Tables: How Case-Oriented Research Challenges Variable-Oriented Research. *Comparative Social Research* 16: 27–42.

Ragin, Charles C., and Howard S. Becker. 1992. *What is a Case? Exploring the Foundations of Social Inquiry.* New York: Cambridge University Press.

Rahnema, Ali. 2000. *An Islamic Utopian: A Political Biography of Ali Shari'ati.* New York: I. B. Tauris.

Rahnema, Saeed. 1996. Continuity and Change in Industrial Policy. In *Iran after the Revolution: Crisis of an Islamic State,* ed. Saeed Rahnema and Sohrab Behdad. New York: I. B. Tauris.

Ramadhan, K. H. 1996. *Soemitro: Former Commander of Indonesian Security Apparatus.* Jakarta: Pustaka Sinar Harapan.

Ramage, Douglas E. 1995. *Politics in Indonesia: Democracy, Islam and the Ideology of Tolerance.* New York: Routledge.

Ramazani, Rouhollah K. 1974. Iran's "White Revolution": A Study in Political Development. *International Journal of Middle East Studies* 5, no. 2: 124–39.

Rasler, Karen. 1996. Concessions, Repression, and Political Protest in the Iranian Revolution. *American Sociological Review* 61: 132–52

Razi, G. Hossein. 1970. Genesis of Party in Iran: A Case Study of the Interaction between the Political System and Political Parties. *Iranian Studies* 3: 58–90.

Razavi, Hossein, and Firouz Vakil. 1987. *The Political Environment of Economic Planning in Iran, 1971–1983: From Monarchy to Islamic Republic.* Boulder, CO: Westview.

Reeve, David. 1985. *GOLKAR of Indonesia: An Alternative to the Party System.* Singapore: Oxford University Press.

Remmer, Karen L. 1999. Regime Sustainability in the Latin Caribbean, 1944–1994. *The Journal of Developing Areas* 33: 331–54.

Republic of Indonesia. N.d. *Proses Kelahiran Undang-Undang Perkawinan* [Process of the birth of the marriage law]. Jakarta.

——. 1974. *Undang-Undang Republik Indonesia Nomor 5 Tahun 1974 Tentang Pokok-pokok Pemerintahan di Daerah* [Republic of Indonesia Law No. 5 1974 regarding principles of governance in the regions]. Jakarta.

Richards, Alan, and John Waterbury. 1996. *A Political Economy of the Middle East.* 2nd ed. Boulder, CO: Westview.

Riphenburg, Carol J. 1998. *Oman: Political Development in a Changing World.* Westport, CT: Praeger.

Robison, Richard. 1986. *Indonesia: The Rise of Capital.* Sydney: Allen and Unwin.

——. 1988. Authoritarian States, Capital-Owning Classes, and the Politics of

Newly Industrializing Countries: The Case of Indonesia. *World Politics* 41, no. 1: 52–74.

——. 1996. The Middle Class and the Bourgeoisie in Indonesia. In *The New Rich in Asia: Mobile Phones, McDonald's, and Middle-Class Revolution,* ed. Richard Robison and David S. G. Goodman. New York: Routledge.

Roeder, Philip G. 2001. Ethnolinguistic Fractionalization (ELF) Indices, 1961 and 1985. February 16. Available at weber.ucsd.edu\~proeder¡lf.htm, accessed November 15, 2001.

Ross, Michael L. 1999. The Political Economy of the Resource Curse. *World Politics* 51 (January): 279–322.

——. 2001a. *Timber Booms and Institutional Breakdown in Southeast Asia.* New York: Cambridge University Press.

——. 2001b. Indonesia's Puzzling Crisis. Manuscript, UCLA.

——. 2001c. Does Oil Hinder Democracy? *World Politics* 53, no. 3: 325–61.

——. 2004a. How Do Natural Resources Influence Civil War? Evidence from 13 Cases. *International Organization* 58 (Winter): 35–67.

——. 2004b. What Do We Know about Natural Resources and Civil War? *Journal of Peace Research* 41 (May): 337–56.

——. 2005. Resources and Rebellion in Aceh, Indonesia. In *Understanding Civil War: Evidence and Analysis,* ed. Paul Collier and Nicholas Sambanis, 35–58. Washington, DC: World Bank.

Rotblat, Howard. 1972. *Stability and Change in an Iranian Provincial Bazaar.* Ph.D. dissertation, University of Chicago.

——. 1975. Social Organization and Development in an Iranian Provincial Bazaar. *Economic Development and Cultural Change* 23: 292–305.

Rouleau, Eric. 1976. Iran: Myth and Reality. *The Guardian,* October 31.

Rubin, Barry. 1981. *Paved with Good Intentions: The American Experience and Iran.* New York: Penguin.

Rueschemeyer, Dietrich, and Peter Evans. 1985. The State and Economic Transformation: Toward an Analysis of the Conditions underlying Effective Intervention. In *Bringing the State Back In,* ed. Peter Evans, Dietrich Rueschemeyer, and Theda Skocpol. New York: Cambridge University Press.

Rueschemeyer, Dietrich, and John D. Stephens. 1997. Comparing Historical Sequences—A Powerful Tool for Causal Analysis: A Reply to John Goldthorpe's "Current Issues in Comparative Macrosociology." *Comparative Social Research* 16: 55–72.

Rueschemeyer, Dietrich, Evelyn H. Stephens, and John D. Stephens. 1992. *Capitalist Development and Democracy.* Chicago: University of Chicago Press.

Rule, James B. 1988. *Theories of Civil Violence.* Berkeley: University of California Press.

Sachs, Jeffrey D., and Andrew W. Warner. 1995. *Natural Resource Abundance and Economic Growth.* Development Discussion Paper 517a. Cambridge: Harvard Institute for International Development.

——. 1999. The Big Push, Natural Resource Booms and Growth. *Journal of Development Economics* 59: 43–76.

Saikal, Amin. 1980. *The Rise and Fall of the Shah.* Princeton: Princeton University Press.

De Saint-Paul, Marc Aicardi. 1989. *Gabon: The Development of a Nation.* Translated by A., F., and T. Palmer. New York: Routledge.

Salehi, M. M. 1988. *Insurgency through Culture and Religion: The Islamic Revolution of Iran.* New York: Praeger.

Sami'i, Ahmad. 1989/1368. *Si Va Haft Sal* [Thirty-seven years]. Tehran: Shabaviz.

Sarraf, Tahmoores. 1990. *Cry of a Nation: The Saga of the Iranian Revolution.* New York: Peter Lang.

Schatzberg, Michael G., and I. William Zartman, eds. 1986. *The Political Economy of Cameroon.* New York: Praeger.

Schiller, Jim. 1996. *Developing Jepara in New Order Indonesia.* Clayton, Australia: Monash Asia Institute.

Schmitter, Philippe. 1973. Still the Century of Corporatism? *Review of Politics* 36 (1974): 85–131.

Schmitz, Hubert. 1984. Industrialization Strategies in Less Developed Countries: Some Lessons of Historical Experience. *Journal of Development Studies* 21, no. 1: 1–21.

Schodt, David W. 1987. *Ecuador: An Andean Enigma.* Boulder, CO: Westview.

Schwartz, Adam. 1994. *A Nation in Waiting: Indonesia in the 1990s.* Boulder, CO: Westview.

Scott, Peter D. 1985. The United States and the Overthrow of Sukarno, 1965–1967. *Pacific Affairs* 53 (Summer): 239–64.

Seale, Patrick. 1988. *Asad of Syria: The struggle for the Middle East.* London: I. B. Taurus.

Shafer, D. Michael. 1994. *Winners and Losers: How Sectors Shape the Developmental Prospects of States.* Ithaca: Cornell University Press.

Shambayati, Hootan. 1994. The Rentier State, Interest Groups, and the Paradox of Autonomy: State and Business in Turkey and Iran. *Comparative Politics* 26: 307–31.

Sheahan, John. 1980. Market-Oriented Economic Policies and Political Repression in Latin America. *Economic Development and Cultural Change* 28, no. 2: 267–91.

Shefter, Martin. 1994. *Political Parties and the State: The American Historical Experience.* Princeton: Princeton University Press.

Shue, Vivienne. 1994. State Power and Social Organization in China. In *State Power and Social Forces,* ed. Joel Migdal, Atul Kohli, and Vivienne Shue. New York: Cambridge University Press.

Skeet, Ian. 1992. *Oman: Politics and Development.* New York: St. Martin's.

Skocpol, Theda. 1979. *States and Social Revolutions.* New York: Cambridge University Press.

——. 1982. Rentier State and Shi'a Islam in the Iranian Revolution. *Theory and Society* 11: 265–83.

——. 1995. Why I Am an Historical Institutionalist. *Polity* 28, no. 1: 104–6.

Smith, Benjamin. 2003a. Collective Action with and without Islam: Mobilizing the Bazaar in Iran. In *Islamic Activism: A Social Movement Theory Approach,* ed. Quintan Wiktorowicz. Indianapolis: Indiana University Press.

——. 2003b. If I Do These Things They Will Throw Me Out: Economic Reform and the Collapse of Indonesia's New Order. *Journal of International Affairs* (Fall): 113–28.

——. 2004. Oil Wealth and Regime Survival in the Developing World, 1960–1999. *American Journal of Political Science* 48, no. 2 (April): 232–48.

——. 2005. Life of the Party: The Origins of Regime Breakdown and Persistence under Single-Party Rule. *World Politics* 57, no. 3 (April): 421–51.

——. 2006. The Wrong Kind of Crisis: Why Oil Booms and Busts Rarely Lead to Authoritarian Breakdown. *Studies in Comparative International Development* 40, no. 4 (Winter): 55–76.

Somerville, Keith. 1986. *Angola: Politics, Economics, and Society.* Boulder, CO: Lynne Rienner.

Spagat, Michael. 2001. The Dynamics of Repressive Dictatorships. Manuscript, University of London.

Soeharto, Pitut. 2000. *Eseiku di Masa Orde Baru: Suato Kritik dan Gagasan* [My essays in the New Order era: Criticism and concept]. Jakarta: Yayasan Nurani Indonesia.

Soejito, Irawan. 1990. *Hubungan Pemerintah Pusat dan Pemerintah Daerah* [Central government–regional government relations]. Jakarta: Rineka Cipta.

Soltan, Karol, Eric M. Uslaner, and Virginia Haufler. 1998. *Institutions and Social Order.* Ann Arbor: University of Michigan Press.

Snyder, Richard. 1992. Explaining Transitions from Neopatrimonial Dictatorships. *Comparative Politics* 24: 379–99.

de Soysa, Indra. 2000. The Resource Curse: Are Civil Wars Driven by Rapacity or Paucity?. In *Greed and Grievance: Economic Agendas in Civil Wars,* ed. Mats Berdal and David Malone, 113–35. Boulder, CO: Lynne Rienner.

Sreberny-Mohammadi, Annabelle, and Ali Mohammadi. 1994. *Small Media, Big Revolution: Communication, Culture, and the Iranian Revolution.* Minneapolis: University of Minnesota Press.

Steinmo, Sven, Kathleen Thelen, and Frank Longstreth, eds. 1992. *Structuring Politics: Historical Institutionalism in Comparative Analysis.* New York: Cambridge University Press.

Stinchcombe, Arthur. 1965. Social Structure and Organizations. In *Handbook of Organizations,* ed. James G. March, 142–93. Chicago: Rand McNally.

——. 1968. *Constructing Social Theories.* Chicago: University of Chicago Press.

Stone, Martin. 1997. *The Agony of Algeria.* New York: Columbia University Press.

Sujanto, Ir. 1991. *Pokok-pokok Pemerintahan di Daerah: Proses Pembuatan Undang-undang No. 5, 1974* [Principles of regional government: The process of making Law No. 5, 1974]. Jakarta: Rineka Cipta.

Sulastomo. 2000. *Hari-Hari Yang Panjang 1963–1966* [Long days, 1963–1966]. Jakarta: Buku Kompas.

Supriatna, Tjahya. 1993. *Sistem Administrasi Pemerintahan di Daerah* [System of government administration in the regions]. Jakarta: Bumi Aksara.

Suryadinata, Leo. 1989. *Military Ascendancy and Political Culture: A Study of Indonesia's GOLKAR.* Athens: Ohio University Center for International Studies.

Suwarno, P. J. 1994. *Hamengku Buwono IX dan Sistem Birokrasi Pemerintahan Yogyakarta 1942–1974* [Hamengku Buwono IX and the bureaucratic system of Yogyakarta government, 1942–1974]. Yogyakarta, Indonesia: Penerbit Kanisius.

Swasono, Sri-Edi. 1973. Some Notes on the Nurturing of the Indonesian Entrepeneur. *Indonesian Quarterly* 1, no. 4 (July): 50–64.

Sydney Morning Herald. 1999. Indonesia: Hidden Holocaust. October 7.

Talu'i, Mahmoud. 1995/1374. *Shah dar Dadgah-he Tarikh* [The Shah in the court of history]. Tehran: Aftab.

Tanter, Richard. 2000. East Timor and the Crisis of the Indonesian Intelligence State. *Bulletin of Concerned Asian Scholars* 32, nos. 1–2: 73–82.

Tapper, Richard. 1979. *Pasture and Politics: Economics, Conflict, and Ritual among Shahsevan Nomads of Northwestern Iran.* London: Academic Press.

Tavanian, Hassan, ed. N.d. *Eqtesad-e Siyasi-ye Towhidi* [Unified political economy]. Tehran: Intisharat-e Sadeq.

Tarrow, Sidney. 1999. Expanding Paired Comparison: A Model Proposal. *APSA-CP* (Summer): 9–12.

Taylor, Charles Lewis, and Michael C. Hudson. 1972. *World Handbook of Political and Social Indicators.* 2nd ed. New Haven: Yale University Press.

Taylor, Charles Lewis, and David A. Jodice. 1982. *World Handbook of Political and Social Indicators.* 3rd ed. New Haven: Yale University Press.

Temple, Jonathan. 2001. Growing into Trouble: Indonesia after 1966. Manuscript, University of Bristol.

Thaiss, Gustav. 1971. The Bazaar as a Case Study of Religion and Social Change. In *Iran Faces the Seventies,* ed. Ehsan Yar-Shater. New York: Praeger.

Thelen, Kathleen. 1999. Historical Institutionalism in Comparative Politics. *Annual Reviews of Political Science* 2, 369–404.

Thompson, Mark R. 1996. Late Industrialisers, Late Democratisers: Developmental States in the Asia-Pacific. *Third World Quarterly* 17, no. 4: 625–47.

Thompson, Virgina, and Richard Adloff. 1984. *Historical Dictionary of the People's Republic of the Congo.* 2nd ed. Metuchen, NJ: Scarecrow Press.

Tilly, Charles, ed. 1975. *The Formation of National States in Western Europe.* Princeton: Princeton University Press.

——. 1978. *From Mobilization to Revolution.* Reading, MA: Addison Wesley.

——. 1984. *Big Structures, Large Processes, Huge Comparisons.* New York: Russell Sage Foundation.

——. 1985. Models and Realities of Popular Collective Action. *Social Research* 52, 717–47.

——. 1990. *Coercion, Capital, and European States.* Cambridge, MA: Basil Blackwell.

——. 1992. Prisoners of the State. *International Social Science Journal* 44, no. 3 (August): 329–42.

——. 1994. The Time of States. *Social Research* 61, no. 2: 269–96.

——. 1997. Means and Ends of Comparison in Macrosociology. *Comparative Social Research* 16: 43–53.

Tlemcani, Rachid. 1986. *State and Revolution in Algeria.* Boulder, CO: Westview.

University of Indonesia [UI]. 1966. *Kebangkitan Semangat '66: Mendjeladjah Tracee Baru* [Resurrection of the soul of '66: Charting a new path]. Jakarta: Jajasan Badan Penerbit, Fakultas Ekonomi Universitas Indonesia.

Uppal, J. S. 1986. *Taxation in Indonesia.* Yogyakarta, Indonesia: Gadjah Mada University Press.

Utomi, Pat. 2002. The Curse of Oil. Niger Delta Congress, available at www.niger deltacongress.com, accessed on April 2, 2002.

'Uyuzi, Muhammad-Rahim. 2001. *Tabaqat-e Ejtema'i va Rezhim-e Shah* (Social classes and the shah's regime). Tehran: Merkez-e Asnad-e Enqelab-e Eslami.

van de Walle, Nicolas. 2001. *African Economies and the Politics of Permanent Crisis*. New York: Cambridge University Press.

Van Evera, Stephen. 1997. *Guide to Methods for Students of Political Science*. Ithaca: Cornell University Press.

Vandewalle, Dirk. 1998. *Libya since Independence: Oil and State Building*. Ithaca: Cornell University Press.

Vatikiotis, Michael. 1993. *Indonesian Politics under Suharto: Order, Development, and Pressure for Change*. New York: Routledge.

Wahid, Nusron. 2000. *Membongkar Hegemoni NU: Di Balik Independensi PMII (1966–1972)* [Demolishing the hegemony of the NU: Behind the independence of the movement of Islamic students of Indonesia, 1966–1972]. Jakarta: PT Bina Rena Pariwara.

Waldner, David. 1999. *State Building and Late Development*. Ithaca: Cornell University Press.

——. 2002. From Intra-Type Variations to the Origins of Types: Recovering the Macro-Analytics of State Building. Presented at the Conference on Asian Political Economy in an Era of Globalization, Dartmouth College, Hanover, New Hampshire, May 10–11, 2002.

——. 2004. Democracy and Dictatorship in the Post-Colonial World. Manuscript, University of Virginia.

——. Forthcoming 2007. Inferences and Explanations at the K/T Boundary . . . and Beyond. In *Theory and Evidence in Comparative Politics and International Relations*, ed. Ned Lebow and Marc Lichbach. New York: Palgrave MacMillan.

Wantchekon, Leonard. 1999. Why do Resource Dependent Countries Have Authoritarian Governments? Leitner Working Paper 1999–11. New Haven: Yale Center for International and Area Studies.

Warr, Peter G. 1986. Indonesia's Other Dutch Disease: Economic Effects of the Petroleum Boom. In *Natural Resources and the Macroeconomy*, ed. J. Peter Neary and Sweder van Wijnbergen. Cambridge: MIT Press.

Warwick, Paul. 1992. Economic Trends and Government Survival in West European Parliamentary Democracies. *American Political Science Review* 86, no. 4 (December): 875–87.

Waterbury, John. 1983. *The Egypt of Nasser and Sadat: The Political Economy of Two Regimes*. Princeton: Princeton University Press.

——. 1992. The Heart of the Matter? Public Enterprise and the Adjustment Process. In *The Politics of Economic Adjustment*, ed. Stephan Haggard and Robert Kaufman. Princeton: Princeton University Press.

——. 1993. *Exposed to Innumerable Delusions: Public Enterprise and State Power in Egypt, India, Mexico, and Turkey*. New York: Cambridge University Press.

Weber, Max. 1978. *Economy and Society*. Trans. G. Roth and C. Wittich. Berkeley: University of California Press.

Weinbaum, Marvin G. 1973. Iran Finds a Party System: The Institutionalization of *Iran Novin*. *Middle East Journal* 27: 439–55.

Wertheim, W. F. 1966. Indonesia before and after the Untung Coup. *Pacific Affairs* 39, nos. 1/2: 115–127.

Wheeler, Douglas L., and René Pélissier. 1978. *Angola*. Westport, CT: Greenwood.

Willis, Michael. 1997. *The Islamist Challenge in Algeria: A Political History*. New York: New York University Press.

Winters, Jeffrey A. 1988. Indonesia: The Rise of Capital: A Review Essay. *Indonesia* 45 (April): 109–28.

——. 1994. Power and the Control of Capital. *World Politics* 46, no. 3 (April): 419–52.

——. 1996. *Power in Motion: Capital Mobility and the Indonesian State*. Ithaca: Cornell University Press.

Wintrobe, Ronald. 1998. *The Political Economy of Dictatorship*. New York: Cambridge University Press.

Woo, Wing Thye, Bruce Glassburner, and Anwar Nasution. 1994. *Macroeconomic Policies, Crises, and Long-Term Growth in Indonesia, 1965–90*. Washington, DC: World Bank Comparative Macroeconomic Studies.

Woods, Patricia. 2004. Gender and the Reproduction and Maintenance of Group Boundaries: Why the "Secular" State Matters to Religious Authorities in Israel. In *Boundaries and Belonging: States and Societies in the Struggle to Shape Identities and Local Practices*, ed. Joel Migdal. New York: Cambridge University Press.

World Bank. 1966. Import Requirements of Indonesia for 1967 in the Sectors of Transport, Agriculture, and Industry. Recommendations by a Mission of the International Bank for Reconstruction and Development, November. Washington, DC.

——. 2001. *World Development Indicators*. CD-Rom. Washington, DC: World Bank.

Yar-Shater, Ehsan, ed. 1971. *Iran Faces the Seventies*. New York: Praeger.

Yates, Douglas. 1995. *The Rentier State in Gabon*. Boston: Boston University Press.

Yergin, Daniel. 1991. *The Prize: The Epic Quest for Oil, Money, and Power*. New York: Simon and Schuster.

Young, Crawford. 1982. *Ideology and Development in Africa*. New Haven: Yale University Press.

Zabih, Sepehr. 1979. *Iran's Revolutionary Upheaval: An Interpretive Essay*. San Francisco: Alchemy Books.

Zacharias, Danny. 1979. The Lurah (Village Head) and Development Programs. *Indonesian Quarterly* 7, no. 2 (April): 94–107.

Zahlan, Rosemarie Said. 1998. *The Making of the Modern Gulf States: Kuwait, Bahrain, Qatar, the United Arab Emirates, and Oman*. Berkshire, U.K.: Ithaca Press.

Zavareei, Manizheh. 1982. Dependent Capitalist Development in Iran and the Mass Uprising of 1979. *Research in Political Economy* 5: 139–88.

Zonis, Marvin. 1971. *The Political Elite of Iran*. Princeton: Princeton University Press.

Zubaida, Sami. 1989. Classes as Political Actors in the Iranian Revolution. In Sami Zubaida, *Islam, the People and the State*. New York: Routledge, 1989.

Periodicals

Angkatan Bersenjata.
Antara.
Bank Markazi Iran. *Gozaresh-e Salaneh va Taraznameh* [Annual Report and Balance Sheet].
Berita Buana.
Berita Yudha.
Economist.
Ettela'at [Persian].
Indonesia Raya.
Iran Almanac. Tehran: Echo of Iran, various editions. In English.
Harian Kami.
Kayhan [Persian].
Kayhan International [English].
Kayhan International, weekly edition [English].
Kompas, daily edition [Indonesian].
Nusantara.
New York Times.
Pedoman.
Pelita.
Rastakhiz [Persian].
Sinar Harapan.
Suara Muhammadiyah.
Tempo.

Index